Non-Fiction

THE GEORGE SAND–
GUSTAVE FLAUBERT LETTERS

George Sand (1804-1876)
(Amantine Aurore Lucile Dupin, Baroness Dudevant)

Gustave Flaubert (1821-1880)

Translator: A.L. McKenzie (1921)
Introduction: Stuart Sherman

Cover Images:
"Still Life with Letter to Thomas B. Clarke," by William Michael Harnett, 1879; George Sand, Photo: Félix Nadar, 1877; Gustave Flaubert, "Bibliothek des allgemeinen und praktischen Wissens. Bd. 5" (1905), Französische Literaturgeschichte, Seite 71.

ISBN-13: 978-1-60762-050-1
ISBN-10: 1-60762-050-2

Original French-to-English Translation Publication: 1921

Reprint Trade Paperback Edition

August 2009

A Publication of
Norilana Books
P. O. Box 2188
Winnetka, CA 91396
www.norilana.com

Printed in the United States of America

The George Sand–Gustave Flaubert Letters

Norilana Books

Classics

www.norilana.com

The George Sand~ Gustave Flaubert Letters

cs⊂Ո৪৪০০০

George Sand
Gustave Flaubert

cs⊂Ո৪৪০০০

Translated from the French by
A.L. McKenzie

Introduction by
Stuart Sherman

Prefatory Note

This translation of the correspondence between George Sand and Gustave Flaubert was undertaken in consequence of a suggestion by Professor Stuart P. Sherman. The translator desires to acknowledge valuable criticism given by Professor Sherman, Ruth M. Sherman, and Professor Kenneth McKenzie, all of whom have generously assisted in revising the manuscript.

A. L. McKenzie

Introduction

The correspondence of George Sand and Gustave Flaubert, if approached merely as a chapter in the biographies of these heroes of nineteenth century letters, is sufficiently rewarding. In a relationship extending over twelve years, including the trying period of the Franco-Prussian War and the Commune, these extraordinary personalities disclose the aspects of their diverse natures which are best worth the remembrance of posterity. However her passionate and erratic youth may have captivated our grandfathers, George Sand in the mellow autumn of her life is for us at her most attractive phase. The storms and anguish and hazardous adventures that attended the defiant unfolding of her spirit are over. In her final retreat at Nohant, surrounded by her affectionate children and grandchildren, diligently writing, botanizing, bathing in her little river, visited by her friends and undistracted by the fiery lovers of the old time, she shows an unguessed wealth of maternal virtue, swift, comprehending sympathy, fortitude, sunny resignation, and a goodness of heart that has ripened into wisdom. For Flaubert, too, though he was seventeen years her junior, the flamboyance of youth was long since past; in 1862, when the correspondence begins, he was firmly settled, a shy, proud, grumpy toiling hermit of forty, in his family seat at

Croisset, beginning his seven years' labor at *L'Education Sentimentale,* master of his art, hardening in his convictions, and conscious of increasing estrangement from the spirit of his age. He, with his craving for sympathy, and she, with her inexhaustible supply of it, meet; he pours out his bitterness, she her consolation; and so with equal candor of self-revelation they beautifully draw out and strengthen each the other's characteristics, and help one another grow old.

But there is more in these letters than a satisfaction for the biographical appetite, which, indeed, finds *its* account rather in the earlier chapters of the correspondents' history. What impresses us here is the banquet spread for the reflective and critical faculties in this intercourse of natural antagonists. As M. Faguet observes in a striking paragraph of his study of Flaubert:

> "It is a curious thing, which does honor to them both, that Flaubert and George Sand should have become loving friends towards the end of their lives. At the beginning, Flaubert might have been looked upon by George Sand as a furious enemy. Emma [*Madame Bovary*] is George Sand's heroine with all the poetry turned into ridicule. Flaubert seems to say in every page of his work: 'Do you want to know what is the real Valentine, the real Indiana, the real Lelia? Here she is, it is Emma Roualt.' 'And do you want to know what becomes of a woman whose education has consisted in George Sand's books? Here she is, Emma Roualt.' So that the terrible mocker of the bourgeois has written a book which is directly inspired by the spirit of the 1840 bourgeois. Their recriminations against romanticism 'which rehabilitates and poetises the courtesan,' against George Sand, the Muse of Adultery, are to be found in acts and facts in *Madame Bovary*."

Now, the largest interest of this correspondence depends precisely upon the continuance, beneath an affectionate personal relationship, of a fundamental antagonism of interests and beliefs, resolutely maintained on both sides. George Sand, with her lifelong passion for propaganda and reformation, labors earnestly to bring Flaubert to her point of view, to remould him nearer to her heart's desire. He, with a playful deference to the sex and years of his friend, addresses her in his letters as "Dear Master." Yet in the essentials of the conflict, though she never gives over her effort, he never budges a jot; he has taken his ground, and in his last unfinished work, Bouvard and Pecuchet, he dies stubbornly fortifying his position. To the last she speaks from a temperament lyrical, sanguine, imaginative, optimistic and sympathetic; he from a temperament dramatic, melancholy, observing, cynical, and satirical. She insists upon natural goodness; he, upon innate depravity. She urges her faith in social regeneration; he vents his splenetic contempt for the mob. Through all the successive shocks of disillusioning experience, she expects the renovation of humanity by some religious, some semi-mystical, amelioration of its heart; he grimly concedes the greater part of humanity to the devil, and can see no escape for the remnant save in science and aristocratic organization. For her, finally, the literary art is an instrument of social salvation— it is her means of touching the world with her ideals, her love, her aspiration; for him the literary art is the avenue of escape from the meaningless chaos of existence—it is his subtly critical condemnation of the world.

The origins of these unreconciled antipathies lie deep beneath the personal relationship of George Sand and Gustave Flaubert; lie deep beneath their successors, who with more or less of amenity in their manners are still debating the same questions today. The main currents of the nineteenth century, with fluent and refluent tides, clash beneath the controversy; and as soon as one hears its "long withdrawing roar," and thinks it is dying away, and is become a part of ancient history, it begins again, and will be heard, no doubt, by the last man as a solemn accompaniment to his final contention with his last adversary.

George Sand was, on the whole, a natural and filial daughter of the French Revolution. The royal blood which she received from her father's line mingled in her veins with that of the Parisian milliner, her mother, and predestined her for a leveller by preparing in her an instinctive ground of revolt against all those inherited prejudices which divided the families of her parents. As a young girl wildly romping with the peasant children at Nohant she discovered a joy in untrammeled rural life which was only to increase with years. At the proper age for beginning to fashion a conventional young lady, the hoyden was put in a convent, where she underwent some exalting religious experiences; and in 1822 she was assigned to her place in the "established social order" by her marriage at seventeen to M. Dudevant. After a few years of rather humdrum domestic life in the country, she became aware that this gentleman, her husband, was behaving as we used to be taught that all French husbands ultimately behave; he was, in fact, turning from her to her maids. The young couple had never been strongly united—the impetuous dreamy girl and her coarse hunting mate; and they had grown wide apart. She should, of course, have adjusted herself quietly to the altered situation and have kept up appearances. But this young wife had gradually become an "intellectual"; she had been reading philosophy and poetry; she was saturated with the writings of Rousseau, of Chateaubriand, of Byron. None of the spiritual masters of her generation counselled acquiescence in servitude or silence in misery. Every eloquent tongue of the time-spirit urged self-expression and revolt. And she, obedient to the deepest impulses of her blood and her time, revolted.

At the period when Madame Dudevant withdrew her neck from the conjugal yoke and plunged into her literary career in Paris, the doctrine that men are created for freedom, equality and fraternity was already somewhat hackneyed. She, with an impetus from her own private fortunes, was to give the doctrine a recrudescence of interest by resolutely applying it to the status of women. We cannot follow her in detail from the point where she abandons the domestic sewing-basket to reappear smoking black cigars in the Latin Quarter. We find her, at about 1831, entering into competition with the brilliant literary generation of

Balzac, Hugo, Alfred de Musset, Merimee, Stendhal, and Sainte-Beuve. To signalize her equality with her brothers in talent, she adopts male attire: "I had a sentry-box coat made, of rough grey cloth, with trousers and waist-coat to match. With a grey hat and a huge cravat of woolen material, I looked exactly like a first-year student." In the freedom of this rather unalluring garb she entered into relations Platonic, fraternal, or tempestuously passionate with perhaps the most distinguished series of friends and lovers that ever fluttered about one flame. There was Aurelien de Seze; Jules Sandeau, her first collaborator, who "reconciled her to life" and gave her a nom de guerre; the inscrutable Merimee, who made no one happy; Musset—an encounter from which both tiger-moths escaped with singed wings; the odd transitional figure of Pagello; Michel Euraed; Liszt; Chopin, whom she loved and nursed for eight years; her master Lamennais; her master Pierre Leroux; her father-confessor Sainte-Beuve; and Gustave Flaubert, the querulous friend of her last decade.

As we have compressed the long and complex story of her personal relationships, so we must compress the intimately related history of her works and her ideas. When under the inspiration of Rousseau, the emancipated George Sand began to write, her purposes were but vaguely defined. She conceived of life as primarily an opportunity for unlimited self-expansion, and of literature as an opportunity for unrestricted self-expression. "Nevertheless," she declares, "my instincts have formed, without my privity, the theory I am about to set down,—a theory which I have generally followed unconsciously.... According to this theory, the novel is as much a work of poetry as of analysis. It demands true situations, and characters not only true but real, grouped about a type intended to epitomize the sentiment or the main conceptions of the book. This type generally represents the passion of love, since almost all novels are love-stories. According to this theory (and it is here that it begins) the writer must idealize this love, and consequently this type,—and must not fear to attribute to it all the powers to which he inwardly aspires, or all the sorrows whose pangs he has observed or felt. This type must in no wise, however, become degraded by the vicissitude of events; it must either die or triumph."

In 1831, when her pen began its fluent course through the lyrical works of her first period—*Indiana, Valentine, Lelia, Jacques,* and the rest—we conceive George Sand's culture, temper, and point of view to have been fairly comparable with those of the young Shelley when, fifteen years earlier, he with Mary Godwin joined Byron and Jane Clairmont in Switzerland—young revoltes, all of them, nourished on eighteenth century revolutionary philosophy and Gothic novels. Both these eighteenth century currents meet in the work of the new romantic group in England and in France. The innermost origin of the early long poems of Shelley and the early works of George Sand is in personal passion, in the commotion of a romantic spirit beating its wings against the cage of custom and circumstance and institutions. The external form of the plot, whatever is fantastic and wilful in its setting and its adventures, is due to the school of Ann Radcliffe. But the quality in Shelley and in George Sand which bewitched even the austere Matthew Arnold in his green and salad days is the poetising of that liberative eighteenth century philosophy into "beautiful idealisms" of a love emancipated from human limitations, a love exalted to the height of its gamut by the influences of nature, triumphantly seeking its own or shattered in magnificent despair. In her novels of the first period, George Sand takes her Byronic revenge upon M. Dudevant. In Indiana and its immediate successors, consciously or unconsciously, she declares to the world what a beautiful soul M. Dudevant condemned to sewing on buttons; in Jacques she paints the man who might fitly have matched her spirit; and by the entire series, which now impresses us as fantastic in sentiment no less than in plot, she won her early reputation as the apologist for free love, the adversary of marriage.

In her middle period—say from 1838 to 1848—of which *The Miller of Aginbault, Consuelo,* and *The Countess of Rudolstadt* are representative works, there is a marked subsidence of her personal emotion, and, in compensation, a rising tide of humanitarian enthusiasm. Gradually satiated with erotic passion, gradually convinced that it is rather a mischief-maker than a reconstructive force in a decrepit society, she is groping, indeed, between her successive liaisons for an elusive felicity, for a larger mission than inspiring Musset's Alexandrines or Chopin's nocturnes. It is somewhat amusing, and at the same time indicative of her vague but deep-seated moral yearnings, to find her writing rebukingly to Sainte-Beuve, as early as 1834, apropos of his epicurean Volupte:

> "Let the rest do as they like; but you, dear friend, you must produce a book which will change and better mankind, do you see? You can, and therefore should. Oh, if poor I could do it! I should lift my head again and my heart would no longer be broken; but in vain I seek a religion: Shall it be God, shall it be love, friendship, the public welfare? Alas, it seems to me that my soul is framed to receive all these impressions, without one effacing another ... Who shall paint justice as it should, as it may, be in our modern society?"

To Sainte-Beuve, himself an unscathed intellectual Odysseus, she declares herself greatly indebted intellectually; but on the whole his influence seems to have been tranquillizing. The material for the radical program, economic, political, and religious, which, like a spiritual ancestor of H. G. Wells, she eagerly sought to popularize by the novels of her middle years, was supplied mainly by Saint-Simon, Lamennais, and Leroux. Her new "religion of humanity," a kind of theosophical socialism, is too fantastically garbed to charm the sober spirits of our age. And yet from the ruins of that time and from the emotional extravagance of books grown tedious, which she has left behind her, George Sand emerges for us with one radiant perception which must be included in whatever religion animates a democratic society: "Everyone must be happy, so that the happiness of a few may not be criminal and cursed by God."

One of George Sand's French critics, M. Caro, a member of the Academy, who deals somewhat austerely with her religiose enthusiasms and with her Utopian projects for social reformation, remarks gravely and not without tenderness:

> "The one thing needful to this soul, so strong, so rich in enthusiasm, is a humble moral quality that she disdains, and when she has occasion to speak of it, even slanders,—namely resignation. This is not, as she seems to think, the sluggish virtue of base souls, who, in their superstitious servitude to force, hasten to crouch beneath every yoke. That is a false and degrading resignation; genuine resignation grows out of the conception of the universal order, weighed against which individual sufferings, without ceasing to be a ground of merit, cease to constitute a right of revolt.... Resignation, in the true, the philosophical, the Christian sense, is a manly acceptance of moral law and also of the laws essential to the social order; it is a free adherence to order, a sacrifice approved by reason of a part of one's private good and of one's personal freedom, not to might nor to the tyranny of a human caprice, but to the exigencies of the common weal, which subsists only by the concord of individual liberty with obedient passions."

Well, resigned in the sense of defeated, George Sand never became; nor did she, perhaps, ever wholly acquiesce in that scheme of things which M. Caro impressively designates as "the universal order." Yet with age, the abandonment of many distractions, the retreat to Nohant, the consolations of nature, and her occupation with tales of pastoral life, beginning with *La Mare au Diable,* there develops within her, there diffuses itself around her, there appears in her work a charm like that which falls upon green fields from the level rays of the evening sun after a day of storms. It is not the charm, precisely, of resignation; it is the charm of serenity—the serenity of an old revolutionist who no longer expects victory in the morning yet is secure in her confidence of a final triumph, and still more secure in the goodness of her cause. "A hundred times in life," she declares, "the good that one does seems to serve no immediate purpose; yet it maintains in one way and another the tradition of well wishing and well doing, without which all would perish." At the outset of her career we compared her with Shelley. In her last phase, she reminds us rather of the authors of *Far from the Madding Crowd* and *The Mill on the Floss,* and of Wordsworth, once, too, a torch of revolution, turning to his Michaels and his leech-gatherers and his Peter Bells. Her exquisite pictures of pastoral life are idealizations of it; her representations of the peasant are not corroborated by Zola's; to the last she approaches the shield of human nature from the golden side. But for herself at least she has found a real secret of happiness in country life, tranquil work, and a right direction given to her own heart and conscience.

It is at about this point in her spiritual development that she turns towards Gustave Flaubert—perhaps a little suspiciously at first, yet resolved from the first, according to her natural instinct and her now fixed principles, to stimulate by believing in his admirable qualities. Writing from Nohant in 1866 to him at Croisset, she epitomises her distinction as a woman and as an author in this playful sally: "Sainte-Beuve, who loves you nevertheless, pretends that you are dreadfully vicious. But perhaps he sees with eyes a bit dirty, like that learned botanist who pretends that the germander is of a *dirty* yellow. The observation was so false that I could not help writing on the margin of his book: '*It is you, whose eyes are dirty.*'"

We have spoken of George Sand as a faithful daughter of the French Revolution; and by way of contrast we may speak of Flaubert as a disgruntled son of the Second Empire. Between his literary advent and hers there is an interval of a generation, during which the proud expansive spirit and the grandiose aspirations imparted to the nation by the first Napoleon dwindled to a spirit of mediocrity and bourgeois smugness under a Napoleon who had inherited nothing great of his predecessor but his name. This change in the time-spirit may help to explain the most significant difference between Flaubert and George Sand. He inherited the tastes and imagination of the great romantic generation; but he inherited none of its social and political enthusiasm. He was disciplined by the romantic writers; yet his reaction to the literary culture of his youth is not ethical but aesthetic; he finds his inspiration less in Rousseau than in Chateaubriand. He is bred to an admiration of eloquence, the poetic phrase, the splendid picture, life in the grand style; with increasing disgust he finds himself entering a society which, he feels, neither understands nor values any of these things, and which threatens their destruction. Consequently, we find him actuated as a writer by two complementary passions—the love of splendor and the hatred of mediocrity—two passions, of which the second sometimes alternates with the first, sometimes inseparably fuses with it, and ultimately almost extinguishes it.

The son of an eminent surgeon of Rouen, Gustave Flaubert may have acquired from his father something of that scientific precision of observation and that cutting accuracy of expression, by which he gained his place at the head of modern French realism and won the discipleship of the Goncourts, Daudet, Zola, and Maupassant and the applause of such connoisseurs of technique as Walter Pater and Henry James. From his mother's Norman ancestry he inherited the physique of a giant, tainted with epilepsy; a Viking countenance, strong-featured with leonine moustaches; and a barbaric temper, habitually somewhat lethargic but irritable, and, when roused, violent and intolerant of opposition. He had a private education at Rouen, with wide desultory reading; went to Paris, which he hated, to study law, which he also hated; frequented the theatres and studios; travelled in Corsica, the Pyrenees, and the East, which he adored, seeing Egypt, Palestine, Constantinople, and

Greece; and he had one, and only one, important love-affair, extending from 1846 to 1854—that with Mme. Louise Colet, a woman of letters, whose difficult relations with Flaubert are sympathetically touched upon in Pater's celebrated essay on "Style." When by the death of his father, in 1845, he succeeded to the family-seat at Croisset, near Rouen, he settled himself in a studious solitude to the pursuit of letters, which he followed for thirty-four years with anguish of spirit and dogged persistence.

Flaubert probably loved glory as much as any man; but he desired to receive it only on his own terms. He profoundly appeals to writers endowed with "the artistic conscience" as "the martyr of literary style." In morals something of a libertine, in matters of art he exhibited the intolerance of weakness in others and the remorseless self-examination and self-torment commonly attributed to the Puritan. His friend Maxime Du Camp, who tried to bring him out and teach him the arts of popularity, he rebuffed with deliberate insult. He developed an aversion to any interruption of his work, and such tension and excitability of nerves that he shunned a day's outing or a chat with an old companion, lest it distract him for a month afterward. His mistress he seems to have estranged by an ill-concealed preference to her of his exacting Muse. To illustrate his "monkish" consecration to his craft we cannot do better than reproduce a passage, quoted by Pater, from his letters to Madame Colet:

> "I must scold you for one thing, which shocks, scandalises me, the small concern, namely, you show for art just now. As regards glory be it so—there I approve. But for art!—the one thing in life that is good and real—can you compare with it an earthly love?—prefer the adoration of a relative beauty to the cultus of the true beauty? Well! I tell you the truth. That is the one thing good in me: the one thing I have, to me estimable. For yourself, you blend with the beautiful a heap of alien things, the useful, the agreeable, what not?
>
> "The only way not to be unhappy is to shut yourself up in art, and count everything else as nothing.

Pride takes the place of all beside when it is established on a large basis. Work! God wills it. That, it seems to me, is clear.

> "I am reading over again the Aeneid, certain verses of which I repeat to myself to satiety. There are phrases there which stay in one's head, by which I find myself beset, as with those musical airs which are forever returning, and cause you pain, you love them so much. I observe that I no longer laugh much, and am no longer depressed. I am ripe, you talk of my serenity, and envy me. It may well surprise you. Sick, irritated, the prey a thousand times a day of cruel pain, I continue my labour like a true working-man, who, with sleeves turned up, in the sweat of his brow, beats away at his anvil, never troubling himself whether it rains or blows, for hail or thunder. I was not like that formerly."

The half-dozen works which Flaubert beat out on his "anvil," with an average expenditure of half-a-dozen years to each, were composed on a theory of which the prime distinguishing feature was the great doctrine of "impersonality." George Sand's fluent improvisations ordinarily originated, as we have noted, in an impulse of her lyrical idealism; she began with an aspiration of her heart, to execute which she invented characters and plot so that she is always on the inside of her story. According to Flaubert's theory, the novel should originate in a desire to present a certain segment of observed life. The author is to take and rigorously maintain a position outside his work. The organ with which he collects his materials is not his heart but his eyes, supplemented by the other senses. Life, so far as the scientific observer can be sure of it, and so far as the artist can control it for representation, is a picture or series of pictures, a dramatic scene or a concatenation of dramatic scenes. Let the novelist first, therefore, with scrupulous fidelity and with minute regard for the possible significance of every observable detail, fill his notebooks, amass his materials, master his subject. After Flaubert, a first-rate sociological investigator is three-fourths of a novelist. The rest of the task is to arrange and set forth these facts so that they shall tell the truth about life impressively, in scene and dramatic spectacle, the meaning of which shall be implicit in the plot and shall reach the reader's consciousness through his senses.

Critics have spent much time in discussing the conflict of "romantic" and "realistic" tendencies in Flaubert's works. And it is obviously easy, so far as subject-matter is concerned, to group his books in two divisions: on the one hand, *The Temptation of St. Anthony, Salammbo,* and two of the *Trois Contes;* on the other hand, *Madame Bovary, L'Education Sentimentale,* and the incomplete *Bouvard and Pecuchet.* We may call the tales in the first group romantic, because the subject-matter is remote in time and place, and because in them Flaubert indulges his passion for splendor—for oriental scenery, for barbaric characters, the pomp of savage war and more savage religion, events strange, terrible, atrocious. We may call the stories in the other group realistic, because the subject-matter is contemporary life in Paris and the provinces, and because in them Flaubert indulges his hatred for mediocrity—for the humdrum existence of the country doctor, the apothecary, the insipid clerk, the vapid sentimental woman, and the charlatans of science. But as a matter of fact, *all* his books are essentially constructed on the same theory: all are just as "realistic" as Flaubert could make them.

Henry James called *Madame Bovary* a brilliantly successful application of Flaubert's theory; he pronounced *L'Education Sentimentale* "elaborately and massively dreary"; and he briefly dismissed *Salammbo* as an accomplished work of erudition. *Salammbo* is indeed a work of erudition; years were spent in getting up its archaeological details. But *Madame Bovary* is also a work of erudition, and *Bouvard and Pecuchet* is a work of enormous erudition; a thousand volumes were read for the notes of the first volume and Flaubert is said to have killed himself by the labor of his unfinished investigations. There is no important distinction to be made between the method or the thoroughness with which he collected his facts in the one case or the other; and the story of the war of the mercenaries against the Carthaginians is evolved with the same alternation of picture and dramatic spectacle and the same hard merciless externality that distinguish the evolution of Emma Bovary's history.

We may go still farther than that towards wiping out the distinction between Flaubert's "romantic" and his "realistic" works; and by the same stroke what is illusory in the pretensions of the realists, namely, their aspiration to an "impersonal art."

If we were seeking to prove that an author can put *nothing but himself* into his art, we should ask for no more impressive illustions than precisely, *Madame Bovary* and *Salammbo*. These two masterpieces disclose to reflection, no less patently than the works of George Sand, their purpose and their meaning. And that purpose and meaning are not a whit less personal to Flaubert than the purpose and meaning of Indiana, let us say, are personal to George Sand. The "meaning" of *Madame Bovary* and *Salammbo* is, broadly speaking, Flaubert's sense of the significance—or, rather, of the insignificance—of human life; and the "purpose" of the books is to express it. The most lyrical of idealists can do no more to reveal herself.

The demonstration afforded by a comparison of *Salammbo* and *Madame Bovary* is particularly striking because the subject-matters are superficially so unlike. But take any characteristic series of pictures or incidents from *Salammbo*: take the passing of the children through the fire to Moloch, or the description of the leprous Hanno, or the physical surrender of the priestess to her country's enemy, or the following picture of the crucified lion:

> "They were marching through a wide defile, hedged in by two chains of reddish hillocks, when a nauseous odor struck their nostrils, and they believed that they saw something extraordinary at the top of a carob tree; a lion's head stood up above the foliage.

"Running towards it, they found a lion attached to a cross by its four limbs, like a criminal; his enormous muzzle hung to his breast, and his forepaws, half concealed beneath the abundance of his mane, were widely spread apart, like a bird's wings in flight; under the tightly drawn skin, his ribs severally protruded and his hind legs were nailed together, but were slightly drawn up; black blood had trickled through the hairs, and collected in stalactites at the end of his tail, which hung straight down the length of the cross. The soldiers crowded around the beast, diverting themselves by calling him 'Consul!' and 'Citizen of Rome!' and threw pebbles into his eyes to scatter the swarming gnats."

And now take any characteristic series of pictures or incidents from *Madame Bovary:* take Bovary's bungling and gruesome operations on the club-footed ostler's leg, with the entire village clustering agape; take the picture of the eyeless, idiotic beggar on the road to Rouen; or the scene in which Emma offers herself for three thousand francs to Rodolphe; or the following bit, only a bit, from the detailed account of the heroine's last hours, after the arsenical poisoning:

"Emma's head was turned towards her right shoulder, the corner of her mouth, which was open, seemed like a black hole at the lower part of her face; her two thumbs were bent into the palms of her hands; a kind of white dust besprinkled her lashes, and her eyes were beginning to disappear in that viscous pallor that looks like a thin web, as if spiders had spun it over. The sheet sunk in from her breast to her knees, and then rose at the tips of her toes, and it seemed to Charles that infinite masses, an enormous load, were weighing upon her.

"The church clock struck two. They could hear the loud murmur of the river flowing in the darkness at the foot of the terrace. Monsieur Bournisien from time to time blew his nose noisily and Homais' pen was scratching over the paper."

In these two detached pictures—the one from a so-called "romantic," the other from a so-called "realistic" book—one

readily observes the likeness in the subjects, which are of a
ghastly repulsiveness; the same minuteness of observation—e.g.,
the lion's hind legs "slightly drawn up," the woman's thumbs
"bent into the palms of her hands"; the same careful notation of
effect on the several senses; the same rhetorical heightening—
e.g., the "stalactites at the end of his tail," the web in the
woman's eyes "as if spiders had spun it over"; and finally, that
celebrated detachment, that air as of a medical examiner,
recording the results of an autopsy. What can we know of such
an author? All, or nearly all, that he knew of himself, provided
we will searchingly ask ourselves what sort of mind is steadily
attracted to the painting of such pictures, to the representation of
such incidents, and what sort of mind expresses a lifetime of
brooding on the significance of life in two such books as
Madame Bovary and *Salammbo.*

    At its first appearance, *Madame Bovary* was prosecuted,
though unsuccessfully, as offensive to public morals. In derision
of this famous prosecution, Henry James with studious
jauntiness, asserts that in the heat of his first admiration he
thought what an excellent moral tract it would make. "It may be
very seriously maintained," he continues, "that M. Flaubert's
masterpiece is the pearl of 'Sunday reading.'" As a work of
fiction and recreation the book lacks, in his opinion, one quite
indispensable quality: it lacks charm. Well, there are momentary
flashes of beauty and grace, dazzling bits of color, haunting
melancholy cadences in every chapter of Flaubert; but a
charming book he never wrote. A total impression of charm he
never gave—he never could give; because his total impression of
life was not charming but atrocious. It is perhaps an accident, as
has been suggested, that one can so readily employ *Madame
Bovary* to illustrate that text on the "wages of sin." Emma, to be
sure, goes down the easy and alluring path to disgrace and ruin.
But that is only an incident in the wider meaning of Flaubert's
fiction, a meaning more amply expressed in *Salammbo,* where
not one foolish woman alone but thousands on thousands of

men, women, and children, mingled with charging elephants and vipers, flounder and fight in indescribable welters of blood and filth, and go down to rot in a common pit. If I read Flaubert's meaning right, all human history is there; you may show it by painting on broad canvas a Carthaginian battle-scene or by photographing the details of a modern bedroom: a brief brightness, night and the odor of carrion, a crucified lion, a dying woman, the jeering of ribald mercenaries, the cackle of M. Homais. It is all one. If Flaubert deserved prosecution, it was not for making vice attractive, but for expressing with invasive energy that personal and desperately pessimistic conception of life by which he was almost overwhelmed.

That a bad physical regimen, bad habits of work in excessive quantities, and the solitude of his existence were contributory to Flaubert's melancholy, his exacerbated egotism, and his pessimism is sufficiently obvious in the letters. This Norman giant with his aching head buried all day long in his arms, groping in anguish for a phrase, has naturally a kindly disposition towards various individuals of his species—is even capable of great generosity; but as he admits with a truth and pathos, deeply appealing to the maternal sympathies of his correspondent, he has no talent for living. He has never been able, like richer and more resourceful souls, to reconcile being a man with being an author. He has made his choice; he has renounced the cheerful sanities of the world:

> "I pass entire weeks without exchanging a word with a human being; and at the end of the week it is not possible for me to recall a single day nor any event whatsoever. I see my mother and my niece on Sundays, and that is all. My only company consists of a band of rats in the garret, which make an infernal racket above my head, when the water does not roar or the wind blow. The nights are black as ink, and a silence surrounds me comparable to that of the desert. Sensitiveness is increased immeasurably in such a setting. I have palpitations of the heart for nothing.

> "All that results from our charming profession. That is what it means to torment the soul and the body. But perhaps this torment is our proper lot here below."

To George Sand, who wrote as naturally as she breathed and almost as easily, seclusion and torment were by no means the necessary conditions of literary activity. Enormously productive, with a hundred books to his half-a-dozen, she has never dedicated and consecrated herself to her profession but has lived heartily and a bit recklessly from day to day, spending herself in many directions freely, gaily, extravagantly. Now that she has definitely said farewell to her youth, she finds that she is twenty years younger; and now that she is, in a sense, dissipating her personality and living in the lives of others, she finds that she is happier than ever before. "It can't be imperative to work so painfully"—such is the burden of her earlier counsels to Flaubert; "spare yourself a little, take some exercise, relax the tendons of your mind, indulge a little the physical man. Live a little as I do; and you will take your fatigues and illnesses and occasional dolours and dumps as incidents of the day's work and not magnify them into the mountainous overshadowing calamities from which you deduce your philosophy of universal misery." No advice could have been more wholesome or more timely. And with what pictures of her own busy felicity she reenforces her advice! I shall produce three of them here in order to emphasize that precious thing which George Sand loved to impart, and which she had the gift of imparting, namely, joy, the spontaneous joyousness of her own nature. The first passage is from a letter of June 14, 1867:

> "I am a little remorseful to take whole days from your work, I who am never bored with loafing, and whom you could leave for whole hours under a tree, or before two lighted logs, with the assurance that I should find there something interesting. I know so well how to live *outside of myself*. It hasn't always been like that. I also was young and subject to indignations. It is over! Since I have dipped into

real nature, I have found there an order, a system, a calmness of cycles which is lacking in mankind, but which man can, up to a certain point, assimilate when he is not too directly at odds with the difficulties of his own life. When these difficulties return, he must endeavor to avoid them; but if he has drunk the cup of the eternally true, he does not get too excited for or against the ephemeral and relative truth."

The second passage is of June 21:

"I love everything that makes up a milieu, the rolling of the carriages and the noise of the workmen in Paris, the cries of a thousand birds in the country, the movement of the ships on the waters. I love also absolute, profound silence, and, in short, I love everything that is around me, no matter where I am."

The last passage gives a glimpse of the seventeenth of January, 1869, a typical day in Nohant:

"The individual named George Sand is well: he is enjoying the marvellous winter which reigns in Berry, gathering flowers, noting interesting botanical anomalies, making dresses and mantles for his daughter-in-law, costumes for the marionettes, cutting out scenery, dressing dolls, reading music, but above all spending hours with the little Aurore, who is a marvellous child. There is not a more tranquil or a happier individual in his domestic life than this old troubadour retired from business, who sings from time to time his little song to the moon, without caring much whether he sings well or ill, provided he sings the motif that runs in his head, and who, the rest of the time, idles deliciously.... This pale character has the great pleasure of loving you with all his heart, and of not passing a day without thinking of the other old troubadour, confined in his solitude of a frenzied artist, disdainful of all the pleasures of the world."

Flaubert did "exercise" a little—once or twice—in compliance with the injunctions of his "dear master"; but he rather resented the implication that his pessimism was personal, that it had any particular connection with his peculiar temperament or habits. He wished to think of himself as a stoic, quite indifferent about his "carcase." His briefer black moods he might acknowledge had transitory causes. But his general and abiding conceptions of humanity were the result of dispassionate reflections. "You think," he cries in half-sportive pique, "that because I pass my life trying to make harmonious phrases, in avoiding assonances, that I too have not my little judgments on the things of this world? Alas! Yes! and moreover I shall burst, enraged at not expressing them." And later: "Yes, I am susceptible to disinterested angers, and I love you all the more for loving me for that. Stupidity and injustice make me roar,— and I howl in my corner against a lot of things 'that do not concern me.'" "On the day that I am no longer in a rage, I shall fall flat as the marionette from which one withdraws the support of the stick."

So far as Flaubert's pessimism has an intellectual basis, it rests upon his researches in human history. For *Salammbo* and *The Temptation of St. Anthony* he ransacked ancient literature, devoured religions and mythologies, and saturated himself in the works of the Church Fathers. In order to get up the background of his *Education Sentimentale* he studied the Revolution of 1848 and its roots in the Revolution of 1789. He found, shall we say? what he was looking for—inexhaustible proofs of the cruelty and stupidity of men. After "gulping" down the six volumes of Buchez and Roux, he declares: "The clearest thing I got out of them is an immense disgust for the French.... Not a liberal idea which has not been unpopular, not a just thing that has not caused scandal, not a great man who has not been mobbed or knifed. 'The history of the human mind is the history of human folly,' as says M. Voltaire. ... Neo-Catholicism on the one hand, and Socialism on the other, have stultified France." In another letter of the same Period and similar provocation: "However much you fatten human cattle, giving them straw as high as their bellies, and even gilding their stable, they will remain brutes, no matter what one says. All the advance that one can hope for, is to make the brute a little less wicked. But as for elevating the ideas of the mass, giving it a larger and therefore a less human conception of God, I have my doubts."

In addition to the charges of violence and cruelty, which he brought against all antiquity as well as against modern times, much in the fashion of Swift or the older Mark Twain, Flaubert nursed four grave causes of indignation, made four major charges of folly against modern "Christian" civilization.

> In religion, we have substituted for Justice the doctrine of Grace. In our sociological considerations we act no longer with discrimination but upon a principle of universal sympathy. In the field of art and literature we have abandoned criticism and research for the Beautiful in favor of universal puffery. In politics we have nullified intelligence and renounced leadership to embrace universal suffrage, which is the last disgrace of the human spirit.

It must be acknowledged that Flaubert's arraignment of modern society possesses the characteristics commended by the late Barett Wendell: it is marked in a high degree by "unity, mass, and coherence." It must be admitted also that George Sand possessed in a high degree the Pauline virtue of being "not easily provoked," or she never could have endured so patiently, so sweetly, Flaubert's reiterated and increasingly ferocious assaults upon her own master passion, her ruling principle. George Sand was one whose entire life signally attested the power of a "saving grace," resident in the creative and recuperative energies of nature, resident in the magical, the miracle-working, powers of the human heart, the powers of love and sympathy. She was a modern spiritual adventurer who had escaped unscathed from all the anathemas of the old theology; and she abounded, like St. Francis, in her sense of the new dispensation and in her benedictive exuberance towards all the creatures of God, including not merely sun, moon, and stars and her sister the lamb but also her brother the wolf. On this principle she loves

Flaubert!—and archly asserts her arch-heresy in his teeth. He complains that her fundamental defect is that she doesn't know how to "hate." She replies, with a point that seems never really to have pierced his thick casing of masculine egotism:

> "Artists are spoiled children and the best are great egotists. You say that I love them too well; I like them as I like the woods and the fields, everything, everyone that I know a little and that I study continually. I make my life in the midst of all that, and as I like my life, I like all that nourishes it and renews it. They do me a lot of ill turns which I see, but which I no longer feel. I know that there are thorns in the hedges, but that does not prevent me from putting out my hands and finding flowers there. If all are not beautiful, all are interesting. The day you took me to the Abbey of Saint-Georges I found the *scrofularia borealis,* a very rare plant in France. I was enchanted; there was much —— in the neighborhood where I gathered it. Such is life!

> "And if one does not take life like that, one cannot take it in any way, and then how can one endure it? I find it amusing and interesting, and since I accept *everything*, I am so much happier and more enthusiastic when I meet the beautiful and the good. If I did not have a great knowledge of the species, I should not have quickly understood you, or known you or loved you."

Two years later the principles and tempers of both these philosophers were put to their severest trial. In 1870, George Sand had opportunity to apply her doctrine of universal acceptance to the Prussians in Paris. Flaubert had opportunity to welcome scientific organization in the Prussian occupation of his own home at Croisset. The first reaction of both was a quite simple consternation and rage, in which Flaubert cries, "The hopeless barbarism of humanity fills me with a black melancholy," and George Sand, for the moment assenting, rejoins: "Men are ferocious and conceited brutes." As the war thickens around him and the wakened militancy of his compatriots presses him hard, Flaubert becomes more and more depressed; he forebodes a general collapse of civilization—

before the century passes, a conflict of races, "in which several millions of men kill one another in one engagement." With the curiously vengeful satisfaction which mortals take in their own misery when it offers occasion to cry "I told you so," he exclaims: "Behold then, the *natural man*. Make theories now! Boast the progress, the enlightenment and the good sense of the masses, and the gentleness of the French people! I assure you that anyone here who ventured to preach peace would get himself murdered."

George Sand in her fields at Nohant—not "above" but a little aside from the conflict—turns instinctively to her peasant doggedly, placidly, sticking at his plow; turns to her peasant with a kind of intuition that he is a symbol of faith, that he holds the keys to a consolation, which the rest of us blindly grope for: "He is imbecile, people say; no, he is a child in prosperity, a man in disaster, more of a man than we who complain; he says nothing, and while people are killing, he is sowing, repairing continually on one side what they are destroying on the other." Flaubert, who thinks that he has no "illusions" about peasants or the "average man," brings forward his own specific of a quite different nature: "Do you think that if France, instead of being governed on the whole by the crowd, were in the power of the mandarins, we should be where we are now? If, instead of having wished to enlighten the lower classes, we had busied ourselves with instructing the higher, we should not have seen M. de Keratry proposing the pillage of the duchy of Baden."

In the great war of our own time with the same foes, our professional advocates of "preparedness," our cheerful chemists, our scientific "intellectuals"—all our materialistic thinkers hardshell and soft-shell,—took the position of Flaubert, just presented; reproached us bitterly for our slack, sentimental pacificism; and urged us with all speed to emulate the scientific spirit of our enemy. There is nothing more instructive in this correspondence than to observe how this last fond illusion falls away from Flaubert under the impact of an experience which demonstrated to his tortured senses the truth of the old Rabelaisian utterance, that "science without conscience is the ruin of the soul."

"What use, pray," he cries in the last disillusion, "is science, since this people abounding in scholars commits abominations worthy of the Huns and worse than theirs, because they are systematic, cold-blooded, voluntary, and have for an excuse, neither passion nor hunger?" And a few months later, he is still in mad anguish of desolation:

> "I had some illusions! What barbarity! What a slump! I am wrathful at my contemporaries for having given me the feelings of a brute of the twelfth century! I'm stifling in gall! These officers who break mirrors with white gloves on, who know Sanskrit, and who fling themselves on the champagne; who steal your watch and then send you their visiting card, this war for money, these civilized savages give me more horror than cannibals. And all the world is going to imitate them, is going to be a soldier! Russia has now four millions of them. All Europe will wear a uniform. If we take our revenge, it will be ferocious in the last degree; and, mark my word, we are going to think only of that, of avenging ourselves on Germany."

Under the imminence of the siege of Paris, Flaubert had drilled men, with an out-flashing of the savage fighting spirit of his ancestors, of which he was more than half ashamed. But at heart he is more dismayed, more demoralized, more thoroughly prostrated than George Sand. He has not fortitude actually to face the degree of depravity which he has always imputed to the human race, the baseness with which his imagination has long been easily and cynically familiar. As if his pessimism had been only a literary pigment, a resource of the studio, he shudders to find Paris painted in his own ebony colors, and his own purely "artistic" hatred of the bourgeois, translated into a principle of action, expressing itself in the horrors of the Commune, with half the population trying to strangle the other half. Hatred, after all, contempt and hatred, are not quite the most felicitous watchwords for the use of human society. Like one whose cruel jest has been taken more seriously than he had intended and has been turned upon his own head, Flaubert considers flight: "I cherish the following dream: of going to live in the sun in a tranquil country." As a substitute for a physical retreat, he buries himself in a study of Buddhism, and so gradually returns to the pride of his intellectual isolation. As the tumult in his senses subsides, he even ventures to offer to George Sand the anodyne of his old philosophical despair: "Why are you so sad? Humanity offers nothing new. Its irremediable misery has filled me with sadness ever since my youth. And in addition I now have no disillusions. I believe that the crowd, the common herd will always be hateful. The only important thing is a little group of minds always the same—which passes the torch from one to another."

There we must leave Flaubert, the thinker. He never passes beyond that point in his vision of reconstruction: a "legitimate aristocracy" established in contempt of the average man—with the Academy of Sciences displacing the Pope.

George Sand, amid these devastating external events, is beginning to feel the insidious siege of years. She can no longer rally her spiritual forces with the "bright speed" that she had in the old days. The fountain of her faith, which has never yet failed of renewal, fills more slowly. For weeks she broods in silence, fearing to augment her friend's dismay with more of her own, fearing to resume a debate in which her cause may be better than her arguments and in which depression of her physical energy may diminish her power to put up a spirited defence before the really indomitable "last ditch" of her position.

When Flaubert himself makes a momentary gesture towards the white flag, and talks of retreat, she seizes the opportunity for a short scornful sally. "Go to live in the sun in a tranquil country! Where? What country is going to be tranquil in this struggle of barbarity against civilization, a struggle which is going to be universal?" A month later she gives him fair warning that she has no intention of acknowledging final defeat: "For me, the ignoble experiment that Paris is attempting or is undergoing, proves nothing against the laws of the eternal progression of men and things, and, if I have gained any principles in my mind, good or bad, they are neither shattered nor changed by it. For a long time I have accepted patience as one accepts the sort of weather there is, the length of winter, old age, lack of success in all its forms." But Flaubert, thinking that he has detected in her public utterances a decisive change of front, privately urges her in a finely figurative passage of a letter which denounces modern republicanism, universal suffrage, compulsory education, and the press—Flaubert urges her to come out openly in renunciation of her faith in humanity and her popular progressivistic doctrines. I must quote a few lines of his attempt at seduction:

> "Ah, dear good master, if you could only hate! That is what you lack, hate. In spite of your great Sphinx eyes, you have seen the world through a golden colour. That comes from the sun in your heart; but so many shadows have risen that now you are not recognizing things any more. Come now! Cry out! Thunder! Take your great lyre and touch the brazen string: the monsters will flee. Bedew us with drops of the blood of wounded Themis."

That summons roused the citadel, but not to surrender, not to betrayal. The eloquent daughter of the people caught up her great lyre—in the public *Reponse a un ami* of October 3, 1871. But her fingers passed lightly over the "brazen string" to pluck again with old power the resonant golden notes. Her reply, with its direct retorts to Flaubert, is not perhaps a very closely reasoned argument. In making the extract I have altered somewhat the order of the sentences:

> "And what, you want me to stop loving? You want me to say that I have been mistaken all my life, that humanity is contemptible, hateful, that it always has been

and always will be so? ... What, then, do you want me to
do, so as to isolate myself from my kind, from my
compatriots, from the great family in whose bosom my own
family is only one ear of corn in the terrestrial field? ... But
it is impossible, and your steady reason puts up with the
most unreasonable of Utopias. In what Eden, in what
fantastic Eldorado will you hide your family, your little
group of friends, your intimate happiness, so that the
lacerations of the social state and the disasters of the
country shall not reach them? ... In vain you are prudent and
withdraw, your refuge will be invaded in its turn, and in
perishing with human civilization you will be no greater a
philosopher for not having loved, than those who threw
themselves into the flood to save some debris of humanity.
... The people, you say! The people is yourself and myself.
It would be useless to deny it. There are not two races....
No, no, people do not isolate themselves, the ties of blood
are not broken, people do not curse or scorn their kind.
Humanity is not a vain word. Our life is composed of love,
and not to love is to cease to live."

This is, if you please, an effusion of sentiment, a chant of
faith. In a world more and more given to judging trees by their
fruits, we should err if we dismissed this sentiment, this faith,
too lightly. Flaubert may have been a better disputant; he had a
talent for writing. George Sand may have chosen her side with a
truer instinct; she had a genius for living. This faith of hers
sustained well the shocks of many long years, and this sentiment
made life sweet.

STUART P. SHERMAN

I. To George Sand 1863

Dear Madam,

I am not grateful to you for having performed what you call a duty. The goodness of your heart has touched me and your sympathy has made me proud. That is the whole of it.

Your letter which I have just received gives added value to your article[1] and goes on still further, and I do not know what to say to you unless it be that *I quite frankly like you.*

It was certainly not I who sent you in September, a little flower in an envelope. But, strange to say, at the same time, I received in the same manner, a leaf of a tree.

As for your very cordial invitation, I am not answering yes or no, in true Norman fashion. Perhaps some day this summer I shall surprise you. For I have a great desire to see you and to talk with you.

It would be very delightful to have your portrait to hang on the wall in my study in the country where I often spend long months entirely alone. Is the request indiscreet? If not, a thousand thanks in advance. Take them with the others which I reiterate.

---

[1] Letter about *Salammbo,* January, 1863, *Questions d'art et de litterature.*

II. TO GUSTAVE FLAUBERT Paris, 15 March, 1864

Dear Flaubert,

I don't know whether you lent me or gave me M. Taine's beautiful book. In the uncertainty I am returning it to you. Here I have had only the time to read a part of it, and at Nohant, I shall have only the time to scribble for Buloz; but when I return, in two months, I shall ask you again for this admirable work of which the scope is so lofty, so noble.

I am sorry not to have said adieu to you; but as I return soon, I hope that you will not have forgotten me and that you will let me read something of your own also.

You were so good and so sympathetic to me at the first performance of Villemer that I no longer admire only your admirable talent, I love you with all my heart.

George Sand

III. To George Sand Paris, 1866

Why of course I am counting on your visit at my own house. As for the hindrances which the fair sex can oppose to it, you will not notice them (be sure of it) any more than did the others. My little stories of the heart or of the senses are not displayed on the counter. But as it is far from my quarter to yours and as you might make a useless trip, when you arrive in Paris, give me a rendezvous. And at that we shall make another to dine informally tête-à-tête.

I sent your affectionate little greeting to Bouilhet.

At the present time I am disheartened by the populace which rushes by under my windows in pursuit of the fatted calf. And they say that intelligence is to be found in the street!

IV. To M. Flobert (Justave) M. of Letters Boulevard du Temple, 42, Paris Paris, 10 May, 1866[2]

M. Flobaire,

You must be a truly dirty oaf to have taken my name and written a letter with it to a lady who had some favors for me which you doubtless received in my place and inherited my hat in place of which I have received yours which you left there. It is the lowness of that lady's conduct and of yours that make me think that she lacks education entirely and all those sentiments which she ought to understand. If you are content to have written Fanie and Salkenpeau I am content not to have read them. You mustn't get excited about that, I saw in the papers that there were outrages against the Religion in whose bosom I have entered again after the troubles I had with that lady when she made me come to my senses and repent of my sins with her and, in consequence if I meet you with her whom I care for no longer you shall have my sword at your throat. That will be the Reparation of my sins and the punishment of your infamy at the same time. That is what I tell you and I salute you.

Coulard

At Palaiseau with the Monks

They told me that I was well punished for associating with the girls from the theatre and with aristocrats.

---

[2] The postage stamp bears the mark Palaiseau 9 May, '66.

V. TO GUSTAVE FLAUBERT 1866

Sir,

After the most scrupulous combined searches I found at last the body of my beloved brother. You are in belles-lettres and you would have been struck by the splendor of that scene. The corpse which was a Brother extended nonchalantly on the edge of a foul ditch. I forgot my sorrow a moment to contemplate he was good this young man whom the matches killed, but the real guilty one was that woman whom passions have separated in this disordered current in which our unhappy country is at the moment when it is more to be pitied than blamed for there are still men who have a heart. You who express yourself so well tell that siren that she has destroyed a great citizen. I don't need to tell you that we count on you to dig his noble tomb. Tell Silvanit also that she can come notwithstanding for education obliges me to offer her a glass of wine. I have the honor to salute you.

I also have the honor to salute Silvanit for whom I am a brother much to be pitied.

Goulard the elder

Have the goodness to transmit to Silvanit the last wishes of my poor Theodore.[3]

---

[3] Letter written by Eugene Lambert.

VI. To GUSTAVE FLAUBERT Palaiseau 14 May, 1866

This is not a letter from Goulard. He is dead! The false Goulard killed him by surpassing him in the real and the comic. But this false Goulard also does not deny himself anything, the rascal!

Dear friend, I must tell you that I want to dedicate to you my novel which is just coming out. But as every one has his own ideas on the subject—as Goulard would say—I would like to know if you permit me to put at the head of my title page simply: to my friend Gustave Flaubert. I have formed the habit of putting my novels under the patronage of a beloved name. I dedicated the last to Fromentin.

I am waiting until it is good weather to ask you to come to dine at Palaiseau with Goulard's Sirenne, and some other Goulards of your kind and of mine. Up to now it has been frightfully cold and it is not worth the trouble to come to the country to catch a cold.

I have finished my novel, and you?

I kiss the two great diamonds which adorn your face.

Jorje Sens

The elder Goulard is my little Lambert, it seems to me that he is quite literary in that way.

VII. To Gustave Flaubert Palaiseau, Wednesday,
16 May, 1866

Well, my dear friend, since you are going away, and as in a fortnight, I am going to Berry for two or three months, do try to find time to come tomorrow Thursday. You will dine with dear and interesting Marguerite Thuillier who is also going away.

Do come to see my hermitage and Sylvester's. By leaving Paris, gare de Sceaux, at I o'clock, you will be at my house at 2 o'clock, or by leaving at 5, you will be there at 6, and in the evening you could leave with my strolling players at 9 or 10. Bring the copy.[4] Put in it all the criticisms which occur to you. That will be very good for me. People ought to do that for each other as Balzac and I used to do. That doesn't make one person alter the other; quite the contrary, for in general, one gets more determined in one's moi, one completes it, explains it better, entirely develops it, and that is why friendship is good, even in literature, where the first condition of any worth is to be one's self.

If you cannot come—I shall have a thousand regrets, but then I am depending upon you Monday before dinner. Au revoir and thank you for the fraternal permission of dedication.

G. Sand

---

[4] This refers to Monsieur Sylveitre, which had just appeared.

VIII. To GEORGE SAND Paris, 17 or 18 May, 1866

Don't expect me at your house on Monday. I am obliged
to go to Versailles on that day. But I shall be at Magny's.
A thousand fond greetings from your
G. Flaubert

IX. To GUSTAVE FLAUBERT Nohant, 31 July, 1866

My good dear comrade,

Will you really be in Paris these next few days as you led me to hope? I leave here the 2nd. What good luck if I found you at dinner on the following Monday. And besides, they are putting on a play[5] by my son and me, on the 10th. Could I possibly get along without you on that day? I shall feel some *emotion* this time because of my dear collaborator. Be a good friend and try to come! I embrace you with all my heart in that hope.

The late Goulard, G. Sand.

---

[5] Les Don Juan de village.

X. TO GUSTAVE FLAUBERT Paris, 4 Aug., 1866

Dear friend, as I'm always out, I don't want you to come and find the door shut and me far away. Come at six o'clock and dine with me and my children whom I expect tomorrow. We dine at Magny's always at 6 o'clock promptly. You will give us 'a sensible pleasure' as used to say, as would have said, alas, the unhappy Goulard. You are an exceedingly kind brother to promise to be at Don Juan. For that I kiss you twice more.

G. Sand

Saturday evening.

XI. To Gustave Flaubert

It is next *Thursday,*
I wrote you last night, and our letters must have crossed.
Yours from the heart,
G. Sand
Sunday, 5 August, 1866.

XII. To Gustave Flaubert
Paris, Wednesday evening, 22 August, 1866

My good comrade and friend, I am going to see Alexandre at Saint-Valery Saturday evening. I shall stay there Sunday and Monday, I shall return Tuesday to Rouen and go to see you. Tell me how that strikes you. I shall spend the day with you if you like, returning to spend the night in Rouen, if I inconvenience you as you are situated, and I shall leave Wednesday morning or evening for Paris. A word in response at once, by telegraph if you think that your answer would not reach me by post before Saturday at 4 o'clock.

I think that I shall be all right but I have a horrid cold. If it grows too bad, I shall telegraph that I cannot stir; but I have hopes, I am already better.

I embrace you.

G. Sand

XIII. To GUSTAVE FLAUBERT
Saint-Valery, 26 August, 1866 Monday, 1 A.M.

Dear friend, I shall be in Rouen on Tuesday at 1 o'clock, I shall plan accordingly. Let me explore Rouen which I don't know, or show it to me if you have the time. I embrace you. Tell your mother how much I appreciate and am touched, by the kind little line which she wrote to me.

G. Sand

XIV. To Gustave Flaubert, at Croissset Paris,
31 August, 1866

First of all, embrace your good mother and your charming niece for me. I am really touched by the kind welcome I received in your clerical setting, where a stray animal of my species is an anomaly that one might find constraining. Instead of that, they received me as if I were one of the family and I saw that all that great politeness came from the heart. Remember me to all the very kind friends. I was truly exceedingly happy with you. And then, you, you are a dear kind boy, big man that you are, and I love you with all my heart. My head is full of Rouen, of monuments and queer houses. All of that seen with you strikes me doubly. But your house, your garden, your *citadel,* it is like a dream and it seems to me that I am still there.

I found Paris very small yesterday, when crossing the bridges.

I want to start back again. I did not see you enough, you and your surroundings; but I must rush off to the children, who are calling and threatening me. I embrace you and I bless you all.

G. Sand

Paris, Friday.

On going home yesterday, I found Couture to whom I said on your behalf that *his* portrait of me was, according to you, the best that anyone had made. He was not a little flattered. I am going to hunt up an especially good copy to send you.

I forgot to get three leaves from the tulip tree, you must send them to me in a letter, it is for something cabalistic.

XV. To Gustave Flaubert Paris, 2 September, 1866

Send me back the lace shawl. My faithful porter will forward it to me wherever I am. I don't know yet. If my children want to go with me into Brittany, I shall go to fetch them, if not I shall go on alone wherever chance leads me. In travelling, I fear only distractions. But I take a good deal on myself and I shall end by improving myself. You write me a good dear letter which I kiss. Don't forget the three leaves from the tulip tree. They are asking me at the Odeon to let them perform a fairy play: *la Nuit de Noel* from the Theatre de Nohant, I don't want to, it's too small a thing. But since they have that idea, why wouldn't they try your fairy play? Do you want me to ask them? I have a notion that this would be the right theatre for a thing of that type. The management, Chilly and Duquesnel, wants to have scenery and *machinery* and yet keep it literary. Let us discuss this when I return here.

You still have the time to write to me. I shall not leave for three days yet. Love to your family.

G. S.

Sunday evening

I forgot! Levy promises to send you my complete works, they are endless. You must stick them on a shelf in a corner and dig into them when your heart prompts you.

XVI. To GUSTAVE FLAUBERT,
at Croissset Nohant, 21 September, 1866

I have just returned from a twelve days trip with my children, and on getting home I find your two letters. That fact, added to the joy of seeing Mademoiselle Aurore again, fresh and pretty, makes me quite happy. And you my Benedictine, you are quite alone in your ravishing monastery, working and never going out? That is what it means *to have already* gone out too much. Monsieur craves Syrias, deserts, dead seas, dangers and fatigues! But nevertheless he can make Bovarys in which every little cranny of life is studied and painted with mastery. What an odd person who can also compose the fight between the Sphinx and the Chimaera! You are a being quite apart, very mysterious, gentle as a lamb with it all. I have had a great desire to question you, but a too great respect for you has prevented me; for I know how to make light only of my own calamities, while those which a great mind has had to undergo so as to be in a condition to produce, seem to me like sacred things which should not be touched roughly nor thoughtlessly.

Sainte-Beuve, who loves you all the same, claims that you are horribly vicious. But perhaps he may see with somewhat unclean eyes, like this learned botanist who asserts that the germander is of *dirty* yellow color. The observation was so false, that I could not refrain from writing on the margin of his book: *It is because you have dirty eyes.*

I suppose that a man of intelligence may have great curiosity.

I have not had it, lacking the courage. I have preferred to leave my mind incomplete, that is my affair, and every one is free to embark either on a great ship in full sail, or on a fisherman's vessel. The artist is an explorer whom nothing ought to stop, and who does neither good nor ill when turning to the right or to the left. His end justifies all.

It is for him to know after a little experience, what are the conditions of his soul's health. As for me, I think that yours is in a good condition of grace, since you love to work and to be alone in spite of the rain.

Do you know that, while there has been a deluge everywhere, we have had, except a few downpours, fine sunshine in Brittany? A horrible wind on the shore, but how beautiful the high surf! and since the botany of the coast carried me away, and Maurice and his wife have a passion for shellfish, we endured it all gaily. But on the whole, Brittany is a famous see-saw.

However, we are a little fed up with dolmens and menhirs and we have fallen on fetes and have seen costumes which they said had been suppressed but which the old people still wear. Well! These men of the past are ugly with their home-spun trousers, their long hair, their jackets with pockets under the arms, their sottish air, half drunkard, half saint. And the Celtic relics, uncontestably curious for the archaeologist, have naught for the artist, they are badly set, badly composed, Carnac and Erdeven have no physiognomy. In short, Brittany shall not have my bones! I prefer a thousand times your rich Normandy, or, in the days when one has dramas in his *head,* a real country of horror and despair. There is nothing in a country where priests rule and where Catholic vandalism has passed, razing monuments of the ancient world and sowing the plagues of the future.

You say *us* a propos of the fairy play. I don't know with whom you have written it, but I still fancy that it ought to succeed at the Odeon under its present management. If I was acquainted with it, I should know how to accomplish for you what one never knows how to do for one's self, namely, to interest the directors. Anything of yours is bound to be too original to be understood by that coarse Dumaine. Do have a copy at your house, and next month I shall spend a day with you in order to have you read it to me. Le Croisset is so near to Palaiseau!—and I am in a phase of tranquil activity, in which I should love to see your great river flow, and to keep dreaming in your orchard, tranquil itself, quite on top of the cliff. But I am joking, and you are working. You must forgive the abnormal intemperance of one who has just been seeing only stones and has not perceived even a pen for twelve days.

You are my first visit to the living on coming out from the complete entombment of my poor Moi. Live! There is my oremus and my benediction and I embrace you with all my heart.

G. Sand

XVII. To George Sand Croisset, 1866

I a mysterious being, dear master, nonsense! I think that I am sickeningly platitudinous, and I am sometimes exceedingly bored with the bourgeois which I have under my skin. Sainte-Beuve, between ourselves, does not know me at all, no matter what he says. I even swear to you (by the smile of your grandchild) that I know few men less vicious than I am. I have dreamed much and have done very little. What deceives the superficial observer is the lack of harmony between my sentiments and my ideas. If you want my confession, I shall make it freely to you. The sense of the grotesque has restrained me from an inclination towards a disorderly life. I maintain that cynicism borders on chastity. We shall have much to say about it to each other (if your heart prompts you) the first time we see each other.

Here is the program that I propose to you. My house will be full and uncomfortable for a month. But towards the end of October or the beginning of November (after Bouilhet's play) nothing will prevent you, I hope, from returning here with me, not for a day, as you say, but for a week at least. You shall have "your little table and everything necessary for writing." Is it agreed?

As for the fairy play, thanks for your kind offers of service. I shall get hold of the thing for you (it was done in collaboration with Bouilhet). But I think it is a trifle weak and I am torn between the desire of gaining a few piasters and the shame of showing such a piece of folly.

I think that you are a little severe towards Brittany, not towards the Bretons who seem to me repulsive animals. A propos of Celtic archaeology, I published in *L'Artiste* in 1858, a rather good hoax on the shaking stones, but I have not the number here and I don't remember the month.

I read, straight through, the 10 volumes of Histoire de ma vie, of which I knew about two thirds but only fragmentarily. What struck me most was the life in the convent. I have a quantity of observations to make to you which occurred to me.

XVIII. To Gustave Flaubert Nohant, 28 September, 1866

It is agreed, dear comrade and good friend. I shall do my best to be in Paris for the performance of your friend's play, and I shall do my fraternal duty there as usual; after which we shall go to your house and I shall stay there a week, but on condition that you will not put yourself out of your room. To be an inconvenience distresses me and I don't need so much bother in order to sleep. I sleep everywhere, in the ashes, or under a kitchen bench, like a stable dog. Everything shines with spotlessness at your house, so one is comfortable everywhere. I shall pick a quarrel with your mother and we shall laugh and joke, you and I, much and more yet. If it's good weather, I shall make you go out walking, if it rains continually, we shall roast our bones before the fire while telling our heart pangs. The great river will run black or grey under the window saying always, *quick! quick!* and carrying away our thoughts, and our days, and our nights, without stopping to notice such small things.

I have packed and sent by *express* a good proof of Couture's picture, signed by the engraver, my poor friend, Manceau. It is the best that I have and I have only just found it. I have sent with it a photograph of a drawing by Marchal which was also like me; but one changes from year to year. Age gives unceasingly another character to the face of people who think and study, that is why their portraits do not look like one another nor like them for long. I dream so much and I live so little, that sometimes I am only three years old. But, the next day I am three hundred, if the dream has been sombre. Isn't it the same with you? Doesn't it seem at moments, that you are beginning life without even knowing what it is, and at other times don't you feel over you the weight of several thousand centuries, of which you have a vague remembrance and a sorrowful impression? Whence do we come and whither do we go? All is possible since all is unknown.

Embrace your beautiful, good mother for me. I shall give myself a treat, being with you two. Now try to find that hoax on the Celtic stones; that would interest me very much. When you saw them, had they opened the galgal of Lockmariaker and cleared away the ground near Plouharnel?

Those people used to write, because there are stones covered with hieroglyphics, and they used to work in gold very well, because very beautifully made torques[6] have been found.

My children, who are, like myself, great admirers of you, send you their compliments, and I kiss your forehead, since Sainte-Beuve lied.

G. Sand

Have you any sun today? Here it is stifling. The country is lovely. When will you come here?

---

[6] Gallic necklaces.

XIX. To GEORGE SAND Croisset, Saturday evening, ... 1866

Good, I have it, that beautiful, dear and famous face! I am going to have a large frame made and hang it on my wall, being able to say, as did M. de Talleyrand to Louis Philippe: "It is the greatest honor that my house has received"; a poor phrase, for we two are worth more than those two amiable men.

Of the two portraits, I like that of Couture's the better. As for Marchal's he saw in you only "the good woman," but I who am an old Romantic, find in the other, "the head of the author" who made me dream so much in my youth.

XX. To GEORGE SAND Croisset, Saturday evening, 1866

Your sending the package of the two portraits made me think that you were in Paris, dear master, and I wrote you a letter which is waiting for you at rue des Feuillantines.

I have not found my article on the dolmens. But I have my manuscript (entire) of my trip in Brittany among my "unpublished works." We shall have to gabble when you are here. Have courage.

I don't experience, as you do, this feeling of a life which is beginning, the stupefaction of a newly commenced existence. It seems to me, on the contrary, that I have always lived! And I possess memories which go back to the Pharaohs. I see myself very clearly at different ages of history, practising different professions and in many sorts of fortune. My present personality is the result of my lost personalities. I have been a boatman on the Nile, a leno in Rome at the time of the Punic wars, then a Greek rhetorician in Subura where I was devoured by insects. I died during the Crusade from having eaten too many grapes on the Syrian shores, I have been a pirate, monk, mountebank and coachman. Perhaps also even emperor of the East?

Many things would be explained if we could know our real genealogy. For, since the elements which make a man are limited, should not the same combinations reproduce themselves? Thus heredity is a just principle which has been badly applied.

There is something in that word as in many others. Each one takes it by one end and no one understands the other. The science of psychology will remain where it lies, that is to say in shadows and folly, as long as it has no exact nomenclature, so long as it is allowed to use the same expression to signify the most diverse ideas. When they confuse categories, adieu, morale!

Don't you really think that since '89 they wander from the point? Instead of continuing along the highroad which was broad and beautiful, like a triumphal way, they stray off by little sidepaths and flounder in mud holes. Perhaps it would be wise for a little while to return to Holbach. Before admiring Proudhon, supposing one knew Turgot? But le Chic, that modern religion, what would become of it!

Opinions chic (or chiques): namely being pro-Catholicism (without believing a word of it) being pro-Slavery, being pro-the House of Austria, wearing mourning for Queen Amelie, admiring Orphee aux Enfers, being occupied with Agricultural Fairs, talking Sport, acting indifferent, being a fool up to the point of regretting the treaties of 1815. That is all that is the very newest.

Oh! You think that because I pass my life trying to make harmonious phrases, in avoiding assonances, that I too have not my little judgments on the things of this world? Alas! Yes! and moreover I shall burst, enraged at not expressing them.

But a truce to joking, I should finally bore you.

The Bouilhet play will open the first part of November. Then in a month we shall see each other.

I embrace you very warmly, dear master.

XXI. To GUSTAVE FLAUBERT,
at Croisset Nohant, Monday evening, 1 October, 1866

Dear friend,

Your letter was forwarded to me from Paris. It isn't lost. I think too much of them to let any be lost. You don't speak to me of the floods, therefore I think that the Seine did not commit any follies at your place and that the tulip tree did not get its roots wet. I feared lest you were anxious and wondered if your bank was high enough to protect you. Here we have nothing of that sort to be afraid of; our streams are very wicked, but we are far from them.

You are happy in having such clear memories of other existences. Much imagination and learning—those are your memories; but if one does not recall anything distinct, one has a very lively feeling of one's own renewal in eternity. I have a very amusing brother who often used to say "at the time when I was a dog. ..." He thought that he had become man very recently. I think that I was vegetable or mineral. I am not always very sure of completely existing, and sometimes I think I feel a great fatigue accumulated from having lived too much. Anyhow, I do not know, and I could not, like you, say, "I possess the past."

But then you believe that one does not really die, since one *lives again?* If you dare to say that to the Smart Set, you have courage and that is good. I have the courage which makes me pass for an imbecile, but I don't risk anything; I am imbecile under so many other counts.

I shall be enchanted to have your written impression of Brittany, I did not see enough to talk about. But I sought a general impression and that has served me for reconstructing one or two pictures which I need. I shall read you that also, but it is still an unformed mass.

Why did your trip remain unpublished? You are very coy. You don't find what you do worth being described. That is a mistake. All that issues from a master is instructive, and one should not fear to show one's sketches and drawings. They are still far above the reader, and so many things are brought down to his level that the poor devil remains common. One ought to love common people more than oneself, are they not the real unfortunates of the world? Isn't it the people without taste and without ideals who get bored, don't enjoy anything and are useless? One has to allow oneself to be abused, laughed at, and misunderstood by them, that is inevitable. But don't abandon them, and always throw them good bread, whether or not they prefer filth; when they are sated with dirt they will eat the bread; but if there is none, they will eat filth in *secula seculorum*.

I have heard you say, "I write for ten or twelve people only." One says in conversation, many things which are the result of the impression of the moment; but you are not alone in saying that. It was the opinion of the Lundi or the thesis of that day. I protested inwardly. The twelve persons for whom you write, who appreciate you, are as good as you are or surpass you. You never had any need of reading the eleven others to be yourself. But, one writes for all the world, for all who need to be initiated; when one is not understood, one is resigned and recommences. When one is understood, one rejoices and continues. There lies the whole secret of our persevering labors and of our love of art. What is art without the hearts and minds on which one pours it? A sun which would not project rays and would give life to no one.

After reflecting on it, isn't that your opinion? If you are convinced of that, you will never know disgust and lassitude, and if the present is sterile and ungrateful, if one loses all influence, all hold on the public, even in serving it to the best of one's ability, there yet remains recourse to the future, which supports courage and effaces all the wounds of pride. A hundred times in life, the good that one does seems not to serve any immediate use; but it keeps up just the same the tradition of wishing well and doing well, without which all would perish.

Is it only since '89 that people have been floundering? Didn't they have to flounder in order to arrive at '48 when they floundered much more, but so as to arrive at what should be? You must tell me how you mean that and I will read Turgot to please you. I don't promise to go as far as Holbach, *although he has some good points, the ruffian!*

Summon me at the time of Bouilhet's play. I shall be here, working hard, but ready to run, and loving you with all my heart. Now that I am no longer a woman, if the good God was just, I should become a man; I should have the physical strength and would say to you: "Come let's go to Carthage or elsewhere." But there, one who has neither sex nor strength, progresses towards childhood, and it is quite otherwhere that one is renewed; *where?* I shall know that before you do, and, if I can, I shall come back in a dream to tell you.

XXII. To GUSTAVE FLAUBERT Nohant, 19 October

Dear friend, they write me from the Odeon that Bouilhet's play is on the 27th. I must be in Paris the 26th. Business calls me in any event. I shall dine at Magny's on that day, and the next, and the day after that. Now you know where to find me, for I think that you will come for the first performance. Yours always, with a full heart,

G. Sand

XXIII. To Gustave Flaubert Nohant, 23 October, 1866

Dear friend, since the play is on the 29th I shall give two more days to my children and I leave here the 28th. You have not told me if you will dine with me and your friend on the 29th informally, at Magny's at whatever hour you wish. Let me find a line at 97 rue des Feuillantines, on the 28th.

Then we shall go to your house, the day you wish. My chief talk with you will be to listen to you and to love you with all my heart. I shall bring what I have *"on the stocks."* That will *give me courage,* as they say here, to read to you my *embryo*. If I could only carry the sun from Nohant. It is glorious.

I embrace and bless you.

G. Sand

XXIV. To GUSTAVE FLAUBERT Paris, 10 November, 1866

On reaching Paris I learn sad news. Last evening, while we were talking—and I think that we spoke of him day before yesterday—my friend Charles Duveyrier died, a most tender heart and a most naive spirit. He is to be buried tomorrow. He was one year older than I am. My generation is passing bit by bit. Shall I survive it? I don't ardently desire to, above all on these days of mourning and farewell. It is as God wills, provided He lets me always love in this world and in the next.

I keep a lively affection for the dead. But one loves the living differently. I give you the part of my heart that he had. That joined to what you have already, makes a large share. It seems to me that it consoles me to make that gift to you. From a literary point of view he was not a man of the first rank, one loved him for his goodness and spontaneity. Less occupied with affairs and philosophy, he would have had a charming talent. He left a pretty play, Michel Perrin.

I travelled half the way alone, thinking of you and your mother at Croisset and looking at the Seine, which thanks to you has become a friendly *goddess*. After that I had the society of an individual with two women, as ordinary, all of them, as the music at the pantomime the other day. Example: "I looked, the sun left an impression like two points in my eyes." *Husband:* "That is called luminous points," and so on for an hour without stopping.

I shall do all sorts of errands for the house, for I belong to it, do I not? I am going to sleep, quite worn out; I wept unrestrainedly all the evening, and I embrace you so much the more, dear friend. Love me *more* than before, because I am sad.

G. Sand

Have you a friend among the Rouen magistrates? If you have, write him a line to watch for the *name* Amedee Despruneaux. It is a civil case which will come up at Rouen in a few days. Tell him that this Despruneaux is the most honest man in the world; you can answer for him as for me. In doing this, if the thing is feasible, you will do me a personal favor. I will do the same for any friend of yours.

XXV. To GUSTAVE FLAUBERT 11 November, 1866

I send you my friend Despruneaux in person. If you know a judge or two,—or if your brother could give him a word of support, do arrange it, I kiss you three times on each eye.
G. Sand
Five minutes' interview and that's all the inconvenience.
Paris, Sunday

XXVI. To George Sand Monday night

You are sad, poor friend and dear master; it was you of whom I thought on learning of Duveyrier's death. Since you loved him, I am sorry for you. That loss is added to others. How we keep these dead souls in our hearts. Each one of us carries within himself his necropolis.

I am entirely *undone* since your departure; it seems to me as if I had not seen you for ten years. My one subject of conversation with my mother is you, everyone here loves you. Under what star were you born, pray, to unite in your person such diverse qualities, so numerous and so rare?

I don't know what sort of feeling I have for you, but I have a particular tenderness for you, and one I have never felt for anyone, up to now. We understood each other, didn't we, that was good.

I especially missed you last evening at ten o'clock. There was a fire at my wood-seller's. The sky was rose color and the Seine the color of gooseberry syrup. I worked at the engine for three hours and I came home as worn out as the Turk with the giraffe.

A newspaper in Rouen, *le Nouvelliste,* told of your visit to Rouen, so that Saturday after leaving you I met several bourgeois indignant at me for not exhibiting you. The best thing was said to me by a former sub-prefect: "Ah! if we had known that she was here ... we would have ... we would have ..." he hunted five minutes for the word; "we would have smiled for her." That would have been very little, would it not?

To "love you more" is hard for me—but I embrace you tenderly. Your letter of this morning, so melancholy, reached the *bottom* of my heart. We separated at the moment when many things were on the point of coming to our lips. All the doors between us two are not yet open. You inspire me with a great respect and I do not dare to question you.

XXVII. To GUSTAVE FLAUBERT, at Croisset Paris,
13 November, 1866. Night from Tuesday to Wednesday.

I have not yet read my play. I have still something to do over. Nothing pressing. Bouilhet's play goes admirably well, and they told me that my little friend Cadol's[7] play would come next. And, for nothing in the world, do I want to step on the body of that child. That puts me quite a distance off and does not annoy me—*nor injure me at all*. What style! Luckily I am not writing for Buloz.

I saw your friend last evening in the foyer at the Odeon. I shook hands with him. He had a happy look. And then I talked with Duquesnel about the fairy play. He wants very much to know it. You have only to present yourself when ever you wish to busy yourself with it. You will be received with open arms.

Mario Proth will give me tomorrow or next day the exact date on the transformation of the journal. Tomorrow I shall go out and buy your dear mother's shoes. Next week I am going to Palaiseau and I shall hunt up my book on faience. If I forget anything, remind me of it.

I have been ill for two days. I am cured. Your letter does my heart good. I shall answer all the questions quite nicely, as you have answered mine. One is happy, don't you think so, to be able to relate one's whole life? It is much less complicated than the bourgeois think, and the mysteries that one can reveal to a friend are always the contrary of what indifferent ones suppose.

---

[7] Edward Cadol, a dramatic author and a friend of Maurice Sand.

I was very happy that week with you: no care, a good nesting-place a lovely country, affectionate hearts and your beautiful and frank face which has a somewhat paternal air. Age has nothing to do with it. One feels in you the protection of infinite goodness, and one evening when you called your mother *"my daughter,"* two tears came in my eyes. It was hard to go away, but I hindered your work, and then,—and then,—a malady of my old age is, not being able to keep still. I am afraid of getting too attached and of wearying others. The old ought to be extremely discreet. From a distance I can tell you how much I love you without the fear of repetition. You are one of the *rare beings* remaining impressionable, sincere, loving art, not corrupted by ambition, not drunk with success. In short you will always be twenty-five years of age because of all sorts of ideas which have become old-fashioned according to the senile young men of today. With them, I think it is decidedly a pose, but it is so stupid! If it is a weakness, it is still worse. They are *men of letters* and not *men*. Good luck to the novel! It is exquisite; but oddly enough there is one entire side of you which does not betray itself in what you do, something that you probably are ignorant of. That will come later, I am sure of it.

I embrace you tenderly, and your mother too, and the charming niece![8] Ah! I forgot, I saw Couture this evening; he told me that in order to be nice to you, he would make your portrait in crayon like mine for whatever price you wish to arrange. You see I am a good commissioner, use me.

---

[8] Madame Caroline Commanville.

XXVIII. To Gustave Flaubert 16 November, 1866

Thanks, dear friend of my heart, for all the trouble that I gave you with my Berrichon Despruneaux. They are friends from the old country, a whole adorable family of fine people, fathers, children, wives, nephews, all in the close circle at Nohant. He must have been *moved* at seeing you. He looked forward to it, all personal interest aside. And I who am not practical, forgot to tell you that the judgment would not be given for a fortnight. That in consequence any preceding within the next two weeks would be extremely useful. If he gains his suit relative to the constructions at Yport, he will settle there and I shall realize the plan formed long since of going every year to his house; he has a delicious wife and they have loved me a long time. You then are threatened with seeing me often scratching at your gate in passing, giving you a kiss on the forehead, crying courage for your labor and running on. I am still awaiting our information on the journal. It seems that it is a little difficult to be exact for '42. I have asked for the most scrupulous exactitude.

For two days I have been taking out to walk my Cascaret,[9] the little engineer of whom I told you. He has become very good looking, the ladies lift their lorgnons at him, and it depends only on him to attain the dignity of a negro "giraffier," but he loves, he is engaged, he has four years to wait, to work to make himself a position, and he has made a vow. You would tell him that he is stupid, I preach to him, on the contrary, my old troubadour doctrine.

---

[9] Francis Laur.

Morality aside, I don't think that the children of this day have sufficient force to manage at the same time, science and dissipation, cocottes and engagements. The proof is that nothing comes from young Bohemia any longer. Good night, friend, work well, sleep well. Walk a little for the love of God and of me. Tell your judges who promised me a smile, to smile on my Berrichon.

XXIX. To Gustave Flaubert 16 November, 1866

Don't take any further steps. Contrary to all anticipations, Despruneaux has gained his suit during the session.

Whether you have done it or not, he is none the less grateful about it and charges me to thank you with all his good and honest heart.

Bouilhet goes from better to better. I have just seen the directors who are delighted.

I love you and embrace you.

Think sometimes of your old troubadour. Friday

G. Sand

XXX. TO GUSTAVE FLAUBERT 18 November (?), 1866

I think that I shall give you pleasure and joy when I tell you that La Conjuration d'Ambroise, thus says my porter, is announced as a real money-maker. There was a line this evening as at Villemer, and Magny which is also a barometer, shows fair weather.

So be content, if that keeps up, Bouilhet is a success. Sunday

G. S.

XXXI. To Gustave Flaubert Palaiseau, 22 November, 1866

I think that it will bring me luck to say good evening to my dear comrade before starting to work.

I am *quite alone* in my little house. The gardener and his family live in the pavilion in the garden and we are the last house at the end of the village, quite isolated in the country, which is a ravishing oasis. Fields, woods, appletrees as in Normandy; not a great river with its steam whistles and infernal chain; a little stream which runs silently under the willows; a silence ... ah! it seems to me that I am in the depths of the virgin forest: nothing speaks except the little jet of the spring which ceaselessly piles up diamonds in the moonlight. The flies sleeping in the corners of my room, awaken at the warmth of my fire. They had installed themselves there to die, they come near the lamp, they are seized with a mad gaiety, they buzz, they jump, they laugh, they even have faint inclinations towards love, but it is the hour of death and paf! in the midst of the dance, they fall stiff. It is over, farewell to dancing!

I am sad here just the same. This absolute solitude, which has always been vacation and recreation for me, is shared now by a dead soul[10] who has ended here, like a lamp which is going out, yet which is here still. I do not consider him unhappy in the region where he is dwelling; but the image that he has left near me, which is nothing more than a reflection, seems to complain because of being unable to speak to me any more.

---

[10] Alexandre Manceau, the engraver, a friend of Maurice Sand.

Never mind! Sadness is not unhealthy. It prevents us from drying up. And you dear friend, what are you doing at this hour? Grubbing also, alone also; for your mother must be in Rouen. Tonight must be beautiful down there too. Do you sometimes think of the "old troubadour of the Inn clock, who still sings and will continue to sing perfect love?" Well! yes, to be sure! You do not believe in chastity, sir, that's your affair. But as for me, I say that *she has some good points, the jade!*

And with this, I embrace you with all my heart, and I am going to, if I can, make people talk who love each other in the old way.

You don't have to write to me when you don't feel like it. No real friendship without *absolute* liberty.

In Paris next week, and then again to Palaiseau, and after that to Nohant. I saw Bouilhet at the Monday performance. I am *crazy* about it. But some of us will applaud at Magny's. I had a cold sweat there, I who am so steady, and I saw everything quite blue.

XXXII. To GEORGE SAND Croisset, Tuesday

You are alone and sad down there, I am the same here.

Whence come these attacks of melancholy that overwhelm one at times? They rise like a tide, one feels drowned, one has to flee. I lie prostrate. I do nothing and the tide passes.

My novel is going very badly for the moment. That fact added to the deaths of which I have heard; of Cormenin (a friend of twenty-five years' standing), of Gavarni, and then all the rest, but that will pass. You don't know what it is to stay a whole day with your head in your hands trying to squeeze your unfortunate brain so as to find a word. Ideas come very easily with you, incessantly, like a stream. With me it is a tiny thread of water. Hard labor at art is necessary for me before obtaining a waterfall. Ah! I certainly know *the agonies of style.*

In short I pass my life in wearing away my heart and brain, that is the real *truth* about your friend.

You ask him if he sometimes thinks of his "old troubadour of the clock," most certainly! and he mourns for him. Our nocturnal talks were very precious (there were moments when I restrained myself in order not to *kiss* you like a big child).

Your ears ought to have burned last night. I dined at my brother's with all his family. There was hardly any conversation except about you, and every one sang your praises, unless perhaps myself, I slandered you as much as possible, dearly beloved master.

I have reread, a propos of your last letter (and by a very natural connection of ideas), that chapter of father Montaigne's entitled "some lines from Virgil." What he said of chastity is precisely what I believe. It is the effort that is fine and not the abstinence in itself. Otherwise shouldn't one curse the flesh like the Catholics? God knows whither that would lead. Now at the risk of repetition and of being a Prudhomme, I insist that your young man is wrong.[11] If he is temperate at twenty years old, he will be a cowardly roue at fifty. Everything has its compensations. The great natures which are good, are above everything generous and don't begrudge the giving of themselves. One must laugh and weep, love, work, enjoy and suffer, in short vibrate as much as possible in all his being.

That is, I think, the real human existence.

---

[11] Refers to Francis Laur.

XXXIII. To GUSTAVE FLAUBERT, at Croisset Palaiseau,
29 November, 1866

One need not be spiritualist nor materialist, you say, but one should be a naturalist. That is a great question.

My Cascaret, that is what I call the little engineer, will decide it as he thinks best. He is not stupid and he will have many ideas, deductions and emotions before realizing the prophecy that you make. I do not catechise him without reserve, for he is stronger than I am on many points, and it is not Catholic spiritualism that stifles him. But the question by itself is very serious, and hovers above our art, above us troubadours, more or less clock-bearing or clockshaped.

Treat it in an entirely impersonal way; for what is good for one might be quite the reverse for another. Let us ask ourselves in making an abstract of our tendencies or of our experiences, if the human being can receive and seek its own full physical development without intellectual suffering. Yes, in an ideal and rational society that would be so. But, in that in which we live and with which we must be content, do not enjoyment and excess go hand in hand, and can one separate them or limit them, unless one is a sage of the first class? And if one is a sage, farewell temptation which is the father of real joys.

The question for us artists, is to know if abstinence strengthens us or if it exalts us too much, which state would degenerate into weakness,—You will say, "There is time for everything and power enough for every dissipation of strength." Then you make a distinction and you place limits, there is no way of doing otherwise. Nature, you think, places them herself and prevents us from abusing her. Ah! but no, she is not wiser than we who are also nature.

Our excesses of work, as our excesses of pleasure, kill us certainly, and the more we are great natures, the more we pass beyond bounds and extend the limits of our powers.

No, I have no theories. I spend my life in asking questions and in hearing them answered in one way or another without any victoriously conclusive reply ever being given me. I await the brilliance of a new state of my intellect and of my organs in a new life; for, in this one, whosoever reflects, embraces up to their last consequences, the limits of pro and con. It is Monsieur Plato, I think, who asked for and thought he held the bond. He had it no more than we. However, this bond exists, since the universe subsists without the pro and con, which constitute it, reciprocally destroying each other. What shall one call it in material nature? *Equilibrium,* that will do, and for spiritual nature? *Moderation,* relative chastity, abstinence from excess, whatever you want, but that is translated by *equilibrium;* am I wrong, my master?

Consider it, for in our novels, what our characters do or do not do, rests only on that. Will they or will they not possess the object of their ardent desires? Whether it is love or glory, fortune or pleasure, ever since they existed, they have aspired to one end. If we have a philosophy in us, they walk right according to us; if we have not, they walk by chance, and are too much dominated by the events which we put in the way of their legs. Imbued by our own ideas and ruled by fatality, they do not always appear logical. Should we put much or little of ourselves in them? Shouldn't we put what society puts in each one of us?

For my part, I follow my old inclination, I put myself in the skin of my good people. People scold me for it, that makes no difference. You, I don't really know if by method or by instinct, take another course. What you do, you succeed in; that is why I ask you if we differ on the question of internal struggles, if the hero ought to have any or if he ought not to know them.

You always astonish me with your painstaking work; is it a coquetry? It does not seem labored. What I find difficult is to choose out of the thousand combinations of scenic action which can vary infinitely, the clear and striking situation which is not brutal nor forced. As for style, I attach less importance to it than you do.

The wind plays my old harp as it lists. It has its *high notes,* its *low notes*, its heavy notes—and its faltering notes, in the end it is all the same to me provided the emotion comes, but I can find nothing in myself. It is *the other* who sings as he likes, well or ill, and when I try to think about it, I am afraid and tell myself that I am nothing, nothing at all. But a great wisdom saves us; we know how to say to ourselves, "Well, even if we are absolutely nothing but instruments, it is still a charming state and like no other, this feeling oneself vibrate."

Now, let the wind blow a little over your strings. I think that you take more trouble than you need, and that you ought to let *the other* do it oftener. That would go just as well and with less fatigue.

The instrument might sound weak at certain moments, but the breeze in continuing would increase its strength. You would do afterwards what I don't do, what I should do. You would raise the tone of the whole picture and would cut out what is too uniformly in the light.

Vale et me ama.

XXXIV. TO GEORGE SAND Saturday morning

Don't bother yourself about the information relative to the journals. That will occupy little space in my book and I have time to wait. But when you have nothing else to do, jot down on paper whatever you can recall of '48. Then you can develop it in talking. I don't ask you for copy of course, but to collect a little of your personal memories.

Do you know an actress at the Odeon who plays Macduff in Macbeth? Dugueret? She would like to have the role of Nathalie in Mont-reveche. She will be recommended to you by Girardin, Dumas and me. I saw her yesterday in Faustine, in which she showed talent. My opinion is that she has intelligence and that one could profit by her.

If your little engineer has made a *vow,* and if that vow does not cost him anything, he is right to keep it; if not, it is pure folly, between you and me. Where should liberty exist if not in passion?

Well! no, *in my day* we didn't take such vows and we loved! and swaggeringly. But all participated in a great eclecticism and when one strayed *from ladies* it was from pride, in defiance of one's self, and for effect. In short, we were Red Romantics, perfectly ridiculous to be sure, but in full bloom. The little good which remains to me comes from that epoch.

XXXV. To GUSTAVE FLAUBERT Palaiseau, 30 November, 1866

There would be a good deal to say on all that, my comrade. My Cascaret, that is to say, the fiance in question, keeps himself for his fiancee. She said to him, "Let us wait till you have accomplished certain definite work," and he works. She said to him, "Let us keep ourselves pure for each other," and he keeps himself pure. It is not that he is choked by Catholic spiritualism; but he has a high ideal of love, and why counsel him to go and lose it when his conscience and his honor depend on keeping it?

There is an equilibrium which Nature, our ruler, herself puts in our instincts, and she sets the limit to our appetites. Great natures are not the most robust. We are not developed in all our senses by a very logical education. We are compressed in every way, and we thrust out our roots and branches when and how we can. Great artists are often weak also, and many are impotent. Some too strong in desire are quickly exhausted. In general I think that we have too intense joys and sorrows, we who work with our brains. The laborer who works his land and his wife hard by day and night is not a forceful nature. His brain is very feeble. You say to develop one's self in every direction? Come, not all at the same time, not without rest.

Those who brag of that, are bluffing a bit, or *if they do* everything, do everything ill. If love for them is a little bread-and-butter and art a little pot-boiler, all right; but if their pleasure is great, verging on the infinite, and their work eager, verging on enthusiasm, they do not alternate these as in sleeping and waking.

As for me, I don't believe in these Don Juans who are Byrons at the same time. Don Juan did not make poems and Byron made, so they say, very poor love. He must have had sometimes—one can count such emotions in one's life—a complete ecstasy of heart, mind and senses. He knew enough about them to be one of the poets of love. Nothing else is necessary for the instrument of our vibration. The continual wind of little appetites breaks them.

Try some day to write a novel in which the artist (the real artist) is the hero, you will see what great, but delicate and restrained, vigor is in it, how he will see everything with an attentive eye, curious and tranquil, and how his infatuations with the things he examines and delves into, will be rare and serious. You will see also how he fears himself, how he knows that he cannot surrender himself without exhaustion, and how a profound modesty in regard to the treasures of his soul prevents him from scattering and wasting them.

The artist is such a fine type to do, that I have never dared really to do him. I do not consider myself worthy to touch that beautiful and very complicated figure; that is aiming too high for a mere woman. But if it could certainly tempt you some day, it would be worth while.

Where is the model? I don't know, I have never *really* known any one who did not show some spot in the sunlight, I mean some side where the artist verged on the Philistine. Perhaps you have not that spot; you ought to paint yourself. As for me I have it. I love classifications, I verge on the pedagogue. I love to sew and to care for children, I verge on the servant. I am easily distracted and verge on the idiot. And then I should not like perfection; I feel it but I shouldn't know how to show it.

But one could give him some faults in his nature. What ones? We shall hunt for them some day. That is not really what you are working on now and I ought not to distract you from it.

Be less cruel to yourself. Go ahead and when the afflatus shall have produced everything you must elevate the general tone and cut out what ought not to come down front stage. Can't that be done? It seems to me that it can. What you do appears so easy, so abundant! It is a perpetual overflow, I do not understand your anguish. Good night, dear brother, my love to all yours. I have returned to my solitude at Palaiseau, I love it. I leave it for Paris, Monday. I embrace you warmly. Good luck to your work.

    G. Sand

XXXVI. Monsieur Gustave Flobert at Croisset, Rouen[12]

Sir the noise that you make in literature by your distinguished talent I also made in my day in the manner that my means permitted me I began in 1804 under the auspices of the celebrated Madame Saqui and bore off palms and left memories in the annals of the tight-rope and coregrafie balancer in all countries where I have been there appreciated by generals and other officers of the Empire by whom I have been solicited up to an advanced age so that wives of prefects and ministers could not have been complimented about it I have read your distinguished works notably Madame Bovarie of which I think I am capable of being a model to you when she breaks the chains of her feet to go where her heart calls her. I am well preserved for my advanced age and if you have a repugnance for an artist in misfortune, I should be content with your ideal sentiments. You can then count on my heart not being able to dispose of my person being married to a man of light character who squandered my wax cabinet wherein were all figures of celebrities, kings, emperors, ancient and modern and celebrated crimes, which if I had had your permission about it you would have been placed in the number I had then a place in the railroad substation to have charge of the cabinets which the jealousy of my rival made me lose, it is in these sentiments that I write you if you deign to write the history of my unhappy life you alone would be worthy of it and would see in it things of which you would be worthy of appreciating I shall present myself at your house in Rouen

---

[12] The postage stamp bears the mark, Paris, 4, December, 1866.

whose address I had from M. Bouilhet who knows me well having come to see me in his youth he will tell you that I have the phthisic still agreeably and always faithful to all who knew me whether in the civil or in the military and in these sentiments for life your affectionate

Victoire Potelet,

called Marengo Lirondelle widow Dodin Rue Lanion, 47, Belleville.

XXXVII. To George Sand Wednesday night,
5th December, 1866

Oh! how lovely the letter of Marengo the Swallow is! Seriously, I think it a masterpiece, not a word which is not a word of genius. I have laughed aloud many times. I thank you very dear master, you are as good as can be.

You never tell me what you are doing. How far has the play gone?

I am not at all surprised that you don't understand my literary agonies. I don't understand them myself. But they exist nevertheless, and violent ones.

I don't in the least know how to set to work to write, and I begin by expressing only the hundredth part of my ideas after infinite gropings. Not one who seizes the first impulse, your friend, no! not at all! Thus for entire days I have polished and re-polished a paragraph without accomplishing anything. I feel like weeping at times. You ought to pity me!

As for our subject under discussion (a propos of your young man), what you write me in your last letter is so my way of thinking, that I have not only practised it but preached it. Ask Theo. However, let us understand one another. Artists (who are priests) risk nothing in being chaste; on the contrary. But the bourgeois, what is the use in it for them? Of course there must be certain ones among humanity who stick to chastity. Happy indeed those who don't depart from it.

I don't agree with you that there is anything worth while to be done with the character of the *ideal artist;* he would be a monster. Art is not made to paint the exceptions, and I feel an unconquerable repugnance to putting on paper something from out of my heart. I even think that a novelist *hasn't the right to express his opinion* on any subject whatsoever. Has the good God ever uttered it, his opinion? That is why there are not a few things that choke me which I should like to spit out, but which I swallow. Why say them, in fact! The first comer is more interesting than Monsieur Gustave Flaubert, because he is more *general* and therefore more typical.

Nevertheless, there are days when I consider myself below imbecility. I have still a globe of goldfish and that amuses me. They keep me company while I dine. Is it stupid to be interested in such simple things? Adieu, it is late, I have an aching head.

I embrace you.

XXXVIII. To GUSTAVE FLAUBERT, at Paris December, 1866

"Not put one's heart into what one writes?" I don't understand at all, oh! not at all! As for me, I think that one cannot put anything else into it. Can one separate one's mind from one's heart? Is it something different? Can sensation itself limit itself? Can existence divide itself? In short, not to give oneself entirely to one's work, seems to me as impossible as to weep with something else than one's eyes, and to think with something else than one's brain.

What was it you meant? You must tell me when you have the time.

XXXIX. To GUSTAVE FLAUBERT Paris, 8 December, 1866

You ask me what I am doing? Your old troubadour is content this evening. He has passed the night in re-doing a second act which did not go properly and which has turned out well, so well that my directors are delighted, and I have good hopes of making the end effective—it does not please me yet, but one must pull it through. In short, I have nothing to tell you about myself which is very interesting. When one has the patience of an ox and the wrist broken from crushing stones well or badly, one has scarcely any unexpected events or emotions to recount. My poor Manceau called me the *road-mender,* and there is nothing less poetic than those beings.

And you, dear friend, are you experiencing the anguish and labors of childbirth? That is splendid and youthful. Those who want them don't always get them!

When my daughter-in-law brings into the world dear little children, I abandon myself to such labor in holding her in my arms that it reacts on me, and when the infant arrives, I am sicker than she is, and even seriously so. I think that your pains now react on me, and I have a headache on account of them. But alas! I cannot assist at any birth and I almost regret the time when one believed it hastened deliverances to burn candles before an image.

I see that that rascal Bouilhet has betrayed me; he promised me to copy the Marengo letter in a feigned hand to see if you would be taken in by it. People have written to me seriously things like that. How good and kind your great friend is. He is adored at the Odeon, and this evening they told me that his play was going better and better. I went to hear it again two or three days ago and I was even more delighted with it than the first time.

Well, well, let's keep up our heart, whatever happens, and when you go to rest remember that someone loves you. Affectionate regards to your mother, brother and niece.

G. Sand

XL. To GEORGE SAND Croisset, Saturday night

I have seen Citizen Bouilhet, who had a real ovation in his own country. His compatriots who had absolutely ignored him up to then, from the moment that Paris applauded him, screamed with enthusiasm.—He will return here Saturday next, for a banquet that they are giving him,—80 covers, at least.

As for Marengo the Swallow, he kept your secret so well, that he read the letter in question with an astonishment which duped me.

Poor Marengo! she is a figure! and one that you ought to put in a book. I wonder what her memoirs would be, written in that style?—Mine (my style) continues to give me no small annoyance. I hope, however, in a month, to have crossed the most barren tract. But at the moment I am lost in a desert; well, by the grace of God, so much the worse for me! How gladly I shall abandon this sort of thing, never to return to it to my dying day! Depicting the modern French bourgeois is a stench in my nostrils! And then won't it be time perhaps to enjoy oneself a bit in life, and to choose subjects pleasant to the author?

I expressed myself badly when I said to you that "one should not write from the heart." I meant to say: not put one's personality into the picture. I think that great art is scientific and impersonal. One should, by an effort of mind, put oneself into one's characters and not create them after oneself. That is the method at least; a method which amounts to this: try to have a great deal of talent and even of genius if you can. How vain are all the poetic theories and criticisms!—and the nerve of the gentlemen who compose them sickens me. Oh! nothing restrains them, those boneheads!

Have you noticed that there is sometimes in the air a current of common ideas? For instance, I have just read my friend Du Camp's new novel: Forces Perdues. It is very like what I am doing, in many ways. His book is very naive and gives an accurate idea of the men of our generation having become real fossils to the young men of today. The reaction of '48 opened a deep chasm between the two Frances.

Bouilhet told me that you had been seriously ill at one of the recent Magny's, although you do pretend to be a "woman of wood." Oh! no you are not of wood, dear good great heart! "Beloved old troubadour," would it not perhaps be opportune to rehabilitate him at the Theatre Almanzor? I can see him with his toque and his guitar and his apricot tunic howling at the black-gowned students from the top of a rock. The talk would be fine. Now, good night; I kiss you on both cheeks tenderly.

XLI. To Gustave Flaubert Paris, 7 December, 1866

Something like a week ago someone came to my house in the morning to ask me the address of the bootmaker, my maid did not want to awaken me, and it was not until noon that I read the letter; the bearer said he came from the Hotel Helder on the rue Helder. I answered at once that Simonin lived at 15 rue Richelieu, I wrote to your mother thinking that it was she who wrote to me. I see that she did not receive my note and I don't understand about it, but it is not my fault.

Your old Troubadour is sick as a dog again today, but it will not prevent him from going to Magny's this evening. He could not die in better company; although he would prefer the edge of a ditch in the spring.

Everything else goes well and I leave for Nohant on Saturday.

I am trying hard to push the entomological work which Maurice is publishing. It is very fine.

I am doing for him what I have never done for myself. I am writing to the newspaper men.

I shall recommend Mademoiselle Bosquet to whom I can, but that appeals to another public, and I don't stand in as well with the literary men as I do with the scholars. But certainly Marengo the Swallow *must be done* and the apricot troubadour also. All that was of the Cadios of the revolution who began to be or who wanted to be something, no matter what. I am of the last comers and you others born of us, you are between the illusions of my time and the crude deception of the new times. It is quite natural that Du Camp should go parallel with you in a series of observations and ideas, that does not mean anything. There will be no resemblance.

Oh no! I have not found a title for you, it is too serious, and then I should need to know everything. In any case I am no good today to do anything except to draw up my epitaph. Et in Arcadia ego, you know, I love you, dear friend brother, and bless you with all my heart.

G. Sand Monday.

XLII. To GUSTAVE FLAUBERT, at Croissset Paris,
9 January, 1867

Dear comrade,

Your old troubadour has been tempted to bite the dust.
He is still in Paris. He should have left the 25th of December; his
trunk was strapped; your first letter was awaiting him every day
at Nohant. At last he is all ready to leave and he goes tomorrow
with his son Alexandre[13] who is anxious to accompany him.

It is stupid to be laid on one's back and to lose
consciousness for three days and to get up as enfeebled as if one
had done something painful and useful. It was nothing after all,
except temporary impossibility of digesting anything whatever.
Cold, or weakness, or work, I don't know. I don't think of it any
longer. Sainte-Beuve is much more disquieting, somebody have
written you about it. He is better also, but there will be serious
trouble, and on account of that, accidents to look out for. I am
very saddened and anxious about it.

I have not worked for two weeks; so my task has not
progressed very much, and as I don't know if I am going to be in
shape very soon, I have given the Odeon *a vacation*. They will
take me when I am ready. I think of going a little to the south
when I have seen my children. The plants of the coast are
running through my head. I am prodigiously uninterested in
anything which is not my little ideal of peaceful work, country
life, and of tender and pure friendship. I really think that I am

---

[13] Alexandre Dumas fils.

not going to live a long time, although I am quite cured and well. I get this warning from the great calm, *continually calmer,* which exists in my formerly agitated soul. My brain only works from synthesis to analysis, and formerly it was the contrary. Now, what presents itself to my eyes when I awaken is the planet; I have considerable trouble in finding again there the *moi* which interested me formerly, and which I begin to' call *you* in the plural. It is charming, the planet, very interesting, very curious but rather backward, and as yet somewhat unpractical; I hope to pass into an oasis with better highways and possible to all. One needs so much money and resources in order to travel here! and the time lost in order to procure. these necessaries is lost to study and to contemplation. It seems to me that there is due me something less complicated, less civilized, more naturally luxurious, and more easily good than this feverish halting-place. Will you come into the land, of my dreams, if I succeed in finding the road? Ah! who can know?

And the novel, is it getting on? Your courage has not declined? Solitude does not weigh on you? I really think that it is not absolute, and that somewhere there is a sweetheart who comes and goes, or who lives near there. But there is something of the anchorite in your life just the same, and if envy your situation. As for me, I am too alone at Palaiseau, with a dead soul; not alone enough at Nohant, with the children whom I love too much to belong to myself,—and at Paris, one does not know what one is, one forgets oneself entirely for a thousand things which are not worth any more than oneself. I embrace you with all my heart, dear friend; remember me to your mother, to your dear family, and write me at Nohant, that will do me good.

The cheeses? I don't know at all, it seems to me that they spoke to me of them, but I don't remember at all. I will tell you that from down there.

XLIII. To GEORGE SAND Croisset, Saturday night

No, dear master, you are not near your end. So much the worse for you perhaps. But you will live to be old, very old, as giants live, since you are of that race: only you *must* rest. One thing astonishes me and that is that you have not died twenty times over, having thought so much, written so much and suffered so much. Do go then, since you have the desire, to the Mediterranean. Its azure sky quiets and invigorates. There are the Countries of Youth, such as the Bay of Naples. Do they make one sadder sometimes? I do not know.

Life is not easy! What a complicated and extravagant affair! I know something about that. One must have money for everything! So that with a modest revenue and an unproductive profession one has to make up one's mind to have but little. So I do! The habit is formed, but the days that work does not go well are not amusing. Yes indeed! I would love to follow you into another planet. And a propos of money, it is that which will make our planet uninhabitable in the near future, for it will be impossible to live here, even for the rich, without looking after one's property; one will have to spend several hours a day fussing over one's *income*. Charming! I continue to fuss over my novel, and I shall go to Paris when I reach the end of my chapter, towards the middle of next month.

And whatever you suspect, no "lovely lady" comes to see me. Lovely ladies have occupied my mind a good deal, but have taken up very little of my time. Applying the term anchorite to me is perhaps a juster comparison than you think.

I pass entire weeks without exchanging a word with a human being, and at the end of the week it is not possible for me to recall a single day nor any event whatsoever. I see my mother and my niece on Sundays, and that is all. My only company consists of a band of rats in the garret, which make an infernal racket above my head, when the water does not roar or the wind blow. The nights are black as ink, and a silence surrounds me comparable to that of the desert. Sensitiveness is increased immeasurably in such a setting. I have palpitations of the heart for nothing.

All that results from our charming profession. That is what it means to torment the soul and the body. But perhaps this torment is our proper lot here below?

I told you, didn't I, that I had reread *Consuelo* and the *Comtesse de Rudolstadt;* it took me four days. We must discuss them at length, when you are willing. Why am I in love with Siverain? Perhaps because I am of both sexes.

XLIV. To GUSTAVE FLAUBERT at Croissset Nohant,
15 January, 1867

Here I am at home, fairly strong except for several hours during the evening. Yet, *that will pass. the evil or he who endures it,* my old cure used to say, *cannot last.* I received your letter this morning, dear friend of my heart. Why do I love you more than most of the others, even more than old and well-tried friends? I am asking, for my condition at this hour, is that of being

Thou who goest seeking, at sunset, fortune!...

Yes, intellectual fortune, *light!* Oh well, here it is: one gets, being old, at the sunset of life,—which is the most beautiful hour of tones and reflections,—a new idea of everything and of affection above all.

In the age of power and of personality, one tests one's friends as one tests the earth, from the point of view of reciprocity. One feels oneself solid, one wants to find that which bears one or leads one, solid. But, when one feels the intensity of the moi fleeing, one loves persons and things for what they are in themselves, for what they represent in the eyes of one's soul, and not at all for what they add further to one's destiny. It is like the picture or the statue which one would like to own, when one dreams at the same time of a beautiful house of one's own in which to put it.

But one has passed through green Bohemia without gathering anything there; one has remained poor, sentimental and troubadourish. One knows very well that it will always be the same, and that one will die without a hearth or a home. Then one thinks of the statue, of the picture which one would not know what to do with and which one would not know where to place with due honor, if one owned it. One is content to know that they are in some temple not profaned by cold analysis, a little far from the eye, and one loves them so much the more. One says: I will go again to the country where they are. I shall see again and I shall love always that which has made me love and understand them. The contact of my personality will not have changed them, it will not be myself that I shall love in them.

And it is thus, truly, that the ideal which one does not dream of grasping, fixes itself in one because it remains *itself*. That is all the secret of the beautiful, of the only truth, of love, friendship, of art, of enthusiasm, and of faith. Consider it, you will see.

That solitude in which you live would be delicious to me in fine weather. In winter I find it stoical, and am forced to recall to myself that you have not the moral need of locomotion *as a habit*. I used to think that was another expenditure of strength during this season of being shut in;—well, it is very fine, but it must not continue indefinitely; if the novel has to last longer, you must interrupt it, or vary it with distractions. Really, my dear friend, think of the life of the body, which gets upset and nervous when you subdue it too much. When I was ill in Paris, I saw a physician, very mad, but very intelligent, who said very true things on that subject. He said that I *spiritualized* myself in a disquieting manner, and when I told him, exactly, a propos of you, that one could abstract oneself from everything except work, and have more rather than less strength, he answered that the danger was as great in accumulating as in losing, and a propos of this, many excellent things which I wish I could repeat to you.

Besides, you know them, but you never pay any attention to them. Then this work which you abuse so in words, is a passion, and a great one! Now, I shall tell you what you tell me.

For our sake and for the sake of your old troubadour, do *spare* yourself a little.

Consuelo, La Comtesse de Rudolstadt, what are they? Are they mine? I don't recall a single word in them. You are reading that, you? Are you really amused? Then I shall read them one of these days and I shall love myself if you love me.

What is being hysterical? I have perhaps been that also, I am perhaps; but I don't know anything about it, never having profoundly studied the thing, and having heard of it without having studied it. Isn't it an uneasiness, an anguish caused by the desire of an impossible *something or other?* In that case, we are all attacked by it, by this strange illness, when we have imagination; and why should such a malady have a sex?

And still further, there is this for those strong in anatomy: *there is only one sex.* A man and a woman are so entirely the same thing, that one hardly understands the mass of distinctions and of subtle reasons with which society is nourished concerning this subject. I have observed the infancy and the development of my son and my daughter. My son was myself, therefore much more woman, than my daughter, who was an imperfect man.

I embrace you. Maurice and Lina who have tasted your cheese, send you their regards, and Mademoiselle Aurore cries to you, *wait, wait, wait!* That is all that she knows how to say while laughing like a crazy person; for, at heart she is serious, attentive, clever with her hands as a monkey and amusing herself better with games she invents, than with those one suggests to her. I think that she will have a mind of her own.

If I do not get cured here, I shall go to Cannes, where some friends are urging me to come. But I cannot yet mention it to my children. When I am with them it is not easy to move. There is passion and jealousy. And all my life has been like that, never my own! Pity yourself then, you who belong to yourself!

XLV. To GEORGE SAND Wednesday evening

I have followed your counsel, dear master, I have *exercised!!!* Am I not splendid; eh?

Sunday night, at eleven o'clock, there was such lovely moonlight along the river and on the snow that I was taken with an itch for movement, and I walked for two hours and a half imagining all sorts of things, pretending that I was travelling in Russia or in Norway. When the tide came in and cracked the cakes of ice in the Seine and the thin ice which covered the stream, it was, without any exaggeration, superb. Then I thought of you and I missed you.

I don't like to eat alone. I have to associate the idea with someone with the things that please me. But this someone is rare. I too wonder why I love you. Is it because you are a great man or a charming being? I don't know. What is certain is that I experience a *particular* sentiment for you and I cannot define it.

And a propos of this, do you think (you who are a master of psychology), that one can love two people in the same way and that one can experience two identical sensations about them? I don't think so, since our individuality changes at every moment of its existence.

You write me lovely things about "disinterested affection." That is true, so is the opposite! We make God always in our own image. At the bottom of all our loves and all our admirations we find ourselves again: ourselves or something approaching us. What is the difference if the *ourselves* is good!

My moi bores me for the moment. How this fool weighs on my shoulders at times! He writes too slowly and is not bluffing at all when he complains of his work. What a task! and what a devil of an idea to have sought such a subject! You should give me a recipe for going faster: and you complain of seeking a fortune! You! I have received a little note from Saint-Beuve which reassures about his health, but it is sad. He seemed to me depressed at not being able to haunt the dells of Cyprus.

He is within the truth, or at least within his own truth, which amounts to the same thing. I shall be like him perhaps, when I am his age. However, I think not. Not having had the same youth, my old age will be different.

That reminds me that I once dreamed a book on Saint Perrine. Champfleury treated that subject badly. For I don't see that he is comic: I should have made him atrocious and lamentable. I think that the heart does not grow old; there are even people whose hearts grow bigger with age. I was much drier and more bitter twenty years ago than now. I am feminized and softened by wear, as others get harder, and that makes me *indignant.* I feel that I am becoming a *cow,* it takes nothing to move me; everything troubles and agitates me, everything is to me as the north wind is to the reed.

A word from you, which I remembered, has made me reread now the Fair Maid of Perth. It is a good story, whatever one says about it. That fellow decidedly had an imagination.

Well, adieu. Think of me. I send you my best love.

XLVI. To Gustave Flaubert, at Croissset Nohant, 1867

Bah! zut! troulala! Well! well! I am not sick any more, or at least I am only half sick. The air of the country restores me, or patience, or *the other* person, the one who wants to work again and to produce. What is my illness? Nothing. Everything is all right, but I have something that they call anemia, an effect without a tangible cause, a breakdown which has been threatening for several years, and which became noticeable at Palaiseau, after my return from Croisset. An emaciation that is too rapid to be within reason, a pulse too slow, too feeble, an indolent or capricious stomach, with a sensation of stifling and a fondness for inertia. I was not able to keep a glass of water on my poor stomach for several days, and that brought me so low that I thought I was hardly curable; but, all is getting on, and I have even been working since yesterday.

You, dear, you go walking in the night, in the snow. That is something which for an exceptional excursion, is rather foolish and might indeed make you ill also. Good Heavens! It is not the moon, it is the sun that I advise; we are not owls, *obviously!* We have just had three spring days. I wager that you have not climbed up to my dear orchard which is so pretty and which I love so much. If it was only in remembrance of me, you ought to climb up every fine day at noon. Your work would flow more abundantly afterward and you would regain the time you lost and more too.

Then you are worrying about money? I don't know what that is, since I have not a sou in the world. I live by my day, work as does the proletarian; when I can no longer do my day's work, I shall be packed up for the other world, and then I shall have no more need of anything. But you must live. How can you live by your pen if you always let yourself be duped and shorn? It is not I who can teach you how to protect yourself But haven't you a friend who knows how to act for you? Alas, yes, the world is going to the devil in that respect; and I was talking of you, the other day, to a very dear friend, while I was showing him the artist, a personage become so rare, and cursing the necessity of thinking of the material side of life. I send you the last page of his letter; you will see that you have in him a friend whom you did not suspect, and whose name will surprise you.

No, I shall not go to Cannes, in spite of a strong temptation! Imagine, I received a little box filled with flowers gathered out-doors, five or six days ago; for the package followed me to Paris and to Palaiseau. Those flowers are adorably fresh, they smell sweetly, they are as pretty as anything.—Ah! to go, go at once to the country of the sun. But I have no money, and besides I have no time. My illness has delayed me and put me off. Let us stay here. Am I not well? If I can't go to Paris next month, won't you come to see me here? Certainly, it is an eight hours' journey. You cannot see this ancient nook. You owe me a week, or I shall believe that I love a big ingrate who does not pay me back.

Poor Sainte-Beuve! More unhappy than we, he who has never had any great disappointments and who has no longer any material worries. He bewails what is the least regrettable and the least serious in life understood as he understood it! And then very proud, having been a Jansenist, his heart has cooled in that direction. Perhaps the intelligence was developed, but that does not suffice to make us live, and does not teach us how to die. Barbes, who has expected for a long time that a stroke would carry him off, is gentle and smiling. It does not seem to him, and it does not seem to his friends, that death will separate him from us. He who quite goes away, is he who believes he ends and does not extend a hand so that anyone can follow him or rejoin him.

And good-night, dear friend of my heart. They are ringing for the performance. Maurice regales us this evening with marionettes. They are very amusing, and the theatre is so pretty! A real artist's jewel. Why aren't you here? It is horrid not to live next door to those one loves.

XLVII. To George Sand Wednesday

I received yesterday your son's book. I shall start it when I have gotten rid of less amusing readings, probably. Meanwhile, don't thank him any the less, dear master.

First, let's talk of you; "arsenic." I am sure of it! You must drink iron, walk, and sleep, and go to the south, no matter what it costs, there! Otherwise the *wooden woman* will break down. As for money, we shall find it; and as for the time, take it. You won't do anything that I advise, of course. Oh! well, you are wrong, and you hurt me.

No, I have not what you call worries about money; my revenues are very small, but they are sure. Only, as it is your friend's habit to anticipate them he finds himself short at times, and he grumbles "in the silence of his closet," but not elsewhere. Unless I have extraordinary reverses, I shall have enough to feed me and warm me until the end of my days. My heirs are or will be rich (for it is I who am the poor one of the family). Then, zut!

As for gaining money by my pen, that is an aspiration that I have never had, recognizing that I was radically incapable of it.

I have to live as a small retired countryman, which is not very amusing. But so many others who are worth more than I am not having the land, it would be unfair for me to complain. Accusing Providence is, moreover a mania so common, that one ought to refrain from it through simple good taste.

Another word about money and one that shall be quite between ourselves. I can, without being inconvenienced at all, as soon as I am in Paris, that is to say from the 20th to the 23rd of the present month, lend you a thousand francs, if you need them in order to go to Cannes. I make you this proposition bluntly, as I would to Bouilhet, or any other intimate friend. Come, don't stand on ceremony!

Between people in society, that would not be correct, I know that, but between troubadours many things are allowable.

You are very kind with your invitation to go to Nohant. I shall go, for I want very much to see your house. I am annoyed not to know it when I think of you. But I shall have to put off that pleasure till next summer. Now I have to stay some time in Paris. Three months are not too long for all I want to do there.

I send you back the page from the letter of your friend Barbes, whose real biography I know very imperfectly. All I know of him is that he is honest and heroic. Give him a handshake for me, to thank him for his sympathy. Is he, *between ourselves,* as intelligent as he is good?

I feel the importance now, of getting men of that class to be rather frank with me. For I am going to start studying the Revolution of '48. You have promised me to hunt in your library at Nohant for (1) an article of yours on faience; (2) a novel by father X——, a Jesuit, on the Holy Virgin.

But what sternness for the father Beuve who is neither Jesuit nor virgin! He regrets, you say, "what is the least regrettable, understood as he understood it." Why so? Everything depends upon the intensity that one puts on the thing.

Men always find that the most serious thing of their existence is enjoyment.

Woman for us all is the highest point of the infinite. That is not noble, but that is the real depth of the male. They exaggerate that unmercifully, God be thanked, for literature and for individual happiness also.

Oh! I have missed you so much. The tides are superb, the wind groans, the river foams and overflows. It blows from the ocean, which benefits one.

XLVIII. TO GUSTAVE FLAUBERT, at Paris Nohant,
8 February, 1867

No, I am not Catholic, but I reject monstrosities. I say that the hideous old man who buys young girls does not make love and that there is in it neither death nor birth, nor infinity, nor male nor female. It is a thing against nature; for it is not desire that drives the young girl into the arms of the ugly old man, and where there is not liberty nor reciprocity there is an attack against holy nature. Therefore that which he regrets is not regrettable, unless he thinks that his little cocottes will regret his person, and I ask you if they will regret anything else than their dirty wages? That was the gangrene in this great and admirable mind, so lucid and so wise on all other subjects. One pardons everything in those one loves, when one is obliged to defend them from their enemies. But what we say between ourselves is buried, and I can tell you that vice has quite spoiled my old friend.

We must believe that we love one another a great deal, dear comrade, for we both had the same thought at the same time. You offer me a thousand francs with which to go to Cannes; you who are as hard up as I am, and, when you wrote to me that you *were bothered* about money matters, I opened my letter again, to offer you half of what I have, which still amounts to about two thousand francs; it is my reserve. And then I did not dare. Why? It is quite stupid; you were better than I, you came straight to the point. Well, I thank you for that kind thought and I do not accept. But I would accept, be sure of it, if I did not have other resources. Only I tell you that if anyone ought to lend to me, it is Buloz who has bought chateaux and lands with my novels. He would not refuse me, I know. He even offers it to me. I shall take from him then, if I have to. But I am not in a condition to leave, I have had a relapse these last few days. I slept thirty-six hours together, exhausted. Now I am on my feet again, but weak. I confess to you that I have not the energy *to wish to live*. I don't care about it; moving from where I am comfortable, to seek new fatigues, working like a dog to renew a dog's life, it is a little stupid, I think, when it would be so sweet to pass away like that, still loving, still loved, at strife with no one, not discontent with oneself and dreaming of the wonders of other worlds—this assumes that the imagination is still fresh. But I don't know why I talk to you of things considered sad, I have too much the habit of looking at them pleasantly. I forget that they appear afflicting to those who seem in the fulness of life. Don't let's talk about them any longer and let spring do the work, spring which perhaps will breathe into me the desire to take up my work again. I shall be as docile to the interior voice that tells me to walk as to that telling me to sit down.

It is not I who promised you a novel on the Holy Virgin. At least I don't think so. I cannot find my article on faience. Do look and see if it was printed at the end of one of my volumes to complete the last sheet. It was entitled Giovanni Freppa ou les Maioliques.

Oh! what luck! While writing to you it has come back to me that there is a corner where I have not looked. I hasten there, I find it! I find something better than my article, and I send you three works which will make you as learned as I am. That of Passeri is charming.

Barbes has intelligence, certainly! but he is a sugar loaf. Brain on a lofty scale, head of an Indian, with gentle instincts, almost impossible to find; all for metaphysical thought which becomes an instinct and a passion that dominates everything. Add to that a character that one can only compare to Garibaldi. A creature of incredible sanctity and perfection. Immense worth without immediate application in France. The setting of another age or another country is what this hero needs. And now good-night,—O God, what a *calf* I am! I leave you the title of *cow,* which you give yourself in your days of weariness. Never mind, tell me when you are to be in Paris. It is probable that I shall have to go there for a few days for one thing or another. We must embrace each other and then you shall come to Nohant this summer. It is agreed, it must be!

My affectionate regards to your mother and to your lovely niece.

Please acknowledge the receipt of the three pamphlets; they would be a loss.

XLIX. To George Sand

Dear master,

You really ought to go to see the sun somewhere; it is foolish to be always suffering; do travel; rest; resignation is the worst of the virtues.

I have need of it in order to endure all the stupidities that I hear! You cannot imagine to what a degree they have reached. France which has been sometimes taken with St. Vitus dance (as under Charles VI), seems to me now to have a paralysis of the brain. They are mad with fear. Fear of the Prussians, fear of the strikes, fear of the Exposition which does not go well, fear of everything. We have to go back to 1849 to find such a degree of imbecility.

There was at the last Magny such inane conversation that I swore to myself never to put foot inside the place again. The only subjects under discussion all the time were Bismarck and the Luxembourg. I was stuffed with it! For the rest I don't find it easy to live. Far from becoming blunted my sensibilities are sharper; a lot of insignificant things make me suffer. Pardon this weakness, you who are so strong and tolerant.

The novel does not go at all well. I am deep in reading the newspapers of '48. I have had to make several (and have not yet finished) journeys to Sevres, to Creil, etc.

Father Sainte-Beuve is preparing a discourse on free thought which he will read at the Senate a propos of the press law. He has been very shrewd, you know.

You tell your son Maurice that I love him very much, first because he is your son and secundo because he is he. I find him good, clever, cultivated, not a poseur, in short charming, and "with talent."

L. TO GUSTAVE FLAUBERT Nohant, 4 March, 1867

Dear good friend, the friend of my heart, the old troubadour is as well as ten thousand men—who are well, and he is gay as a finch, because the sun shines again and copy is progressing.

He will probably go to Paris soon for the play by his son Dumas, let us try to be there together.

Maurice is very proud to be declared *cock* by an eagle. At this moment he is having a spree with veal and wine in honor of his firemen.

The *American*[14] in question is charming. He has, literally speaking, a passion for you, and he writes me that after seeing you he loves you more, that does not surprise me.

Poor Bouilhet! Give him this little note enclosed here. I share his sorrow, I knew her.

Are you amused in Paris? Are you as sedentary there as at Croisset?

In that case I shall hardly see you unless I go to see you.

Tell me the hours when you do not receive the fair sex, and when sexagenarian troubadours do not incommode you.

Cadio is entirely redone and rewritten up to the part I read to you, it is less offensive.

I am not doing Montreveche. I will tell you about that. It is quite a story. I love you and I embrace you with all my heart.

Your old George Sand

---

[14] Henry Harrisse.

Did you receive my pamphlets on the faience? You have not acknowledged them. They were sent to Croisset the day after I got your last letter.

LI. To Gustave Flaubert 14 March, 1867

Your old troubadour is again prostrate. Every moment his guitar threatens to be broken. And then he sleeps forty-eight hours and is cured—but feeble, and he cannot be in Paris on the 16th as he had intended. Maurice went alone a little while ago, I shall go to join him in five or six days.

Little Aurore consoles me for this mischance. She twitters like a bird along with the birds who are twittering already as in full spring time.

The anemone Sylvia which I brought from the woods into the garden and which I had a great deal of trouble in acclimating is finally growing thousands of white and pink stars among the blue periwinkle. It is warm and damp. One cannot break one's guitar in weather like this. Good-bye, dear good friend.

G. Sand

LII. To GUSTAVE FLAUBERT Friday, 22 March, 1867

Your old troubadour is here, not so badly off. He will go to dine on Monday at Magny's, we shall agree on a day for both of us to dine with Maurice. He is at home at five o'clock but not before Monday.

He is running around!

He embraces you.

LIII. To Gustave Flaubert 1867 (?)

Then Wednesday, if you wish, my dear old fellow. Whom do you want to have with us? Certainly, the dear Beuve if that is possible, and no one if you like.

We embrace you.

G. S. Maurice Saturday evening.

LIV. TO GUSTAVE FLAUBERT Nohant, 11 April, 1867

Here I am back again in my nest, and almost cured from a bad fever which attacked me in Paris, the day before my departure.

Really your old troubadour has had ridiculous health for six months. March and April have been such stupid months for him. It makes no difference, however, for he is recovering again, and is seeing once more the trees and the grass grow, it is always the same thing and that is why it is beautiful and good. Maurice has been touched by the friendship that you have shown him; you have seduced and ravished him, and he is not demonstrative.

He and his wife,—who is not at all an ordinary woman,—desire absolutely that you come to our house this year, I am charged to tell you so very seriously and persistently if need be. And is that hateful grip gone? Maurice wanted to go to get news of you; but on seeing me so prostrated by the fever, he thought of nothing except packing me up and bringing me here like a parcel. I did nothing except sleep from Paris to Nohant and I was revived on receiving the kisses of Aurore who knows now how to give great kisses, laughing wildly all the while; she finds that very funny.

And the novel? Does it go on its way the same in Paris as in Croisset? It seems to me that everywhere you lead the same hermitlike existence. When you have the time to think of friends, remember your old comrade and send him two lines to tell him that you are well and that you don't forget him.

LV. To George Sand

I am worried at not having news from you, dear master. What has become of you? When shall I see you?

My trip to Nohant has fallen through. The reason is this: my mother had a little stroke a week ago. There is nothing left of it, but it might come on again. She is anxious for me, and I am going to hurry back to Croisset. If she is doing well towards the month of August, and I am not worried, it is not necessary to tell you that I shall rush headlong towards your home.

As regards news, Sainte-Beuve seems to me very ill, and Bouilhet has just been appointed librarian at Rouen.

Since the rumours of war have quieted down, people seem to me a little less foolish. My nausea caused by the public cowardice is decreasing.

I went twice to the Exposition; it is amazing. There are splendid and extraordinary things there. But man is made to swallow the infinite. One would have to know all sciences and all arts in order to be interested in everything that one sees on the Champ de Mars. Never mind; someone who had three entire months to himself, and went every morning to take notes, would save himself in consequence much reading and many journeys.

One feels oneself there very far from Paris, in a new and ugly world, an enormous world which is perhaps the world of the future. The first time that I lunched there, I thought all the time of America, and I wanted to speak like a negro.

LVI. To Gustave Flaubert, at Croisset Nohant, 9 May, 1867

Dear friend of my heart,

I am well, I am at work, I am finishing Cadio. It is warm, I am alive, I am calm and sad, I hardly know why. In this existence so even, so tranquil, and so gentle as I have here, I am in an element that weakens me morally while strengthening me physically; and I fall into melancholies of honey and roses which are none the less melancholy. It seems to me that all those I love forget me, and that it is justice, because I live a selfish life having nothing to do for any one of them.

I have lived with tremendous attachments which overwhelmed me, which exceeded my strength and which I often used to curse. And it happens that having nothing more to carry them on with, I am bored by being well. If the human race went on very well or very ill, one would reattach oneself to a general interest, would live with an idea, wise or foolish. But you see where we are now, you who storm so fiercely against cowards. That disappears, you say? But only to recommence! What kind of a society is it that becomes paralyzed in the midst of its expansions, because tomorrow can bring a storm? The thought of danger has never produced such demoralizations. Have we declined to such an extent that it is necessary to beg us to eat, telling us at the same time that nothing will happen to disturb our digestion? Yes, it is silly, it is shameful. Is it the result of prosperity, and does civilization involve this sickly and cowardly selfishness?

My optimism has had a rude jolt of late. I worked up a joy, a courage at the idea of seeing you here. It was like a cure that I carefully contrived, but you are worried about your dear, old mother, and certainly I cannot protest.

Well, if, before your departure from Paris, I can finish Cadio, to which I am bound under pain of having nothing wherewith to pay for my tobacco and my shoes, I shall go with Maurice to embrace you. If not, I shall hope for you about the middle of the summer. My children, quite unhappy by this delay, beg to hope for you also, and we hope it so much the more because it would be a good sign for the dear mother.

Maurice has plunged again into Natural History; he wants to perfect himself in the *micros;* I learn on the rebound. When I shall have fixed in my head the name and the appearance of two or three thousand imperceptible varieties, I shall be well advanced, don't you think so? Well, these studies are veritable *octopuses,* which entwine about you and which open to you I don't know what infinity. You ask if it is the destiny of man to *drink the infinite;* my heavens, yes, don't doubt it, it is his destiny, since it is his dream and his passion.

Inventing is absorbing also; but what fatigue afterwards! How empty and worn out intellectually one feels, when one has scribbled for weeks and months about that animal with two legs which has the only right to be represented in novels! I see Maurice quite refreshed and rejuvenated when he returns from his beasts and his pebbles, and if I aspire to come out from my misery, it is to bury myself also in studies, which in the speech of the Philistines, are not of any use. Still it is worth more than to say mass and to ring the bell for the adoration of the Creator.

Is it true what you tell me of G——? Is it possible? I cannot believe it. Is there in the atmosphere which the earth engenders nowadays, a gas, laughing or otherwise, which suddenly seizes the brain, and carries it on to commit extravagances, as there was under the first revolution a maddening fluid which inspired one to commit cruelties? We have fallen from the Hell of Dante into that of Scarron.

Of what are you thinking, good head and good heart, in the midst of this bacchanal? You are wrathful, oh very well, I like that better than if you were laughing at it; but when you are calmer and when you reflect?

Must one find some fashion of accepting the honor, the duty, and the fatigue of living? As for me, I revert to the idea of an everlasting journey through worlds more amusing, but it would be necessary to go there quickly and change continually. The life that one fears so much to lose is always too long for those who understand quickly what they see. Everything repeats itself and goes over and over again in it.

I assure you that there is only one pleasure: learning what one does not know, and one happiness: loving the exceptions. Therefore I love you and I embrace you tenderly.

Your old troubadour G. Sand

I am anxious about Sainte-Beuve. What a loss that would be! I am content if Bouilhet is content. Is it really a good position?

LVII. To George Sand Paris, Friday morning

I am returning to my mother next Monday, dear master. I have little hope of seeing you before then!

But when you are in Paris, what is to prevent you from pushing on to Croisset where everyone, including myself, adores you? Sainte-Beuve has finally consented to see a specialist and to be seriously treated. And he is better anyway. His morale is improving.

Bouilhet's position gives him four thousand francs a year and lodging. He now need not think of earning his living, which is a real luxury.

No one talks of the war any more, they don't talk of anything.

The Exposition alone is what "everybody is thinking about," and the cabmen exasperate the bourgeois.

They were beautiful (the bourgeois) during the strike of the tailors. One would have said that *society* was going to pieces.

Axiom: Hatred of the bourgeois is the beginning of virtue. But I include in the word bourgeois, the bourgeois in blouses as well the bourgeois in coats.

It is we and we alone, that is to say the literary men, who are the people, or to say it better: the tradition of humanity.

Yes, I am susceptible to disinterested angers and I love you all the more for loving me for that. Stupidity and injustice make me roar,—and I *howl* in my corner against a lot of things "that do not concern me."

How sad it is not to live together, dear master, I admired you before I knew you. From the day I saw your lovely and kind face, I loved you. There you are.—And I embrace you warmly.

Your old

Gustave Flaubert

I shall have the package of pamphlets about faience sent to the rue des Feuillantines. A good handshake to Maurice. A kiss on the four cheeks of Mademoiselle Aurore.

LVIII. To George Sand

I stayed thirty-six hours in Paris at the beginning of this week, in order to be present at the Tuileries ball. Without any exaggeration, it was splendid. Paris on the whole turns to the colossal. It is becoming foolish and unrestrained. Perhaps we are returning to the ancient Orient. It seems to me that idols will come out of the earth. We are menaced with a Babylon.

Why not? The *individual* has been so denied by democracy that he will abase himself to a complete effacement, as under the great theocratic despotisms.

The Tsar of Russia displeased me profoundly; I found him a rustic. On a parallel with Monsieur Floquet who cries without any danger: "Long live Poland!" We have chic people who have had themselves registered at the Elysee. Oh! what a fine epoch!

My novel goes piano. The further I get on the more difficulties arise. What a heavy cart of sandstone to drag along! And you pity yourself for a labor that lasts six months!

I have enough more for two years, at least *(of mine)*. How the devil do you find the connection between your ideas? It is that that delays me. Moreover this book demands tiresome researches. For instance on Monday; I was at the Jockey Club, at the Cafe Anglais, and at a lawyer's in turn.

Do you like Victor Hugo's preface to the Paris-Guide? Not very much, do you? Hugo's philosophy seems to me always vague.

I was carried away with delight, a week ago, at an encampment of Gypsies who had established at Rouen. This is the third time that I have seen them and always with a new pleasure. The great thing is that they excite the hatred of the bourgeois, although they are as inoffensive as sheep.

I appeared very badly before the crowd because I gave them a few sous, and I heard some fine words a la Prudhomme. That hatred springs from something very profound and complex. One finds it among all orderly people.

It is the hatred that one feels for the bedouin, for the heretic, the philosopher, the solitary, the poet; and there is a fear in that hate. I, who am always for the minority, am exasperated by it. It is true that many things exasperate me. On the day that I am no longer outraged, I shall fall flat as the marionette from which one withdraws the support of the stick.

Thus, *the stake* that has supported me this winter, is the indignation that I had against our great national historian, M. Thiers, who had reached the condition of a demi-god, and the pamphlet Trochu, and the everlasting Changarnier coming back over the water. God be thanked that the Exposition has delivered us momentarily from these *great men*.

LIX. To GUSTAVE FLAUBERT, at Croisset Nohant, 30 May, 1867

Here you are at home, old friend of my heart, and I and Maurice must go to embrace you. If you are still buried in work, we shall only come and go. It is so near to Paris, that you must not hesitate to tell us. I have finished Cadio, hurray! I have only to *polish* it a little. It is like an illness, carrying this great affair for so long in one's *head*. I have been so interrupted by real illnesses that I have had great trouble in setting to work again at it. But I am wonderfully well since the fine weather and I am going to take a bath of botany.

Maurice will take one of entomology. He walks three leagues with a friend of like energy in order to hunt in a great plain for an animal which has to be looked at with a magnifying glass. That is happiness! That is being really infatuated. My gloom has disappeared in making Cadio; at present I am only fifteen years old, and everything to me appears for the best in the best possible of worlds. That will last as long as it can. These are the intervals of innocence in which forgetfulness of evil compensates for the inexperience of the golden age.

How is your dear mother? She is fortunate to have you again near her! And the novel? Good heavens! it must get on! Are you walking a little? Are you more reasonable?

The other day, some people not at all stupid were here who spoke highly of *Madame Bovary*, but with less zest of *Salammbo*. Lina got into a white heat, not being willing that those wretches should make the slightest objection to it; Maurice had to calm her, and moreover he criticised the work very well, as an artist and as a scholar; so well that the recalcitrants laid down their arms. I should like to have written what he said. He speaks little and often badly; but that time he succeeded extraordinarily well.

I shall then not say adieu, but au revoir, as soon as possible. I love you much, much, my dear old fellow, you know it. My ideal would be to live a long life with a good and great heart like yours. But then, one would want never to die, and when one is really *old,* like me, one must hold oneself ready for anything.

I embrace you tenderly, so does Maurice. Aurore is the sweetest and the most ridiculous person. Her father makes her drink while he says: *Dominus vobiscum!* then she drinks and answers: Amen! How she is getting on! What a marvel is the development of a little child! No one has ever written about that. Followed day by day, it would be precious in every respect. It is one of those things that we all see without noticing.

Adieu again; think of your old troubadour who thinks unceasingly of you.

G. Sand

LX. To Gustave Flaubert Nohant, 14 June, 1867

Dear friend of my heart, I leave with my son and his wife the 20th of the month to stay two weeks in Paris, perhaps more if the revival of Villemer delays me longer. Therefore your dear good mother, whom I do not want to miss, has all the time she needs to go to see her daughters. I shall wait in Paris until you tell me if she has returned, or rather, if I make you a real visit, you shall tell me the time that suits you best.

My intention, for the moment, was quite simply to go to pass an hour with you, and Lina was tempted to accompany me; I should have shown her Rouen, and then we should have embraced you in time to return in the evening to Paris; for the dear little one has always her ear and her heart listening when she is away from Aurore, and her holidays are marked by a continual uneasiness which I quite understand. Aurore is a treasure of gentleness which absorbs us all. If it can be arranged, we shall then go on the run to grasp your hands. If it cannot, I shall go alone later when your heart says so, and, if you are going south, I shall put it off until everything can be arranged without disturbing whatever may be the plans of your mother or yourself. I am very free. So, don't disturb yourself, and arrange your summer without bothering about me.

I have thirty-six plans also, but I don't incline to any one; what amuses me is what seizes me and takes me off suddenly. It is with a journey as with a novel: those who travel are those who command. Only when one is in Paris, Rouen is not a journey, and I shall always be ready when I am there, to respond to your call. I am a little remorseful to take whole days from your work,

I who am never bored with loafing, and whom you could leave for whole hours under a tree, or before two lighted logs, with the assurance that I should find there something interesting. I know so well how to live *outside of myself!* It hasn't always been like that. I also was young and subject to indignations. It is over!

Since I have dipped into real nature, I have found there an order, a system, a calmness of cycles which is lacking in mankind, but which man can, up to a certain point, assimilate when he is not too directly at odds with the difficulties of his own life. When these difficulties return he must endeavor to avoid them; but if he has drunk the cup of the eternally true, he does not get too excited for or against the ephemeral and relative truth.

But why do I say this to you? Because it comes to my pen-point; for in considering it carefully, your state of overexcitement is probably truer, or at least more fertile and more human than my *senile* tranquillity. I would not like to make you as I am, even if by a magical operation I could. I should not be interested in myself if I had the honor to meet myself. I should say that one troubadour is enough to manage and I should send the other to Chaillot.

A propos of gypsies, do you know that there are gypsies of the sea? I discovered in the outskirts of Tamaris, among the furthest rocks, great boats well sheltered, with women and children, a coast settlement, very restricted, very tanned; fishing for food without trading; speaking a language that the people of the country do not understand; living only in these great boats stranded on the sand, when the storms troubled them in their rocky coves; intermarrying, inoffensive and sombre, timid or savage; not answering when any one speaks to them. I don't even know what to call them. The name that I have been told has escaped me but I could get some one to tell me again. Naturally the country people hate them and that they have no religion; if that is so they ought to be superior to us. I ventured all alone among them. "Good day, sirs." Response, a slight bend of the head. I looked at their encampment, no one moved. It seemed as if they did not see me. I asked them if my curiosity annoyed them. A shrug of the shoulders as if to say, "What do we care?" I spoke to a young man who was mending the meshes in a net very cleverly; I showed him a piece of five francs in gold. He looked the other way. I showed him one in silver. He deigned to look at it. "Do you want it?" He bent his head on his work. I put it near him, he did not move. I went away, he followed me with his eyes. When he thought that I could not see him any longer, he took the piece and went to talk with a group. I don't know what happened. I fancy that they put it in the common exchequer. I began botanizing at some distance within sight to see if they would come to ask me something or to thank me. No one moved. I returned as if by chance towards them; the same silence, the same indifference. An hour later, was at the top of the cliff, and I asked the coast-guard who those people were who spoke neither French, nor Italian, nor patois. He told me their name, which I have not remembered.

He thought that they were Moors, left on the coast since the time of the great invasions from Provence, and perhaps he is not mistaken. He told me that he had seen me among them from his watch tower, and that I was wrong, for they were a people capable of anything; but when I asked him what harm they did he confessed to me that they had done none. They lived by their fishing and above all on the things cast up by the sea which they knew how to gather up before the most alert. They were an object of perfect scorn. Why? Always the same story. He who does not do as all the world does can only do evil.

If you go into the country, you might perhaps meet them at the end of the Brusq. But they are birds of passage, and there are years when they do not appear at all. I have not even seen the Paris Guide. They owe me a copy, however; for I gave something to it without receiving payment. It is because of that no doubt that they have forgotten me.

To conclude, I shall be in Paris from the 20th of June to the 5th of July. Send me a word always to 97 rue des Feuillantines. I shall stay perhaps longer, but I don't know. I embrace you tenderly, my splendid old fellow. Walk a little, I beg of you. I don't fear anything for the novel; but I fear for the nervous system taking too much the place of the muscular system. I am very well, except for thunder bolts, when I fall on my bed for forty-eight hours and don't want any one to speak to me. But it is rare and if I do not relent so that they can nurse me, I get up perfectly cured.

Maurice's love. Entomology has taken possession of him this year; he discovers marvels. Embrace your mother for me, and take good care of her. I love you with all my heart.

G. Sand

LXI. To Gustave Flaubert Nohant, 24 July, 1867

Dear good friend, I spent three weeks in Paris with my children, hoping to see you arriving or to receive a line from you which would tell me to come and embrace you. But you were *head over heels* and I respect these crises of work; I know them! Here am I back again in old Nohant, and Maurice at Nerac terminating by a compromise the law-suit which keeps him from his inheritance. His agreeable father stole about three hundred thousand francs from his children in order to please his cook; happily, although Monsieur used to lead this edifying life, I used to work and did not cut into my capital. I have nothing, but I shall leave the daily bread assured.

They write me that Villemer goes well. Little Aurore is as pretty as anything and does a thousand gracious tricks. My daughter Lina is always my real daughter. The *other* is well and is beautiful, that is all that I ask of her.

I am working again; but I am not strong. I am paying for my energy and activity in Paris. That does not make any difference, I am not angry against life, I love you with all my heart. I see, when I am gloomy, your kind face, and I feel the radiant power of your goodness. You are a charm in the Indian summer of my sweet and pure friendships, without egoisms, and without deceptions in consequence.

Think of me sometimes, work well and call me when you are ready to loaf. If you are not ready, never mind. If your heart told you to come here, there would be feasting and joy in the family. I saw Sainte-Beuve, I am content and proud of him.

Good night, friend of my heart. I embrace you as well as your mother.

G. Sand

LXII. To GUSTAVE FLAUBERT, at Paris Nohant, 6 August, 1867

When I see how hard my old friend has to work in order to write a novel, it discourages my facility, and I tell myself that I write *botched* literature. I have finished Cadio; it has been in Buloz' hands a long time. I am writing another thing,[15] but I don't see it yet very clearly; what can one do without sun and without heat? I ought to be in Paris now, to see the Exposition again at my leisure, and to take your mother to walk with you; but I really must work, since I have only that to live on. And then the children; that Aurore is a wonder. You really must see her, perhaps I shall not see her long, If I don't think I am destined to grow very old; I must lose no time in loving!

Yes, you are right, it is that that sustains me. This hypocritical fit has a rough disillusionment in store for it, and one will lose nothing by waiting. On the contrary, one will gain. You will see that, you who are old though still quite young. You are my son's age. You will laugh together when you see this heap of rubbish collapse.

You must not be a Norman, you must come and see us for several days, you will make us happy; and it will restore the blood in my veins and the joy in my heart.

Love your old troubadour always and talk to him of Paris; a few words when you have the time.

Outline a scene for Nohant with four or five characters, we shall enjoy it. We embrace you and summon you.

G. Sand

---

[15] Mademoiselle Merquem.

LXIII. To GUSTAVE FLAUBERT, at Croisset Nohant,
18 August, 1867

Where are you, my dear old fellow? If by chance you should be in Paris, during the first few days of September, let us try to see each other. I shall stay there three days and I shall return here. But I do not hope to meet you there. You ought to be in some lovely country, far from Paris and from its dust. I do not know even if my letter will reach you. Never mind, if you can give news of yourself, do so. I am in despair. I have lost suddenly, without even knowing that he was ill, my poor dear, old friend, Rollinat, an angel of goodness, of courage, of devotion. It is a heavy blow for me. If you were here you would give me courage; but my poor children are as overwhelmed as I am. We adored him, all the countryside adored him.

Keep well, and think sometimes of your absent friends. We embrace you affectionately. The little one is very well, she is charming.

LXIV. To GUSTAVE FLAUBERT, at Paris Nohant, August, 1867

I bless you, my dear old fellow, for the kind thought that you had of coming; but you were right not to travel while you were ill. Ah! my God, I dream of nothing but illness and unhappiness: take care of yourself, my old comrade. I shall go to see you if I can pull myself together; for, since this new dagger-thrust, I am feeble and crushed and I have a sort of fever. I shall write you a line from Paris. If you are prevented, you must answer me by telegram. You know that with me there is no need of explanation: I know every hindrance in life and I never blame the hearts that I know.—I wish that, right away, if you have a moment to write, you would tell me where I should go for three days to see the coast of Normandy without striking the neighborhood where *"the world"* goes. In order to go on with my novel, I must see a countryside near the Channel, that all the world has not talked about, and where there are real natives at home, peasants, fisherfolk, a real village in a corner of the rocks. If you are in the mood we will go there together. If not, don't bother about me. I go everywhere and I am not disturbed by anything. You told me that the population of the coasts was the best in the country, and that there were real dyed-in-the-wool simple-hearted men there. It would be good to see their faces, their clothes, their houses, and their horizons. That is enough for what I want to do, I need only accessories; I hardly want to describe; *seeing* it is enough in order not to make a false stroke. How is your mother? Have you been able to take her to walk and to distract her a little? Embrace her for me as I embrace you.

G. Sand

Maurice embraces you; I shall go to Paris without him: he is drawn on the jury for the 2 September till ... no one knows. It is a tiresome task. Aurore is very cunning with her arms, she offers them to you to kiss; her hands are marvels and they are incredibly clever for her age.

Au revoir, then, if I can only pull myself out of the state I am now in. Insomnia is the devil; in the daytime one makes a lot of effort not to sadden others. At night one falls back on oneself.

LXV. To GUSTAVE FLAUBERT, at Croisset Nohant,
10 September, 1867

Dear old fellow,

I am worried at not having news of you since that illness of which you spoke. Are you well again? Yes, we shall go to see the rollers and the beaches next month if you like, if your heart prompts you. The novel goes on apace; but I shall besprinkle it with local color afterwards.

While waiting, I am still here, stuck up to my chin in the river every day, and regaining my strength entirely in this cold and shady stream which I adore, and where I have passed so many hours of my life reviving myself after too long sessions in company with my ink-well. I go definitely to Paris, the 16th; the 17th at one o'clock, I leave for Rouen and Jumieges, where my friend Madame Lebarbier de Tinan awaits me at the house of M. Lepel-Cointet, the landowner; I shall stay there the 18th so as to return to Paris the 19th. Will it be inconvenient if I come to see you? I am sick with longing to do so; but I am so absolutely forced to spend the evening of the 19th in Paris that I do not know if I shall have the time. You must tell me. I can get a word from you the 16th in Paris, 97 rue des Feuillantines. I shall not be alone; I have as a travelling companion a charming young literary woman, Juliette Lamber. If you were lovely, lovely, you would walk to Jumieges the 19th. We would return together so that I could be in Paris at six o'clock in the evening at the latest. But if you are even a little bit ill still, or are *plunged* in ink, pretend that I have said nothing, and prepare to see us next month. As for the *winter* walk on the Norman coast, that gives me a cold in my back, I who plan to go to the Gulf of Juan at that time.

I have been sick over the death of my friend Rollinat. My body is cured, but my soul! I should have to stay a week with you to refresh myself in your affectionate strength; for cold and purely philosophical courage to me, is like cauterizing a wooden leg.

I embrace you and I love you (also your mother). Maurice also, what French! One is happy to forget it, it is a tiresome thing.

Your troubadour

G. Sand

LXVI. To George Sand

Dear master,

What, no news?

But you will answer me since I ask you a service. I read this in my notes: "National of 1841. Bad treatments inflicted on Barbes, kicks on his breast, dragged by the beard and hair in order to put him in an in-pace. Consultation of lawyers signed: E. Arago, Favre, Berryer, to complain of these abominations."

Find out from him if all that is true; I shall be obliged.

LXVII. To Gustave Flaubert, at Croisset Paris,
Tuesday, 1st October, 1867

Dear friend, you shall have your information. I asked
Peyrat last evening, I am writing today to Barbes who will
answer directly to you.

Where do you think I have come from? From Normandy.
A charming opportunity took me there six days ago. I had been
enchanted with Jumieges. This time I saw Etretat, Yport, the
prettiest of all the villages, Fecamp, Saint-Valery, which I knew,
and Dieppe, which dazzled me; the environs, the chateau
d'Arques, Limes, what a country! And I went back and forth
twice within two steps of Croisset and I sent you some big
kisses; always ready to return with you to the seaside or to talk
with you at your house when you are free. If I had been alone, I
should have bought an old guitar and should have sung a ballad
under your mother's window. But I could not take a large family
to you.

I am returning to Nohant and I embrace you with all my
heart.

G. Sand

I think that the Bois-Dore is going well, but I don't know
anything about it. I have a way of my own of being in Paris,
namely, being at the seaside, which does not keep me informed
of what is going on. But I gathered gentians in the long grass of
the immense Roman fort of Limes where I had quite a *stunning*
view of the sea. I walked out like an old horse, but I am
returning quite frisky.

LXVIII. To George Sand

At last, at last, I have news of you, dear master, and good news, which is doubly agreeable.

I am planning to return to my home in the country with Madame Sand, and my mother hopes that will be the case. What do you say? For, with all that goes on, we never see each other, confound it!

As for my moving, it is not that I lack the desire of being free to move about. But I should be lost if I stirred before I finish my novel. Your friend is a man of wax; everything gets imprinted on him, is encrusted on him, penetrates him. If I should visit you, I should think of nothing but you and yours, your house, your country, the appearance of the people I had met, etc. I require great efforts to gather myself together; I always tend to scatter myself. That is why, dear adored master, I deprive myself of going to sit down to dream aloud in your house. But, in the summer or autumn of 1869, you shall see what a fine commercial traveller I am, once let loose to the open air. I am abject, I warn you.

As to news, there is a quiet once more since the Kerveguen incident has died its beautiful death. Was it not a farce? and silly?

Sainte-Beuve is preparing a lecture on the press law. He is better, decidedly. I dined Tuesday with Renan. He was marvellously witty and eloquent, and artistic! as I have never seen him. Have you read his new book? His preface causes talk. My poor Theo worries me. I do not think him strong.

LXIX. To GUSTAVE FLAUBERT, at Paris Nohant,
12 October, 1867

I have sent your letter to Barbes; it is fine and splendid,
as you are. I know that the worthy man will be glad of it. But as
for me, I want to throw myself out of the window; for my
children are unwilling to hear of my leaving so soon. Yes, it is
horrid to have seen your house four times without going to see
you. But I am cautious to the point of fear. To be sure the idea of
summoning you to Rouen for twenty minutes did occur to me.
But you are not, as I am, on tiptoe, all ready to start off. You live
in your dressing gown, the great enemy of liberty and activity.
To force you to dress, to go out, perhaps in the middle of an
absorbing chapter, and only to see someone who does not know
how to say anything quickly, and who, the more he is content,
the stupider he is,—I did not dare to. Here I am obliged to finish
something which drags along, and before the final touch I shall
probably go to Normandy. I should like to go by the Seine to
Honfleur. It will be next month, if the cold does not make me ill,
and I shall try this time to carry you away in passing. If not, I
shall see you at least, and then I shall go to Provence.

Ah! if I could only take you there! And if you could, if
you would, during the second week in October when you are
going to be free, come to see me here! You promised, and my
children would be so happy if you would! But you don't love us
enough for that, scoundrel that you are! You think that you have
a lot of better friends: you are very much mistaken; it is always
one's best friends whom one neglects or ignores.

Come, a little courage; you can leave Paris at a quarter past nine in the morning, and get to Chateauroux at four, there you would find my carriage and be here at six for dinner. It is not bad, and once here, we all laugh together like good-natured bears; no one dresses; there is no ceremony, and we all love one another very much. Say yes!

I embrace you. And I too have been bored at not seeing you, *for a year.*

Your old troubadour

LXX. To GUSTAVE FLAUBERT, at Croisset Nohant, 27 October, 1867

I have just made a resume in a few pages of my impressions as a landscape painter, gathered in Normandy: it has not much importance, but I was able to quote three lines from *Salammbo,* which seemed to me to depict the country better than all my phrases, and which had always struck me as a stroke from a master brush. In turning over the pages to find these lines, I naturally reread almost all, and I remain convinced that it is one of the most beautiful books that have been made since they began to make books.

I am well, and I am working quickly and much, so as to live on my *income* this winter in the South. But what will be the delights of Cannes and where will be the heart to engage in them? My spirits are in mourning while thinking that at this hour people arc fighting for the pope. Ah! *Isidore!*[16]

I have tried in vain this month to go again to see ma Normandie, that is to say, my great, dear heart's friend. My children have threatened me with death if I leave them so soon. Just at present friends are coming. You are the only one who does not talk of coming on. Yet, that would be so fine! Next month I shall move heaven and earth to find you wherever you are, and meanwhile I love you tremendously. And you. Your work? your mother's health? I am worried at not having news of you.

G. Sand

---

[16] Name applied to Napoleon III.

LXXI. To George Sand 1st November, 1867

Dear master,

I was as much ashamed as touched, last evening, when I received your "very nice" letter. I am a wretch not to have answered the first one. How did that happen? For I am usually prompt.

My work does not go very well. I hope that I shall finish my second part in February. But in order to have it all finished in two years, I must not budge from my arm-chair till then. That is why I am not going to Nohant. A week of recreation means three months of revery for me. I should do nothing but think of you, of yours in Berry, of all that I saw. My unfortunate spirit would navigate in strange waters. I have so little resistance.

I do not hide the pleasure that your little word about *Salammbo* gives me. That old book needs to be relieved from a few inversions, there are too many repetitions of *alors, mais* and *et*. The labor is too evident.

As for the one I am doing, I am afraid that the idea is defective, an irremediable fault; will such weak characters be interesting? Great effects are reached only through simple means, through positive passions. But I don't see simplicity anywhere in the modern world.

A sad world! How deplorable and how lamentably grotesque are affairs in Italy! All these orders, counter-orders of counter-orders of the counter-orders! The earth is a very inferior planet, decidedly.

You did not tell me if you were satisfied with the revivals at the Odeon. When shall you go south? And where shall you go in the south?

A week from today, that is to say, from the 7th to the 10th of November, I shall be in Paris, because I have to go sauntering in Auteuil in order to discover certain little nooks. What would be nice would be for us to come back to Croisset together. You know very well that I am very angry at you for your two last trips in Normandy.

Then, I shall see you soon? No joking? I embrace you as I love you, dear master, that is to say, very tenderly.

Here is a bit that I send to your dear son, a lover of this sort of fluff:

"One evening, expected by Hortense, Having his eyes fixed on the clock, And feeling his heart beat with eager throbs, Young Alfred dried up with impatience." *(Memoires de l'Academie de Saint-Quentin.)*

LXXII. To Gustave Flaubert Nohant, 5 December, 1867

Your old troubadour is no good, I admit it. He has been working like an ox to have the money to go away with this winter to the gulf of Juan, and at the moment of leaving he would like to stay behind. He is worried at leaving his children and the little Aurore, but he suffers with the cold, he fears anemia, and he thinks he is doing his duty in going to find a land which the snow does not render impracticable, and a sky under which one can breathe without having dagger-thrusts in one's lungs.

So you see.

He has thought of you, probably much more than you think of him; for he has stupid and easy work, and his thoughts run elsewhere very far from him, and from his task, when his hand is weary of writing. As for you, you work for truth, and you become absorbed, and you have not heard my spirit, which more than once has *tapped* at your study door to say to you: "It is I." Or else you have said: "It is a spirit tapping let him go to the devil!"

Aren't you coming to Paris? I am going there between the 15th and the 20th. I shall stay there only a few days, and then flee to Cannes. Will you be there? God grant it! On the whole I am pretty well; I am furious with you for not wanting to come to Nohant; I won't reproach you for I don't know how. I have scribbled a lot; my children are always good and kind to me in every sense of the word. Aurore is a love.

We have *raved* politically; now we try not to think of it any more and to have patience. We often speak of you and we love you. Your old troubadour especially who embraces you with all his heart, and begs to be remembered to your good mother.

    G. Sand

LXXIII. To GEORGE SAND Wednesday night

Dear master, dear friend of the good God, "let us talk a little of Dozenval," let us roar at M. Thiers! Can a more triumphant imbecile, a more abject dabster, a more stercoraceous bourgeois be found! No, nothing can give the idea of the puking with which this old diplomatic idiot inspires me in piling up his stupidity on the dung-hill of bourgeoisie! Is it possible to treat philosophy, religion, peoples, liberty, the past and future, history, and natural history, everything and more yet, with an incoherence more inept and more childish! He seems to me as everlasting as mediocrity! He overwhelms me!

But the fine thing is the brave national guards whom he stuffed in 1848, who are beginning to applaud him again! What infinite madness! That proves that everything consists of temperament. Prostitutes,—like France,—always have a weakness for old buffoons.

Furthermore, I shall try in the third part of my novel (when I reach the reaction that followed the days of June) to insert a panegyric about him a propos of his book: *De la propriete,* and I hope that he will be pleased with me.

What form should one take to express occasionally one's opinion on the things of this world, without the risk of passing later for an imbecile? It is a tough problem. It seems to me that the best thing is simply to depict the things which exasperate one. To dissect is to take vengeance. Well! it is not he with whom I am angry, nor with the others but with *ours.*

If they had paid more attention to the education of the *superior* classes, delaying till later the agricultural meetings; in short, if the head had been put above the stomach, should we have been likely to be where we are now?

I have just read, this week, Buchez' Preface to his Histoire parlementaire. Many inanities which burden us today come from that among other things.

And now, it is not good of you to say that I do not think of "my old Troubadour"; of whom then, do I think? perhaps of my wretched book? but that is more difficult and less agreeable.

How long do you stay at Cannes?

After Cannes shan't you return to Paris? I shall be their towards the end of January.

In order to finish my book in the spring of 1869, I must not give myself a week of holiday; that is why I do not go to Nohant. It is always the story of the Amazons. In order to draw the bow better they crushed their breast. It is a fine method after all.

Adieu, dear master, write to me, won't you?

I embrace you tenderly.

LXXIV. To GUSTAVE FLAUBERT, at Croisset Nohant,
31 December, 1867

I don't agree with you at all that it is necessary to destroy the breast to draw a bow. I have quite a contrary belief which I follow, and I think that it is good for many others, probably for the majority. I have just developed my idea on that subject in a novel which has been sent to the Revue and will appear after About's. I think that the artist ought to live according to his nature as much as possible. To him who loves struggle, warfare; to him who loves women, love; to an old fellow like me who loves nature, travel and flowers, rocks, fine landscapes, children also, the family, all that stirs the emotions, that combats moral anemia.

I think that art always needs a palette overflowing with soft or striking colors according to the subject of the picture; the artist is an instrument on which everything ought to play before he plays on others; but all that is perhaps not applicable to a mind like yours which has acquired much and now has only to digest. I shall insist on one point only, that the physical being is necessary to the moral being and that I fear for you some day a deterioration of health which will force you to suspend your work and let it grow cold.

Well, you are coming to Paris the beginning of January and we shall see each other; for I shall not go until after the New Year. My children have made me promise to spend that day with them, and I could not resist, in spite of the great necessity of moving. They are so sweet! Maurice has an inexhaustible gaiety and invention. He has made for his marionette theatre, marvelous scenery, properties, and machinery and the plays which they give in that ravishing box are incredibly fantastic.

The last one was called 1870. One sees in it, Isidore with Antonelli commanding the brigands of Calabria, trying to regain his throne and to re-establish the papacy. Everything is in the future; at the end the widow Euphemia marries the Grand Turk, the only remaining sovereign. It is true that he is a former *democrat* and is recognized as none other than the great tumbler Coquenbois when unmasked. These plays last till two o'clock in the morning and we are crazy on coming out of them. We sup till five o'clock. There is a performance twice a week, and the rest of the time they make the properties, and the play continues with the same characters, going through the most incredible adventures.

The public is composed of eight or ten young people, my three great nephews, and sons of my old friends. They get excited to the point of yelling. Aurore is not admitted; the plays are not suited to her age. As for me, I am so amused that I become exhausted. I am sure that you would be madly amused by it also; for there is a splendid fire and abandon in these improvisations; and the characters done by Maurice have the appearance of living beings, of a burlesque life that is real and impossible at the same time; it seems like a dream. That is how I have been living for the ten days that I have not been working.

Maurice gives me this recreation in my intervals of repose that coincide with his. He brings to it as much ardor and passion as to his science. He has a truly charming nature and one never gets bored with him. His wife is also charming, quite large just now, always moving, busying herself with everything, lying down on the sofa twenty times a day, getting up to run after her child, her cook, her husband, who demands a lot of things for his theatre, coming back to lie down again; crying out that she feels ill and bursting into shrieks of laughter at a fly that circles about; sewing layettes, reading the papers with fervor, reading novels which make her weep; weeping also at the marionettes when there is a little sentiment, for there is some of that too. In short a personality and a type: she sings ravishingly, she gets angry, she gets tender, she makes succulent dainties *to surprise us with,* and every day of our vacation there is a little fete which she organizes.

Little Aurore promises to be very sweet and calm, understanding in a marvelous manner what is said to her and *yielding to reason* at two years of age. It is very extraordinary and I have never seen it before. It would be disquieting if one did not feel a great serenity in that little brain.

But how I am gossiping with you! Does all this amuse you? I should like this chatty letter to substitute for one of those suppers of ours which I too regret, and which would be so good here with you, if you were not a stick-in-the-mud, who won't let yourself be dragged away to *life for life's sake.* Ah! when one is on a vacation, how work, logic, reason seem strange *contrasts!* One asks whether one can ever return to that ball and chain.

I tenderly embrace you, my dear old fellow, and Maurice thinks your letter so fine that he is going to put the phrases and words at once in the mouth of his first philosopher. He bids me embrace you for him.

Madame Juliette Lambert[17] is really charming; you would like her a great deal, and then you have it 18 degrees above zero down there, and here we are in the snow. It is severe; moreover, I rarely go out, and my dog himself doesn't want to go out. He is not the least amazing member of society. When he is called Badinguet, he lies on the ground ashamed and despairing, and sulks all the evening.

---

[17] Afterwards, Madame Edmond Adam.

LXXV. TO GEORGE SAND 1st January, 1868

It is unkind to sadden me with the recital of the amusements at Nohant, since I cannot share them. I need so much time to do so little that I have not a minute to lose (or gain), if I want to finish my dull old book by the summer of 1869.

I did not say it was necessary to suppress the heart, but to restrain it, alas! As for the regime that I follow which is contrary to the laws of hygiene, I did not begin yesterday. I am accustomed to it. I have, nevertheless, a fairly seasoned sense of fatigue, and it is time that my second part was finished, after which I shall go to Paris. That will be about the end of the month. You don't tell me when you return from Cannes.

My rage against M. Thiers is not yet calmed, on the contrary! It idealizes itself and increases.

LXXVI. To GUSTAVE FLAUBERT Nohant, 12 January, 1868

No, it is not silly to embrace each other on New Year's day: on the contrary, it is good and it is nice. I thank you for having thought of it and I kiss you on your beautiful big eyes. Maurice embraces you also. I am housed here by the snow and the cold, and my trip is postponed. We amuse ourselves madly at home so as to forget that we are prisoners, and I am prolonging my holidays in a ridiculous fashion. Not an iota of work from morning till night. What luck if you could say as much!—But what a fine winter, don't you think so? Isn't it lovely, the moonlight on the trees covered with snow? Do you look at that at night while you are working?—If you are going to Paris the end of the month, I shall still have a chance to meet you.

From far, or from near, dear old fellow, I think of you and I love you from the depth of my old heart which does not know the flight of years.

G. Sand

My love to your mother always. I imagine that she is in Rouen during this severe cold.

LXXVII. TO GUSTAVE FLAUBERT Paris, 10 May, 1868

Yes, friend of my heart, am I not in the midst of terrible things; that poor little Madame Lambert[18] is severely threatened.

I saw M. Depaul today. One must be prepared for anything!—If the crisis is passed or delayed, for there is question of bringing on the event, I shall be happy to spend two days with my old troubadour, whom I love tenderly.

G. Sand.

---

[18] Madame Eugene Lambert, the wife of the artist.

LXXVIII. To GUSTAVE FLAUBERT Paris, 11 May, 1868

If you were to be at home Wednesday evening, I should go to chat an hour alone with you after dinner in your quarters. I despair somewhat of going to Croisset; it is tomorrow that that they decide the fate of my poor friend.

A word of response, and above all do not change any plan. Whether I see you or not, I know that two old troubadours love each other devotedly!

G. Sand Monday evening.

LXXIX. TO GUSTAVE FLAUBERT Paris, 17 May, 1868

I have a little respite, since they are not going to bring on the confinement. I hope to go to spend two days at that dear Croisset. But then don't go on Thursday, I am giving a dinner for the prince[19] at Magny's and I told him that I would detain you by force. Say yes, at once. I embrace you and I love you.

G. Sand

---

[19] Prince Jerome Napoleon.

LXXX. To Gustave Flaubert

I shall not go with you to Croisset, for you must sleep, and we talk too much. But on Sunday or Monday if you still wish it; only I forbid you to inconvenience yourself. I know Rouen, I know that there are carriages at the railway station and that one goes straight to your house without any trouble.

I shall probably go in the evening.

Embrace your dear mamma for me, I shall be happy to her again.

G. Sand

If those days do not suit you, a word, and I shall communicate with you again. Have the kindness to put the address on the *enclosed* letter and to put it in the mail.

LXXXI. To GUSTAVE FLAUBERT Paris,
21 Thursday—May, 1868

I see that the day trains are very slow, I shall make a
great effort and shall leave at eight o'clock Sunday, so as to
lunch with you; if it is too late don't wait for me, I lunch on two
eggs made into an omelet or shirred, and a cup of coffee. Or dine
on a little chicken or some veal and vegetables.

In giving up trying to eat *real meat,* I have found again a
strong stomach. I drink cider with enthusiasm, no more
champagne! At Nohant, I live on sour wine and galette, and
since I am not trying any more to *thoroughly nourish* myself, no
more anemia; believe then in the logic of physicians!

In short you must not bother any more about me than
about the cat and not even so much. Tell your little mother, just
that. Then I shall see you at last, all I want to for two days. Do
you know that you are *inaccessible* in Paris? Poor old fellow, did
you finally sleep like a dormouse in your cabin? I would like to
give you a little of my sleep that nothing, not even a cannon, can
disturb.

But I have had bad dreams for two weeks about my poor
Esther, and now at last, here are Depaul, Tarnier, Gueniaux and
Nelaton who told us yesterday that she will deliver easily and
very well, and that the child has every reason to be superb. I
breathe again, I am born anew, and I am going to embrace you
so hard that you will be scandalised. I shall see you on Sunday
then, and don't inconvenience yourself.

G. Sand

LXXXII. To GUSTAVE FLAUBERT Paris, 26 May, 1868

Arrived while dozing. Dined with your delightful and charming friend Du Camp. We talked of you, only of you and your mother, and we said a hundred times that we loved you. I am going to sleep so as to be ready to move tomorrow morning.

I am charmingly located on the Luxembourg garden.

I embrace you, mother and son, with all my heart which is entirely yours.

G. Sand

Tuesday evening, rue Gay-Lussac, 5.

LXXXIII. To GUSTAVE FLAUBERT Paris, 28 May, 1868

My little friend gave birth this morning after two hours of labor, to a boy who seemed dead but whom they handled so well that he is very much alive and very lovely this evening. The mother is very well, what luck!

But what a sight! It was something to see. I am very tired, but very content and tell you so because you love me.

G. Sand

Thursday evening. I leave Tuesday for Nohant.

LXXXIV. To GUSTAVE FLAUBERT, at Croisset Nohant,
21 June, 1868

Here I am again, *bothering* you for M. Du Camp's
address which you never gave me, although you forwarded a
letter for me to him, and from *whom* I never thought of asking
for it when I dined with him in Paris. I have just read his *Forces
Perdues;* I promised to tell him my opinion and I am keeping my
word. Write the address, then give it to the postman and thank
you.

There you are alone at odds with the sun in your
charming villa!

Why am I not the ... river which cradles you with its
sweet *murmuring* and which brings you freshness in your den! I
would chat discreetly with you between two pages of your novel,
and I would make that fantastic grating of the chain[20] which you
detest, but whose oddity does not displease me, keep still. I love
everything that makes up a milieu, the rolling of the carriages
and the noise of the workmen in Paris, the cries of a thousand
birds in the country, the movement of the ships on the waters; I
love also absolute, profound silence, and in short, I love
everything that is around me, no matter where I am; it is
auditory idiocy, a new variety. It is true that I choose my milieu
and don't go to the Senate nor to other disagreeable places.

Everything is going on well at our house, my troubadour.
The children are beautiful, we adore them; it is warm, I adore
that. It is always the same old story that I have to tell you and I

---

[20] The chain of the tug-boat going up or coming down the Seine.

love you as the best of friends and comrades. You see that is not new. I have a good and strong impression of what you read to me; it seemed to me so beautiful that it must be good. As for me, I am not sticking to anything. Idling is my dominant passion. That will pass, what does not pass, is my friendship for you.

G. Sand

Our affectionate regards.

LXXXV. To GEORGE SAND Croisset, Sunday, 5 July, 1868

I have sawed wood hard for six weeks. The patriots won't forgive me for this book, nor the reactionaries either! What do I care! I write things as I feel them, that is to say, as I think they are. Is it foolish of me? But it seems to me that our unhappiness comes exclusively from people of our class. I find an enormous amount of Christianity in Socialism.

There are two notes which are now on my table.

"This system (his) is not a system of disorder, for it has its source in the Gospels, and from this divine source, hatred, warfare, the clashing of every interest, *cannot proceed!* for the doctrine formulated from the Gospel, is a doctrine of peace, union and love." (L. Blanc).

"I shall even dare to advance the statement that together with the respect for the Sabbath, the last spark of poetic fire has been extinguished in the soul of our rhymesters. It has been said that without religion, there is no poetry!" (Proudhon).

A propos of that, I beg of you, dear master, to read at the end of his book on the observance of the Sabbath, a love-story entitled, I think, Marie et Maxime. One must know that to have an idea of the style of les Penseurs. It should be placed on a level with Le Voyage en Bretagne by the great Veuillot, in Ca et La. That does not prevent us from having friends who are great admirers of these two gentlemen.

When I am old, I shall write criticism; that will console me, for I often choke with suppressed opinions. No one understands better than I do, the indignation of the great Boileau against bad taste: "The senseless things which I hear at the Academy hasten my end." There was a man!

Every time now that I hear the chain of the steam-boats, I think of you, and the noise irritates me less, when I say to myself that it pleases you. What moonlight there is tonight on the river!

LXXXVI. To GUSTAVE FLAUBERT, at Croisset Nohant,
31 July, 1868

I am writing to you at Croisset in any case, because I
doubt if you are in Paris during this Toledo-like heat; unless the
shade of Fontainebleau has kept you. What a lovely forest, isn't
it? but it is especially so in winter, without leaves, with its fresh
moss, which has chic. Did you see the sand of Arbonne? There
is a little Sahara there which ought to be lovely now.

We are very happy here. Every day a bath in a stream
that is always cold and shady; in the daytime four hours of work,
in the evening, recreation, and the life of Punch and Judy. *A
travelling theatrical company* came to us; it was part of a
company from the Odeon, among whom were several old friends
to whom we gave supper at La Chatre, two successive nights
with all their friends, after the play;—songs, laughter, with
champagne frappe, till three o'clock in the morning to the great
scandal of the bourgeois, who would have committed any crime
to have been there. There was a very comic Norman, a real
Norman, who sang real peasant songs to us, in the real language.
Do you know that they have quite a Gallic wit and mischief?
They contain a mine of master-pieces of genre. That made me
love Normandy still more. You may know that comedian. His
name is Freville. It is he who is charged in the repertory with the
parts of the dull valets, and with being kicked from behind. He is
detestable, impossible, but out of the theatre, he is as charming
as can be. Such is fate!

We have had some delightful guests at our house, and we
have had a joyous time without prejudice to the Lettres d'un

Voyageur in the Revue, or to botanical excursions in some very surprising wild places. The little girls are the loveliest thing about it all. Gabrielle is a big lamb, sleeping and laughing all day; Aurore, more spiritual, with eyes of velvet and fire, talking at thirty months as others do at five years, and adorable in everything. They are keeping her back so that she shall not get ahead too fast.

You worry me when you tell me that your book will blame the patriots for everything that goes wrong. Is that really so? and then the victims! it is quite enough to be undone by one's own fault without having one's own foolishness thrown in one's teeth. Have pity! There are so many fine spirits among them just the same! Christianity has been a fad and I confess that in every age it is a lure when one sees only the tender side of it; it wins the heart. One has to consider the evil it does in order to get rid of it. But I am not surprised that a generous heart like Louis Blanc dreamed of seeing it purified and restored to his ideal. I also had that illusion; but as soon as one takes a step in this past, one sees that it cannot be revived, and I am sure that now Louis Blanc smiles at his dream. One should think of that also.

One must remind oneself that all those who had intelligence have progressed tremendously during the last twenty years and that it would not be generous to reproach them with what they probably reproach themselves.

As for Proudhon, I never thought him sincere. He is a rhetorician of *genius,* as they say. But I don't understand him. He is a specimen of perpetual antithesis, without solution. He affects one like one of the old Sophists whom Socrates made fun of.

I am trusting you for *generous* sentiments. One can say a word more or less without wounding, one can use the lash without hurting, if the hand is gentle in its strength. You are so kind that you cannot be cruel.

Shall I go to Croisset this autumn? I begin to fear not, and to fear that Cadio is not being rehearsed. But I shall try to escape from Paris even if only for one day.

My children send you their regards. Ah! Heavens! there was a fine quarrel about *Salammbo;* some one whom you do not know, went so far as not to like it, Maurice called him *bourgeois,* and to settle the affair, little Lina, who is high tempered, declared that her husband was wrong to use such a word, for he ought to have said *imbecile.* There you are. I am well as a Turk. I love you and I embrace you.

Your old Troubadour,

G. Sand

LXXXVII. To GEORGE SAND Dieppe, Monday

But indeed, dear master, I was in Paris during that tropical heat (trop picole, as the governor of the chateau of Versailles says), and I perspired greatly. I went twice to Fontainebleau, and the second time by your advice, saw the sands of Arboronne. It is so beautiful that it made me almost dizzy.

I went also to Saint-Gratien. Now I am at Dieppe, and Wednesday I shall be in Croisset, not to stir from there for a long time, the novel must progress.

Yesterday I saw Dumas: we talked of you, of course, and as I shall see him tomorrow we shall talk again of you.

I expressed myself badly if I said that my book "will blame the patriots for everything that goes wrong." I do not recognize that I have the right to blame anyone. I do not even think that the novelist ought to express his own opinion on the things of this world. He can communicate it, but I do not like him to say it. (That is a part of my art of poetry.) I limit myself, then, to declaring things as they appear to me, to expressing what seems to me to be true. And the devil take the consequences; rich or poor, victors or vanquished, I admit none of all that. I want neither love, nor hate, nor pity, nor anger. As for sympathy, that is different; one never has enough of that. The reactionaries, besides, must be less spared than the others, for they seem to be more criminal.

Is it not time to make justice a part of art? The impartiality of painting would then reach the majesty of the law,—and the precision of science!

Well, as I have absolute confidence in your great mind, when my third part is finished, I shall read it to you, and if there is in my work, something that seems *mean* to you, I will remove it.

But I am convinced beforehand that you will object to nothing.

As for allusions to individuals, there is not a shadow of them.

Prince Napoleon, whom I saw at his sister's Thursday, asked for news of you and praised Maurice. Princess Matilde told me that she thought you "charming," which made me like her better than ever.

How will the rehearsals of Cadio prevent you from coming to see your poor old friend this autumn? It is not impossible. I know Freville. He is an excellent and very cultivated man.

LXXXVIII. TO GEORGE SAND
Croisset, Wednesday evening, 9 September, 1868

Is this the way to behave, dear master? Here it is nearly two months since you have written to your old troubadour! you in Paris, in Nohant, or elsewhere? They say that Cadio is now being rehearsed at the Porte Saint-Martin (so you have fallen out with Chilly?) They say that Thuillier will make her re-appearance in your play. (But I thought she was dying). And when are they to play this Cadio? Are you content? etc., etc.

I live absolutely like an oyster. My novel is the rock to which I attach myself, and I don't know anything that goes on in the world.

I do not even read, or rather I have not read La Lanterne! Rochefort bores me, between ourselves. It takes courage to venture to say even hesitatingly, that possibly he is not the first writer of the century. O Velches! Velches! as M. de Voltaire would sigh (or roar)! But a propos of the said Rochefort, have they been somewhat imbecilic? What poor people!

And Sainte-Beuve? Do you see him? As for me, I am working furiously. I have just written a description of the forest of Fontainebleau that made me want to hang myself from one of its trees. As I was interrupted for three weeks, I am having terrible trouble in getting back to work. I am like the camels, which can't be stopped when they are in motion, nor started when they are resting. It will take me a year to finish the book. After that I shall abandon the bourgeois definitely. He is too difficult and on the whole too ugly. It will be high time to do something beautiful and that I like.

What would please me well for the moment, would be to embrace you. When will that be? Till then, a thousand affectionate thoughts.

LXXXIX. To Gustave Flaubert, at Croisset Paris,
10 September, 1868

Just at present, dear friend, there is a truce to my correspondence. On all sides I am reproached, *wrongly,* for not answering letters. I wrote you from Nohant about two weeks ago that I was going to Paris, on business about Cadio:—and now, I am returning to Nohant tomorrow at dawn to see my Aurore. I have written during the last week, four acts of the play, and my task is finished until the end of the rehearsals which will be looked after by my friend and collaborator, Paul Meurice. All his care does not prevent the working out of the first part from being a horrible bungle. One needs to see the putting-on of a play in order to understand that, and if one is not armed with humor and inner zest for the study of human nature in the actual individuals whom the fiction is to mask, there is much to rage about. But I don't rage any more, I laugh; I know too much of all that to get excited about it, and I shall tell you some fine stories about it when we meet.

However, as I am an optimist just the same, I look at the good side of things and people; but the truth is that everything is bad and everything is good in this world.

Poor Thuillier has not sparkling health; but she hopes to carry the burden of the work once more. She needs to earn her living, she is cruelly poor. I told you in my lost letter that Sylvanie[21] had been several days at Nohant. She is more beautiful than ever and quite well again after a terrible illness.

---

[21] Madame Arnould-Plessy.

Would you believe that I have not seen Sainte-Beuve? That I have had only the time here to sleep a little, and to eat in a hurry? It is just that. I have not heard anyone whatsoever talked about outside of the theatre and of the players. I have had mad desires to abandon everything and to go to surprise you for a couple of hours; but I have not been a day without being kept at *forced labor*.

I shall return here the end of the month, and when they play Cadio, I shall beg you to spend twenty-four hours here for me. Will you do it? Yes, you are too good a troubadour to refuse me. I embrace you with all my heart, and your mother too. I am happy that she is well.

G. Sand

XC. To GUSTAVE FLAUBERT Nohant, 18 September, 1868

It will be, I think, the 8th or 10th of October. The management announces it for the 26th of September. But that seems impossible to everyone. Nothing is ready; I shall be advised, I shall advise you. I have come to spend the days of respite that my very conscientious and very devoted collaborator allows me. I am taking up again a novel on the *theatre,* the first part of which I had left on my desk, and I plunge every day in a little icy torrent which tumbles me about and makes me sleep like a top. How comfortable one is here with these two little children who laugh and chatter from morning till night like birds, and how foolish it is to go to compose and to put on *made up things* when the reality is so easy and so fine! But one gets accustomed to regarding all that as a military order, and goes to the front without asking oneself if it means wounds or death. Do you think that that bothers me? No, I assure you; but it does not amuse me either. I go straight ahead, stupid as a cabbage and patient as a Berrichon. Nothing is interesting in my life except *other people*. Seeing you soon in Paris will be more of a pleasure than my business will be an annoyance to me. Your novel interests me more than all mine. Impersonality, a sort of idiocy which is peculiar to me, is making a noticeable progress. If I were not well, I should think that it was a malady. If my old heart did not become each day more loving, I should think it was egotism; in short, I don't know what it is, and there you are. I have had trouble recently. I told you of it in the letter which you did not receive. A person whom you know, whom I love greatly,

Celimene,[22] has become a religious enthusiast, oh! indeed, an ecstatic, mystic, molinistic religious enthusiast, I don't know what, imbecile! I have exceeded my limits. I have raged, I have said the hardest things to her, I have laughed at her. Nothing made any difference, it was all the same to her. Father Hyacinthe replaces for her every friendship, every good opinion; can you understand that? Her very noble mind, a real intelligence, a worthy character! and there you are! Thuillier is also religious, but without being changed; she does not like priests, she does not believe in the devil, she is a heretic without knowing it. Maurice and Lina are furious against I They don't like her at all. As for me, it gives me much sorrow not to love her any more.

We love you, we embrace you.

I thank you for coming to see Cadio.

G. Sand

---

[22] Madame Arnould-Plessy.

XCI. To George Sand

Does that astonish you, dear master? Oh well! it doesn't me! I told you so but you would not believe me.

I am sorry for you. For it is sad to see the friends one loves change. This replacement of one soul by another, in a body that remains the same as it was, is a distressing sight. One feels oneself betrayed! I have experienced it, and more than once.

But then, what idea have you of women, O, you who are of the third sex? Are they not, as Proudhon said, "the desolation of the Just"? Since when could they do without delusions? After love, devotion; it is in the natural order of things. Dorine has no more men, she takes the good God. That is all.

The people who have no need of the supernatural, are rare. Philosophy will always be the lot of the aristocrats. However much you fatten human cattle, giving them straw as high as their bellies, and even gilding their stable, they will remain brutes, no matter what one says. All the advance that one can hope for, is to make the brute a little less wicked. But as for elevating the ideas of the mass, giving it a larger and therefore a less human conception of God, I have my doubts.

I am reading now an honest book (written by one of my friends, a magistrate), on the Revolution in the Department of Eure. It is full of extracts from writings of the bourgeois of the time, simple citizens of the small towns. Indeed I assure you that there is now very little of that strength! They were literary and fine, full of good sense, of ideas, and of generosity.

Neo-catholicism on the one hand, and Socialism on the other, have stultified France. Everything moves between the

Immaculate Conception and the dinner pails of the working people.

I told you that I did not flatter the democrats in my book. But I assure you that the conservatives are not spared. I am now writing three pages on the abominations of the national guard in June, 1848, which will cause me to be looked at favorably by the bourgeois. I am rubbing their noses in their own dirt as much as I can. But you don't give me any details about Cadio. Who are the actors, etc.? I mistrust your novel about the theatre. You like those people too much! Have you known any well who love their art? What a quantity of artists there are who are only bourgeois gone astray!

We shall see each other in three weeks at the latest. I shall be very glad of it and I embrace you.

And the censorship? I really hope for you that it will make some blunders. Besides, I should be distressed if it was wanting in its usual habits.

Have you read this in the paper? "Victor Hugo and Rochefort, the greatest writers of the age." If Badinguet now is not avenged, it is because he is hard to please in the matter of punishments.

XCII. To Gustave Flaubert

The halcyons skim over the water and are common every where. The name is pretty and sufficiently well known.

I embrace you.

Your troubadour.

Paris, Friday evening, 28 August or 4 September, 1868. In October, yes, I will try!

XCIII. To GEORGE SAND Saturday evening

I received your two notes, dear master. You send me "halcyon" to replace the word, "dragonfly." Georges Pouchet suggested gerre of the lakes (genus, Gerris). Well! neither the one nor the other suits me, because they do not immediately make a picture for the ignorant reader.

Must I then describe that little creature? But that would retard the movement! That would fill up all the landscape I shall put "insects with large feet" or "long insects." That would be clear and short.

Few books have gripped me more than Cadio, and I share entirely Maxime's[23] admiration.

I should have told you of it sooner if my mother and my niece had not taken my copy. At last, this evening, they gave it back to me; it is here on my table, and I am turning the pages as I write you.

In the first place, it seems to me as if *it ought to have been the way it is!* It is plain, it gets you and thrills you. How many people must be like Saint-Gueltas, like Count de Sauvieres, like Rebec! and even like Henri, although the models are rarer. As for the character of Cadio, which is more of an invention than the others, what I like best in him is his ferocious anger. In it is the special truth of the character. Humanity turned to fury, the guillotine become mystic, life only a sort of bloody dream, that is what must take place in such heads. I think you have one Shakespearean scene: that of the delegate to the

---

[23] Maxime Du Camp.

Convention with his two secretaries, is of an incredible strength. It makes one cry out! There is one also which struck me very much at the first reading: the scene where Saint-Gueltas and Henri each have the pistols in their pockets: and many others. What a fine page (I open by chance) is page 161!

In the play won't you have to give a longer role to the wife of the good Saint-Gueltas? The play ought not to be very hard to cut. It is only a question of condensing and shortening it. If it is played, I'll guarantee a terrific success. But the censorship?

Well, you have written a masterpiece, that's true! and a very amusing one. My mother thinks it recalls to her stories that she heard while a child. A propos of Vendee, did you know that her paternal grandfather was, after M. Lescure, the head of the Vendee army? The aforesaid head was named M. Fleuriot d'Argentan. I am not any the prouder for that; besides the thing is doubtful, for my grandfather, a violent republican, hid his political antecedents.

My mother is going in a few days to Dieppe, to her grandchild's. I shall be alone a good part of the summer, and I plan to grub.

"I labor much and shun the world. It is not at balls that the future is founded." (Camilla Doucet.)

But my everlasting novel bores me sometimes in an incredible manner! These tiny details are stupid to bother with! Why annoy oneself about such a miserable subject?

I would write you at length about Cadio; but it is late and my eyes are smarting.

So, thank you, very kindly, my dear master.

XCIV. To M. GUSTAVE FLAUBERT, at Croisset Paris,
end of September, 1868

Dear friend,

It is for Saturday next, 3rd October. I am at the theatre
every evening from six o'clock till two in the morning. They talk
of putting mattresses behind the scenes for the actors who are
not in front. As for me, as used to wakefulness as you are, I
experience no fatigue; but I should be very much bored if I had
not the resource that one has always, of thinking of other things.
I am sufficiently accustomed to it to be writing another play
while they are rehearsing, and there is something quite exciting
in these great dark rooms where mysterious characters move,
talking in low tones, in unexpected costumes; nothing is more
like a dream, unless one imagines a conspiracy of patients
escaped from Bicetre.

I don't at all know what the performance will be. If one
did not know the prodigies of harmony and of vim which occur
at the last moment, one would judge it all impossible, with
thirty-five or forty speaking actors of whom only five or six
speak well. One spends hours over the exits and entrances of the
characters in blue or white blouses who are to be the soldiers or
the peasants, but who, meanwhile perform incomprehensible
manoeuvres. Still the dream. One has to be a madman to put on
these things. And the frenzy of the actors, pale and worn out,
who drag themselves to their place yawning, and suddenly start
like crazy people to declaim their tirade; continually the
assembling of insane people.

The censorship has left us alone as regards the manuscript; tomorrow these gentlemen will inspect the costumes, which perhaps will frighten them.

I left my dear world very quiet at Nohant. If Cadio succeeds, it will be a little *dot* for Aurore; that is all my ambition. If it does not succeed, I shall have to begin over again, that is all.

I shall see you. Then, in any case, that will be a happy day. Come to see me the night before, if you arrive the night before, or even the same day. Come to dine with me the night before or the same day; I am at home from one o'clock to five. Thank you; I embrace you and I love you.

G. Sand

XCV. To GUSTAVE FLAUBERT Paris, 5 October, 1868

Dear good friend, I recommend again to your good offices, my friend Despruneaux, so that you will again do what you can to be of use to him in a very just suit which has already been judged in his favor.

Yours,

G. Sand

XCVI. To Gustave Flaubert Nohant, 15 October, 1868

Here I am "ter hum" where, after having hugged my children and my grandchildren, I slept thirty-six hours at one stretch. You must believe that I was tired and did not notice it. I am waking from that animal-hibernation and you are the first person to whom I want to write. I did not thank you enough for coming to Paris for my sake, you who go about so little: and I did not see you enough either; when I knew that you had supped with Plauchut,[24] I was angry at having stayed to take care of my sickly Thuillier, to whom I was of no use, and who was not particularly pleased about it.

Artists are spoiled children and the best are great egoists. You say that I like them too well; I like them as I like the woods and the fields, everything, every one that I know a little and that I study continually. I make my life in the midst of all that, and as I like my life I like all that nourishes it and renews it. They do me a lot of ill turns which I see, but which I no longer feel. I know that there are thorns in the hedges, but that does not prevent me from putting out my hands and finding flowers there. If all are not beautiful, all are interesting. The day you took me to the Abbey of Saint-Georges I found the scrofularia borealis, a very rare plant in France. I was enchanted; there was much...in the neighborhood where I gathered it. Such is life!

And if one does not take life like that, one cannot take it in any way, and then how can one endure it? I find it amusing and interesting, and since I accept *everything,* I am so much happier and more enthusiastic when I meet the beautiful and the

---

[24] Edmond Plauchut, a writer and a friend of George Sand.

good. If I did not have a great knowledge of the species, I should not have quickly understood you, or known you or loved you. I can have an enormous indulgence, perhaps banal, for I have had to practice it so much; but appreciation is quite another thing, and I do not think that it is entirely worn out in your old troubadour's mind.

I found my children still very good and very tender, my two little grandchildren still pretty and sweet. This morning I dreamed, and I woke up saying this strange sentence: "There is always a youthful great first part in the drama of life. First part in mine: Aurore." The fact is that it is impossible not to idolize that little one. She is so perfect in intelligence and goodness, that she seems to me like a dream.

You also, without knowing it, *you are a dream* ... like that. Plauchut saw you once, and he adored you. That proves that he is not stupid. When he left me in Paris, he told me to remember him to you.

I left Cadio in doubt between good and average receipts. The cabal against the new management relaxed after the second day. The press was half favorable, half hostile. The good weather is against it. The hateful performance of Roger is also against it. So that we don't know yet if we shall make money or not. As for me, when money comes, I say, "So much the better," without excitement, and if it does not come, I say, "So much the worse," without any chagrin. Money not being the aim, ought not to be the preoccupation. It is, moreover, not the real proof of success, since so many vapid or poor things make money.

Here I am with another play already underway, so as to keep my hand in. I have a novel also on the stocks, on the *strolling players*. I have studied them a good deal this time without learning anything new. I already had the plot. It is not complicated and is very logical.

I embrace you tenderly as well as your little mother. Give me some sign of life. Does the novel get on?

G. Sand

XCVII. To GEORGE SAND Saturday evening

I am remorseful for not having answered at length your last letter, my dear master. You told me of the "ill turns" that people did you. Did you think that I did not know it? I confess to you even (between ourselves), that I was hurt on account of them more because of my good taste, than because of my affection for you. I did not think that several of your friends were warm enough towards you. "My God! my God! how mean literary men are!" A bit out of the correspondence of the first Napoleon. What a nice bit, eh? Doesn't it seem to you that they belittle him too much?

The infinite stupidity of the masses makes me indulgent to individualities, however odious they may be. I have just gulped down the first six volumes of Buchez and Roux. The clearest thing I got out of them is an immense disgust for the French. My Heavens! Have we always been bunglers in this fair land of ours? Not a liberal idea which has not been unpopular, not a just thing that has not caused scandal, not a great man who has not been mobbed or knifed! "The history of the human mind is the history of human folly!" as says M. de Voltaire.

And I am convinced more and more of this truth: the doctrine of grace has so thoroughly permeated us that the sense of justice has disappeared. What terrified me so in the history of '48 has quite naturally its origins in the Revolution, which had not liberated itself from the middle ages, no matter what they say. I have re-discovered in Marat entire fragments of Proudhon (sic) and I wager that they would be found again in the preachers of the League.

What is the measure that the most advanced proposed after Varennes? Dictatorship and military dictatorship. They close the churches, but they raise temples, etc.

I assure you that I am becoming stupid with the Revolution. It is a gulf which draws me in.

However, I work at my novel like a lot of oxen. I hope on New Year's Day not to have over a hundred pages more to write, that is to say, still six good months of work. I shall go to Paris as late as possible. My winter is to pass in complete solitude, good way of making life run along rapidly.

XCVIII. TO GUSTAVE FLAUBERT, in Paris Nohant,
20 November, 1868

You say to me, "When shall we see each other?" About
the 15th of December, we are baptizing here our two little girls
as Protestants. It is Maurice's idea; he was married before the
pastor, and does not want the persecution and influence of the
Catholic church about his children. Our friend Napoleon is the
godfather of Aurore, and I am the godmother. My nephew is the
godfather of the other. All that takes place just among ourselves,
in the family. You must come, Maurice wants you to, and if you
say no, you will disappoint him greatly. You shall bring your
novel, and in a free moment, you shall read it to me; it will do
you good to read it to one who listens well. One gets a
perspective and judges one's work better. I know that. Say yes to
your old troubadour, he will be *exceedingly grateful* to you for it.
I embrace you six times if you say yes.
G. Sand

XCIX. To George Sand Tuesday

Dear master,

You cannot imagine the sorrow you give me! In spite of the longing I have, I answer "no." Yet I am distracted with my desire to say "yes." It makes me seem like a gentleman who cannot be disturbed, which is very silly. But I know myself: if I go to your house at Nohant, I shall have a month of dreaming about my trip. Real pictures will replace in my brain the fictitious pictures which I compose with great difficulty. All my house of cards will topple over.

Three weeks ago because I was foolish enough to accept an invitation to dinner at a country place nearby, I lost four days (sic). What would it be on leaving Nohant? You do not understand that, you strong Being! I think that you will be a little vexed with your old troubadour for not coming to the baptism of the two darlings of his friend Maurice? The dear master must write to me if I am wrong, and to give me the news!

Here is mine! I work immoderately and am absolutely *enchanted* by the prospect of the end which begins to be visible.

So that it may arrive more quickly, I have made the resolution to live here all winter, probably until the end of March. Even admitting that everything goes perfectly, I shall not have finished all before the end of May. I don't know anything that goes on and I read nothing, except a little of the French Revolution, after my meals, to aid digestion. I have lost my former good habit of reading every day in Latin. Therefore I don't know a word of it any more! I shall polish it up again when I am freed from my odious bourgeois, and I am nowhere near it.

My only excitement consists in going to dine on Sundays at Rouen with my mother. I leave at six o'clock, and I am home at ten. Such is my life.

Did I tell you that I had a visit from Tourgueneff? How you would love him!

Sainte-Beuve gets along. Anyway, I shall see him next week when I am in Paris for two days, to get necessary information What is the information about? The national guard!!!

Listen to this: *le Figaro* not knowing with what to fill its columns, has had the idea of saying that my novel tells the life of Chancellor Pasquier. Thereupon, fear of the aforesaid family, which wrote to another part of the same family living in Rouen, which latter has been to find a lawyer from whom my brother received a visit, so that ... in short, I was very stupid not to "get some benefit from the opportunity." Isn't it a fine piece of idiocy, eh?

C. To Gustave Flaubert, at Ceoisset Nohant,
21 December, 1868

Certainly, I am cross with you and angry with you, not
from unreasonableness nor from selfishness, but on the contrary,
because we were joyous and *hilarious* and you would not
distract yourself and amuse yourself with us. If it was to amuse
yourself elsewhere, you would be pardoned in advance; but it
was to shut yourself up, to get all heated up, and besides for a
work which you curse, and which—wishing to do and being
obliged to do anyhow,—you ought to be able to do at your ease
and without becoming too absorbed in it.

You tell me that you are like that. There is nothing more
to say; but one may well be distressed at having an adored
friend, a captive in chains far away, whom one may not free. It is
perhaps a little coquettish on your part, so as to make yourself
pitied and loved the more. I, who have not buried myself alive in
literature, have laughed and lived a great deal during these
holidays, but always thinking of you and talking of you with our
friend of the Palais Royal,[25] who would have been happy to see
you and who loves you and appreciates you a great deal.
Tourgueneff has been more fortunate than we, since he was able
to snatch you from your ink-well. I know him personally very
little, but I know his work by heart. What talent! and how
original and polished! I think that the foreigners do better than
we do. They do not pose, while we either put on airs or grovel:

---

[25] Jerome Napoleon.

the Frenchman has no longer a social milieu, he has no longer an intellectual milieu.

I except you, you who live a life of exception, and I except myself, because of the foundation of careless unconventionally which was bestowed upon me; but I, I do not know how to be "careful" and to polish, and I love life too much, and I am amused too much by the mustard and all that is not the real "dinner," to ever be a litterateur. I have had flashes of it, but they have not lasted. Existence where one ignores completely one's "moi" is so good, and life where one does not play a role is such a pretty performance to watch and to listen to! When I have to give of myself, I live with courage and resolution, but I am no longer amused.

You, oh! fanatical troubadour, I suspect you of amusing yourself at your profession more than at anything in the world. In spite of what you say about it, art could well be your sole passion, and your shutting yourself up, at which I mourn like the silly that I am, your state of pleasure. If it is like that then, so much the better, but acknowledge it to console me.

I am going to leave you in order to dress the marionettes, for the plays and the laughter have been resumed with the bad weather, and that will keep us busy for a part of the winter, I fancy. Behold! here I am, the imbecile that you love, and that you call *master*. A fine master who likes to amuse himself better than to work!

Scorn me profoundly, but love me still. Lina tells me to tell you that you are not much, and Maurice is furious too; but we love you in spite of ourselves and embrace you just the same. Our friend Plauchut wants to be remembered to you; he adores you too.

Yours, you huge ingrate,

G. Sand

I had read the hoax of *le Figaro* and had laughed at it. It turns out to have assumed grotesque proportions. As for me, they gave me a grandson instead of two granddaughters, and a

Catholic baptism instead of a Protestant. That does not make any difference. One really has to lie a little to divert oneself.

CI. To Georges Sand Saint Sylvester's night, one o'clock, 1869

Why should I not begin the year of 1869 in wishing to you and to yours "Happy New Year and many of them"? It is rococo, but it pleases me. Now, let us talk.

No, I don't get into a heat, for I have never been better. They thought me, in Paris, "fresh as a young girl," and those people who don't know my life attributed that appearance of health to the air of the country. That is what conventional ideas are. Every one has his system. For my part, when I am not hungry, the only thing I can eat is dry bread. And the most indigestible food, such as apples in sour cider, and bacon, are what cure me of the stomach-ache. And so on. A man who has no common sense ought not to try to live according to common-sense rules.

As for my frenzy for work, I will compare it to an attack of herpes. I scratch myself while I cry. It is both a pleasure and a torture at the same time. And I am doing nothing that I want to! For one does not choose one's subjects, they force themselves on one. Shall I ever find mine? Will an idea fall from Heaven suitable to my temperament? Can I write a book to which I shall give myself heart and soul? It seems to me in my moments of vanity, that I am beginning to catch a glimpse of what a novel ought to be. But I still have three or four of them to write before that one (which is, moreover, very vague), and at the rate I am going, if I write these three or four, that will be the most I can do. I am like M. Prudhomme, who thinks that the most beautiful church would be one which had at the same time the spire of Strasbourg, the colonnade of Saint Peter's, the portico of the

Parthenon, etc. I have contradictory ideals. Thence embarrassment, hesitation, impotence.

As to whether the "claustration" to which I condemn myself may be a "state of joy," no. But what can I do? To get drunk with ink is more worth while than to get drunk with brandy. The muse, cross-grained as she is, gives less trouble than a woman. I cannot harmonize the one with the other. I must choose. My choice was made a long time ago. There remains the matter of the senses. They have always been my servants. Even at the time of my earliest youth, I did exactly as I wanted with them. I have reached my fiftieth year, and it is not their ardor that troubles me.

This regime is not amusing, I agree to that. There are moments of empty and horrible boredom. But they become more and more rare in proportion as one grows older. In short, *living* seems to me a business for which I was not made, and yet...!

I stayed in Paris for three days, which I made use of in hunting up information, and in doing errands about my book. I was so worn out last Friday, that I went to bed at seven o'clock in the evening. Such are my mad orgies at the capital.

I found the Goncourts in a frenzied (sic) admiration over a book entitled Histoire de ma vie by George Sand. Which proves more good taste than learning on their part. They even wanted to write to you to express all their admiration. (In return I found —— stupid. He compares Feydeau to Chateaubriand, admires very much the Lepreux de la cite d'Aoste, finds Don Quichotte tedious, etc.).

Do you notice how rare literary sense is? The knowledge of language, archeology, history, etc., all that should be useful however! Well! well! not at all! The so-called enlightened people are becoming more and more incompetent in the matter of art. Even what art means escapes them. The glosses for them are more important than the text. They pay more attention to the crutches than to the legs themselves.

CII. To Gustave Flaubert 1st January, 1869

It is one o'clock, I have just embraced my children. I am tired from having spent the night in making a complete costume for a large doll for Aurore; but I don't want to turn in without embracing you also, my great friend, and my dear, big child. May '69 be easy for you, and may it see the end of your novel. May you keep well and be always yourself! I don't know anything better, and I love you.

G. Sand

I have not the address of the Goncourts. Will you put the enclosed answer in the mail?

CIII. To GUSTAVE FLAUBERT, at Croissset Nohant,
17 January, 1869

The individual named George Sand is well: he is
enjoying the marvelous winter which reigns in Berry, gathering
flowers, noting interesting botanical anomalies, making dresses
and mantles for his daughter-in-law, costumes for the
marionettes, cutting out scenery, dressing dolls, reading music,
but above all spending hours with the little Aurore who is a
marvelous child. There is not a more tranquil or a happier
individual in his domestic life than this old troubadour retired
from business, who sings from time to time his little song to the
moon, without caring much whether he sings well or ill,
provided he sings the motif that runs in his head, and who, the
rest of the time, idles deliciously. It has not always been as nice
as this. He had the folly to be young; but as he did no evil nor
knew evil passions, nor lived for vanity, he is happy enough to
be peaceful and to amuse himself with everything.

This pale character has the great pleasure of loving you
with all his heart, and of not passing a day without thinking of
the other old troubadour, confined in his solitude of a frenzied
artist, disdainful of all the pleasures of this world, enemy of the
magnifying glass and of its attractions. We are, I think, the two
most different workers that exist; but since we like each other
that way, it is all right. The reason each of us thinks of the other
at the same hour, is because each of us has a need of his
opposite; we complete ourselves, in identifying ourselves at
times with what is not ourselves.

I told you, I think, that I had written a play on returning from Paris. They liked it; but I don't want them to play it in the spring, and the end of the winter is filled up, unless the play they are rehearsing fails. As I do not know how to *wish* my colleagues ill luck, I am in no hurry and my manuscript is on the shelf. I have the time. I am writing my little annual novel, when I have one or two hours a day to get to work on it; I am not sorry to be prevented from thinking of it. That develops it. Always before going to sleep, I have an agreeable quarter of an hour to continue it in my head; there you have it.

I know nothing, nothing at all of the Sainte-Beuve incident. I get a dozen newspapers, whose wrappers I respect to such an extent that without Lina, who tells me the chief news from time to time, I would not know if Isidore were still among us.

Sainte-Beuve is very high tempered, and, as regards opinions, so perfectly skeptical, that I should never be astonished at anything he did, in one sense or the other. He was not always like that, at least not so much so. I have known him to be more credulous and more republican than I was then. He was thin and pale, and gentle; how people change! His talent, his knowledge, his mind have increased enormously, but I used to like his character better. Just the same, there is still much good in him. There is still love and reverence for letters—and he will be the last of the critics. Criticism rightly so-called, will disappear. Perhaps there is no longer any reason for its existence. What do you think about it?

It appears that you are studying the boor (pignouf). As for me, I avoid him. I know him too well. I love the Berrichon peasant who is not, who never is, a boor, even when he is of no great account; the word pignouf has its depths; it was created exclusively for the bourgeois, wasn't it? Ninety out of a hundred provincial middle-class women are boorish (pignouf lardes) to a high degree, even with pretty faces that ought to give evidence of delicate instincts. One is surprised to find a basis of gross self-sufficiency in these false ladies. Where is the woman now? She is becoming a freak in society.

Good night, my troubadour: I love you, and I embrace you warmly; Maurice also.

G. Sand

CIV. TO GEORGE SAND Croisset, Tuesday, 2 February, 1869

My dear master,

You see in your troubadour a worn-out man. I have spent a week in Paris, looking up wearisome information (from seven to nine hours in fiacres every day, which is a fine way to make money out of literature). Oh, well!

I have just reread my outline. All that I have still to write horrifies me, or rather disgusts me, so that I want to vomit. It is always so, when I get to work. It is then that I am bored, bored, bored! But this time exceeds all others. That is why I dread so much interruptions in the daily grind. I could not do otherwise, however. I dragged about at funerals at Pere-Lachaise, in the valley of Montmorency, through shops of religious objects, etc.

In short, I have enough material for four or five months now. What a big "Hooray" I shall utter, when it is finished, and when I am not in the midst of remaking the bourgeois! It is high time that I enjoyed life.

I saw Sainte-Beuve and the Princess Mathilde, and I know thoroughly the story of their break, which seems to me irrevocable. Sainte-Beuve was outraged against Dalloz and has gone to *le Temps*. The princess begged him not to do anything about it. He did not listen to her. That is all. My opinion on it, if you wish to know it, is this. The first wrong was done by the princess, who was hasty; but the second and the worst was by pere Beuve, who did not behave as a courteous man. If one has a friend, a rather good fellow, and that friend has given one thirty thousand francs a year income, one owes him some consideration. It seems to me that in Sainte-Beuve's place I should have said, "That displeases you, let us talk no more about it." He lacked manners and poise. What disgusted me a little, between ourselves, was the way he praised the emperor to me! yes, he praised Badinguet, to me!—And we were alone!

The princess had taken the thing too seriously from the beginning. I wrote to her, saying that Sainte-Beuve was right; he, I am sure, found me rather cold. It was then, in order to justify himself to me, that he made these protestations of isidorian love, which humiliated me a little; for it was as if he took me for a complete imbecile.

I think that he is preparing for a funeral like Beranger's, and that Hugo's popularity makes him jealous. Why write for the papers, when one can make books, and when one is not perishing of hunger? He's no sage, Sainte-Beuve. Not like you!

Your strength charms me and amazes me. I mean the strength of your entire being, not only that of your brain.

You speak of criticism in your last letter to me, telling me that it will soon disappear. I think, on the contrary, that it is, at most, only at its dawning. They are on a different tack from before, but nothing more. At the time of La Harpe, they were grammarians; at the time of Sainte-Beuve and of Taine, they are historians. When will they be artists, only artists, but really artists? Where do you know a criticism? Who is there who is anxious about the work in itself, in an intense way? They analyze very keenly the setting in which it was written, and the causes that produced it; but the *unconscious* poetic expression? Where it comes from? its composition, its style? the point of view of the author? Never.

That criticism would require great imagination and great sympathy. I mean a faculty of enthusiasm that is always ready, and then *taste,* a rare quality, even among the best, so much so that one does not talk about it any longer.

What irritates me every day, is to see a master-piece and a disgrace put on the same level. They exalt the little, and they lower the great, nothing is more imbecile nor more immoral.

At Pere-Lachaise I was seized with a profound and sorrowful disgust for humanity. You cannot imagine the fetichism of the tombs. The real Parisian is more of an idolater than a negro is! It made me long to lie down in one of the graves.

And the *progressives* think that there is nothing better than to rehabilitate Robespierre! Note Hamel's book! If the Republic returned they would bless the liberty poles out of policy and believing that measure strong.

When shall I see you? I plan to be in Paris from Easter to the end of May, This spring I shall go to see you at Nohant, I swear it.

CV. To Gustave Flaubert Nohant, 11 February, 1869

While you are running around to get material for your novel, I am inventing all sorts of pretexts not to write mine. I let myself be distracted by guilty fancies, something I am reading fascinates me and I set myself to scribbling on paper that will be left in my desk and bring me no return. That has amused me, or rather that has compelled me, for it would be in vain for me to struggle against these caprices; they interrupt me and force me...you see that I have not the strength of mind that you think.

As for our masculine friend, he is ungrateful, while our feminine friend is too exacting. You were right; they are both wrong and it is not their fault, it is the social machinery which insists on it. The kind of recognition, that is to say, submission that she exacts, depends on a tradition that the present time still profits by (there lies the evil); but does not accept any longer as a duty. The notions of the obliged are changed, those of the obliger ought to change also. It must be said that one does not buy moral liberty by any kindness,—and as for him, he should have foreseen that he would be considered enchained. The simplest thing would have been not to care about having thirty thousand francs a year. It is so easy to do without it. Let him extricate himself. They won't entangle us in it: we aren't so foolish!

You say very good things about criticism. But in order to do as you say, there must be artists, and the artist is too much occupied with his own work, to forget himself in estimating that of others.

Heavens, what fine weather! Don't you enjoy it, at least from your window? I'll wager that the tulip tree is in bud. Here, the peaches and the apricots are in flower. It is said that they will be ruined; that does not stop them from being pretty and not tormenting themselves about it.

We have had our family carnival: my niece, my grandchildren, etc. We all put on fancy dress; it is not difficult here, one only has to go to the wardrobe and one comes down again as Cassandra, Scapin, Mezzetin, Figaro, Basile, etc., all that is very pretty. The pearl was Lolo as a little Louis XIII in crimson satin, trimmed with white satin fringed and laced with silver. I spent three days in making this costume, which was very chic; it was so pretty and so funny on that little girl of three years, that we were all amazed in looking at her.

Then we played charades, had supper, and frolicked till daylight. You see that banished to a desert, we keep up a good deal of vitality. And that I delay all I can, the trip to Paris and the chapter of business. If you were there, I would not need to be urged. But you are going there the end of March if and I cannot afford to wait till then. To conclude, you swear to come this summer and we count on it absolutely. Sooner than not have you come I shall go to drag you here by the hair.

I embrace you most warmly on this good hope.

G. Sand

CVI. To GUSTAVE FLAUBERT, at Croissset Nohant,
24 February, 1869

I am all alone at Nohant as you are all alone at Croisset.
Maurice and Lina have gone to Milan, to see Calamatta who is
dangerously ill. Should they have the misfortune to lose him,
they will have to go to Rome to settle his estate, an irksome task
added to a sorrow, it is always like that. That sudden separation
was sad, my poor Lina weeping at leaving her daughters and
weeping at not being with her father. They left me the care of the
children whom I rarely leave and who only let me work when
they sleep; but I am happier at having this care on my shoulders
to console me. I have, every day, in two hours news from Milan
by telegram. The patient is better; my children are only as far as
Turin today and do not know yet what I know. How this
telegraph changes one's idea of life, and when the formalities
and formulas are still more simplified, how full existence will be
of facts and how free from uncertainties.

Aurore, who lives on adorations in the lap of her father
and mother and who weeps every day when I am away, has not
asked a single time where they are. She plays and laughs, then
she stops; her great eyes stare, she says: *my father?* another time
she says: *mamma?* I distract her, she thinks no more of it, and
then she begins again. They are very mysterious, children! They
think without understanding. Only one sad word is needed to
bring out their sorrow. She carries it unconsciously. She looks in
my eyes to see if I am sad or anxious; I laugh and she laughs, I
think that we must keep her sensitiveness asleep as long as

possible, and that she never would weep for me if they did not speak of me.

What is your advice, you who have brought up an intelligent and charming niece? Is it wise to make them loving and affectionate early? I thought so formerly: I was afraid when I saw Maurice too impressionable and Solange too much the opposite, and resisting affection. I would like little ones to be shown only the sweet and the good of life, until the time when reason can help them to accept or to fight the bad. What do you say?

I embrace you and ask you to tell me when you are going to Paris, my trip is delayed as my children may be absent a month; I shall be able, perhaps, to meet you in Paris.

Your old solitary,

G. Sand

What an admirable definition I rediscover with surprise in the fatalist Pascal!

"Nature acts progressively, itus et reditus. It goes on and returns, then it goes still further, then half as far, then further than ever."[26]

What a way of speaking, eh? How the language turns, is twisted, made supple, is condensed under this grandiose "hand."

---

[26] George Sand had copied this and fastened it over her work table at Nohant.

CVII. To George Sand Tuesday night

What do I say about it, dear master? Should one excite or repress the sensitiveness of children? It seems to me that one should not have any set rule about it. It is according as they have a tendency to too much or too little. Moreover, the basis isn't changed. There are tender natures and hard natures, irremediably so. And then the same sight, the same lesson can produce opposite effects. Could anything have hardened me more than having been brought up in a hospital and having played, as a child, in a dissecting amphitheatre? But no one is more sensitive than I am to physical suffering. It is true that I am the son of an extremely humane man, sensitive in the true meaning of the word. The sight of a suffering dog made tears come to his eyes. He did his surgical operations none the less well, and he invented some dreadful ones.

"Show little ones only the sweet and the good of life until the time when reason can help them to accept or to fight the bad." Such is not my opinion. For then something terrible, an infinite disenchantment is bound to be produced in their hearts. And then, how could reason form itself, if it does not apply itself (or if one does not apply it daily) to distinguish good from evil? Life ought to be a continual education; one must learn everything—from talking to dying.

You tell me very true things about the unconsciousness of children. He who could read clearly in these little brains would grasp in them the roots of the human race, the origin of the gods, the sap which produces actions later on, etc. A negro who talks to his idol, and a child who talks to her doll seem to me close together.

The child and the savage (the primitive) do not distinguish the real from the fantastic. I remember very clearly that at five or six years of age I wanted to "send my heart" to a little girl with whom I was in love (I mean my material heart). I could see it in the middle of straw, in a basket, an oyster basket.

But no one has been so far as you in these analyses. There are some infinitely profound pages about it in the Histoire de ma vie. What I say is true, since minds quite opposite to yours have been amazed at them. For instance, the Goncourts.

The good Tourgueneff ought to be in Paris at the end of March. What would be fine, would be for us all three to dine together.

I am thinking again of Sainte-Beuve. Without doubt one can get along without thirty thousand francs a year. But there is something easier yet: that is, when one has them, not to launch into abuse, every week, in the papers. Why doesn't he write books, since he is rich and has talent?

I am just now reading *Don Quichotte* again. What a tremendous old book! Is there any more beautiful?

CVIII. To GUSTAVE FLAUBERT Nohant, 7 March, 1869

Still alone with my grandchildren; my nephews and friends come to spend two out of every three days with me, but I miss Maurice and Lina. Poor Calamatta is at the last gasp.

Give me the address of the Goncourts, you have never given it to me. Shall I never know it? My letter is still waiting there for them.

I love you and embrace you. I love you much, much, and I embrace you very warmly.

G. Sand

CIX. To GUSTAVE FLAUBERT Nohant, 12 March, 1869

Poor Calamatta died the 9th, my children are coming back. My Lina must be distressed. I have news from them only by telegraph. From Milan here in an hour and a half. But there are no details, and I am anxious. I embrace you tenderly,

G. Sand

Thank you for the address.

CX. To GUSTAVE FLAUBERT, at Croissset Nohant, 2 April, 1869

Dear friend of my heart, here we are once more calm again. My children returned to me very exhausted. Aurore has been a little ill. Lina's mother has come to get into touch with her about their affairs. She is a loyal and excellent woman, very artistic, and very amiable. I too have had a bad cold, but everything is getting better now, and our charming little girls console their little mother. If it were less bad weather, and I had a less bad cold, I would go at once to Paris, for I want to see you there. How long do you stay there? Tell me quickly.

I shall be very glad to renew my acquaintance with Tourgueneff, whom I knew a little without having read him, and whom I have since read with a whole-hearted admiration. You seem to me to love him a great deal; then I love him too, and I wish when your novel is finished, that you would bring him to our house. Maurice also knows him and appreciates him greatly, he who likes whatever does not resemble anything else.

I am working at my novel about *traveling actors*[27] like a convict. I am trying to have it amusing and to explain art; it is a new form for me and amuses me. Perhaps it will not have any success. The taste of the day is for marquises and courtesans; but what difference does that make?—You must find me a title, which is a resume of that idea: *the modern roman comique.*

My children send you affectionate greetings; your old troubadour embraces his old troubadour.

G. Sand

---

[27] Pierre qui roule.

Answer quickly how long you expect to stay in Paris. You say that you are paying bills and that you are vexed. If you have need of quibus, I have at the moment a few sous I can lend you. You know that you offered once to lend me some. If I had been in a hole I would have accepted. Give all my regards to Maxime Du Camp and thank him for not forgetting me.

CXI. To Gustave Flaubert Nohant, 17 April, 1869

I am well, I am finishing (today, I hope) my modern Roman comique which will be called I don't know what. I am a little tired, for I have done a lot of other things. But I am going to Paris in eight or ten days to rest, to embrace you, to talk of you, of your work, to forget mine, God be thanked! and to love you as always very much and very tenderly.

G. Sand

Regards from Maurice and his wife.

CXII. To GUSTAVE FLAUBERT Monday, 26 April, 1869

I arrived last night, I am running around like a rat, but every day at 6 o'clock one is sure of finding me at Magny's, and the first day that you are free, come to dine with your old troubadour who loves you and embraces you.

Send word ahead to me, however, so that by an exceptional chance, I do not have the ill luck to miss you.

Monday.

CXIII. To Gustave Flaubert
Thursday evening, 29 April, 1869

I am back from Palaiseau and I find your letter. Saturday I am not sure of being free; I have to read my play with Chilly on account of some objections of detail, and I had told you so. But I see him tomorrow evening, and I shall try to get him to give me another day. I shall write you then, tomorrow evening, Friday, and if he frees me, I shall go to your house about three o'clock on Saturday so that we can read before and after dinner; I dine on a little fish, a chicken wing, an ice and a cup of coffee, never anything else, by which means my stomach keeps well. If I am kept by Chilly, we shall postpone till next week after Friday.

I sold Palaiseau today to a master shoemaker who has a *leather* plaster on his right eye, and who calls the sumachs of the garden, the schumakre.

Then Saturday morning you shall have word from your old comrade.

G. Sand

CXIV. To Gustave Flaubert 30 April, 1869

No way of going out today. This slavery to one's profession is horrid, isn't it? Between now and Friday I shall write to you so that we can again settle on a day. I embrace you, my old beloved troubadour.

G. Sand

CXV. To Gustave Flaubert 3 May, 1869

They are encroaching upon my time more and more. All my days are full until and including next Sunday.—Tell me quickly if you want me Monday, a week from today—or if it is another day. Let us fix it for it is a fact that I don't really know whom to listen to.

Your troubadour who does not want *this state of affairs* to continue!

G. Sand
Monday.

CXVI. To Gustave Flaubert Paris, 4 May, 1869

On Monday then, and if I have an hour free I shall try to embrace my troubadour before that. But don't disturb yourself, I know very well that one does nothing here that one would like to do. Anyway, on Monday between three and four, clear out your windpipe so as to read me a part before dinner.

G. Sand

Tues. evening.

CXVII. To GUSTAVE FLAUBERT Sunday, 9 May, 1869

Tomorrow, your reverence, I shall go to dine at your house. I shall be at home every day at five o'clock, but you might meet some guys whom you dislike. You would much better come to Magny's where you would find me alone, or with Plauchut, or with friends who are also yours.

I embrace you. I received today the letter which you wrote to me at Nohant.

G. Sand

CXVIII. To GUSTAVE FLAUBERT Paris, 18 May, 1869

I saw Levy today, I tested him at first; I saw that he would not give up his contract at any price. I then said to him many good things about the book and made the remark that he had gotten it very cheap. But he said to me, if the book is in two volumes, it will be 20,000 francs, that is agreed. So I suppose that you will have two volumes, won't you?

However, I persisted and he said to me: If the book is a success, I shall not begrudge two or three thousand francs more. I said that you would not demand anything, that it was not your way of acting, but that for *my part,* I should insist for you without your knowledge, and he left me saying: Be easy, I don't say no. Should the book succeed I will make the author profit by it.

That is all that I have been able to do now, but I will take it up again at the proper time and place. Leave that to me, I will return your contract. What day next week will you dine with me at Magny's? I am a little weary.

You would be very kind to come to read at my house, we should be alone and one evening will be enough for the rest. Set the day, and *at six thirty* if that does not bother you. My stomach is beginning to suffer a little from Paris habits. Your troubadour who loves you,

G. Sand

The rest of the week will finish up Palaiseau, but Sunday if you like, I am free. Answer if you want Sunday at Magny's at half past six.

CXIX. To Gustave Flaubert

Then Monday, I count on you, at half past six; but as I am going to Palaiseau, I may be a few minutes late or early. The first one at Magny's must wait for the other. I am looking forward with pleasure to hearing *the rest*. Don't forget the manuscript.

Your troubadour

Thursday evening, 20 May, 1869.

CXX. To GUSTAVE FLAUBERT Paris, 29 May, 1869

Yes, Monday, my dear good friend, I count on you and I embrace you.

G. Sand

I am off for Palaiseau *and it is ten o'clock in the morning!*

CXXI. To George Sand

My prophecy is fulfilled; my friend X—— has gained only ridicule with his candidacy. That serves him right. When a man of style debases himself to practical life, he loses caste and should be punished. And then, is it a question of politics, now! The citizens who are excited for or against the Empire or the Republic seem to me as useful as those who discuss efficacious or efficient grace. Politics are as dead as theology! They have had three hundred years of existence, that is quite enough.

Just now I am lost in the Church Fathers. As for my novel *l'Education sentimentale,* I am paying no more attention to it, God be thanked! It is recopied. Other hands have gone over it. So, the thing is no longer mine. It does not exist any longer, good night. I have taken up again my old hobby of Saint Antoine. I have reread my notes, I am making another new plan and I am devouring the ecclesiastical memoirs of the Nain de Tillemont. I hope to succeed in finding a logical connection (and therefore a dramatic interest) between the different hallucinations of the Saint. This extravagant setting pleases me and I am absorbed in it, there you are!

My poor Bouilhet bothers me. He is in such a nervous state that they have advised him to take a little trip to the south of France. He is overwhelmed by an unconquerable melancholy. Isn't it queer! He who was so gay, formerly!

My Heavens! What a beautiful and farcical thing is the life of the desert Fathers! But without doubt they were all Buddhists. That is a stylish problem to work at, and its solution would be more important than the election of an academician. Oh! ye men of little faith! Long live Saint Polycarp!

Fangeat, who has reappeared recently, is the citizen who, on the 25th day of February, 1848, demanded the death of Louis-Philippe "without a trial." That is the way one serves the cause of progress.

CXXII. To George Sand

What a good and charming letter was yours, adored master! There is no one but you! upon my word of honor! I am ending by believing it. A wind of stupidity and folly is now blowing over the world. Those who stand up firm and straight against it are rare.

This is what I meant when I wrote that the times of politics were over. In the 18th century the chief business was diplomacy. "The secrecy of the cabinets" really existed. The peoples still were sufficiently amenable to be separated and to be combined. That order of things seems to me to have said its last word in 1815. Since then, one has hardly done anything except dispute about the external form that it is fitting to give the fantastic and odious being called the State.

Experience proves (it seems to me) that no form contains the best in itself; orleanism, republic, empire do not mean anything anymore, since the most contradictory ideas can enter into each one of these pigeon holes. All the flags have been so soiled with blood and with filth that it is time not to have any at all. Down with words! No more symbols nor fetiches! The great moral of this reign will be to prove that universal suffrage is as senseless as the divine right although a little less odions!

The question is then out of place. One is concerned no longer with dreaming of the best form of government, since all are equal, but with making science prevail. That is the most important. The rest will follow inevitably. Purely intellectual men have rendered more service to the human race than all the Saint Vincent de Pauls in the world! And politics will be an everlasting folly so long as it is not subordinate to science. The government of a country ought to be a section of the Institute, and the last section of all.

Before concerning yourself with relief funds, and even with agriculture, send to all the villages in France, Robert Houdins to work miracles! The greatest crime of Isidore is the wretched condition in which he leaves our beautiful country. Dixi.

I admire Maurice's occupations and his healthy life. But I am not capable of imitating him. Nature, far from fortifying me, drains my strength. When I lie on the grass I feel as if I am already under the earth and that the roots of green things are beginning to grow in my belly. Your troubadour is naturally an unhealthy man. I do not like the country except when travelling, because then the independence of my individuality causes me to rise above the knowledge of my nothingness.

CXXIII. To Gustave Flaubert Nohant, 6 August, 1869

Well, dear good friend, here it is August, and you have promised to come. We don't forget it, we count on it, we dream of it, and we talk of it every day. You were to take a trip to the seashore first if I am not mistaken. You must need to shake up your gloom. That does not dispel it, but it does force it to live with us and not be too oppressive. I have thought a great deal about you lately, I would have hastened to see you if I had not thought I should find you surrounded by older and better friends than I am. I wrote you at the same time that you wrote me, our letters crossed.

Come to see us, my dear old friend, I shall not go to Paris this month, I do not want to miss you. My children will be happy to spoil you and to try to distract you. We all love you, and I love you *passionately,* as you know.

CXXIV. To Gustave Flaubert Nohant, 14 August, 1869

Your change of plans distresses us, dear friend, but we do not dare to complain in the face of your anxieties and sorrows. We ought to wish you to do what would distract you the most, and take the least out of you. I am in hopes of finding you in Paris, as you are staying there some time and I always have business there. But it is so hard to see friends in Paris and one is so overwhelmed by so many tedious duties! Well, it is a real sorrow to me not to have to expect you any more at our house, where each one of us would have tried to love you better than the others and where you would have been at home; sad when you wanted to be, busy if you liked. I resign myself on condition that you will be better off somewhere else and that you will make it good to us when you can.

Have you at least arranged your affairs with Levy? Is he paying you for two volumes? I would like you to have something on which to live independently and as master of your time. Here there is repose for the mind in the midst of the exuberant activities of Maurice, and of his brave little wife who sets herself to love all he loves and to help him eagerly in all he undertakes. As for me, I have the appearance of incarnate idleness in the midst of this hard work. I botanize and I bathe in a little icy torrent. I teach my servant to read, I correct proof and I am well. That is my life and nothing bores me in this world where I think that *as far as i am concerned* all is for the best. But I am afraid of becoming more of a bore than I used to be. People don't like such as I am very much. We are too inoffensive. However, love me still a little, for I feel by the disappointment of not seeing you, that it would have gone hard with me if you had meant to break your word.

And I embrace you tenderly, dear old friend.

G. Sand

CXXV. To GUSTAVE FLAUBERT Thursday

I know nothing either of Chilly or la petite Fadette. In a few days I am going to make a tour of Normandy. I shall go through Paris. If you want to come around with me,—oh! but no, you don't travel about; well, we shall see each other in passing. I have certainly earned a little holiday. I have worked like a beast of burden. I need too to see some blue, but the blue of the sea will do, and you would like the blue of the artistic and literary firmament over our heads. Bah! that doesn't exist. Everything is prose, flat prose in the environment in which mankind has settled itself. It is only in isolating oneself a little that one can find in oneself the normal being again.

I am resuming my letter interrupted for two days by my wounded hand which inconveniences me a good deal. I am not going to Normandy at all, my Lamberts whom I was going to see in Yport came back to Paris and my business calls me there too. I shall then see you next week probably, and I shall embrace you as if you were my dear big child. Why can't I put the rosy, tanned face of Aurore in the place of mine! She is not what you would call pretty, but she is adorable and so quick in comprehending that we all are astonished. She is as amusing in her chatter as a person,—who might be amusing. So I am going to be forced to start thinking about my business! It is the one thing of which I have a horror and which really troubles my serenity. You must console me by joking with me a little when you have the time.

I shall see you soon, have courage in the sickening work of proof-reading. As for me I hurry over it quickly and badly, but you must not do as I do.

My children send you their love and your troubadour loves you.

G. Sand

Saturday evening

I have just received news from the Odeon. They are at work putting on my play and do not speak of anything else.

CXXVI. To GUSTAVE FLAUBERT Paris, 6 September, 1869

They wrote me yesterday to come because they wanted me at the Opera-Comique. Here I am rue Gay-Lussac. When shall we meet? Tell me. All my days, are still free.

I embrace you.

G. Sand

CXXVII. To GUSTAVE FLAUBERT Paris, 8 September, 1869

I send you back your handkerchief which you left in the carriage. It is surely tomorrow *Thursday* that we dine together? I have written to the big Marchal to come to Magny's too.

Your troubadour

G. Sand

Wednesday morning.

CXXVIII. To GUSTAVE FLAUBERT Paris, Tuesday,
5 October, 1869

Where are you now, my dear troubadour? I am still writing to you at the boulevard du Temple, but perhaps you have taken possession of your delightful lodgings. I don't know the address although I have seen the house, the situation and the view.—I have been twice in the Ardennes and in a week or ten days, if Lina or Maurice does not come to Paris, as they have a slight desire to do, I shall leave again for Nohant.

We must then meet and see each other. Here am I a little sfogata (eased) from my need for travel, and enchanted with what I have seen. Tell me what day except tomorrow, Wednesday, you can give me for dinner at Magny's or elsewhere with or without Plauchut, with whomever you wish provided I see you and embrace you.

Your old comrade who loves you.

G. Sand

CXXIX. To George Sand

Dear good adored master,

I have wanted for several days to write you a long letter in which I should tell you all that I have felt for a month. It is funny. I have passed through different and strange states. But I have neither the time nor the repose of mind to gather myself together enough.

Don't be disturbed about your troubadour. He will always have "his independence and his liberty" because he will always do as he has always done. He has left everything rather than submit to any obligation whatsoever, and then, with age, one's needs lessen. I suffer no longer from not living in the Alhambra.

What would do me good now, would be to throw myself furiously into *Saint-Antoine,* but I have not even the time to read.

Listen to this: in the very beginning, your play was to come after Aisse; then it was agreed that it should come *before.* Now Chilly and Duquesnel want it to come after, simply and solely "to profit by the occasion," to profit by my poor Bouilhet's death. They will give you a "sort of compensation." Well, I am the owner and the master of Aisse just as if I were the author, and I do not want that. You understand, I do not want you to inconvenience yourself in anything.

You think that I am as sweet as a lamb! Undeceive yourself, and act as if Aisse had never existed; and above all no sensitiveness?

That would offend me. Between simple friends, one needs manners and politenesses; but between you and me, that would not seem at all suitable; we do not owe each other anything at all except to love each other.

I think that the directors of the Odeon will regret Bouilhet in every way. I shall be less easy than he was at rehearsals. I should very much like to read Aisse to you so as to talk a little about it; some of the actors whom they propose are, to my way of thinking, impossible. It is hard to have to do with uneducated people.

CXXX. To Gustave Flaubert
Wednesday evening, 13 October, 1869

Our poor friend is not to be buried till the day after tomorrow, they will let me know where and when we ought to be there, I shall tell you by telegram.

I have seen the directors twice. It was agreed this morning with Duquesnel that they should make an attempt with de la T(our) Saint-Y(bars). I yielded my turn to Aisse. I was not to come till March. I went back there this evening, Chilly IS *unwilling,* and Duquesnel, better informed than this morning, regards the step as useless and harmful. I then quoted my contract, my right. What a fine thing, the theatre! M. Saint-Ybars' contract antedates mine. They had thought le Batard would last two weeks and it will last forty days longer. Then La Tour Saint-Ybars precedes us[28] and I cannot give up my turn to Aisse without being postponed till next year, which I'll do if you want me to; but it would do me a good deal of harm, for I have gotten into debt with the Revue and I must refill my purse.—Are directors rascals in all that? No, but incompetents who are always afraid of not having enough plays, and accept too many, foreseeing that they will have failures.—When they are successful, if the authors contracted for are *angry* they have to go to court. I have no taste for disputes and the scandals of the side-scenes and the newspapers; and neither have you. What would be the result? Inadequate compensation and a deal of uproar for nothing. One needs patience in any event, I have it,

---

[28] This refers to l'Affranchi.

and I tell you again if you are really upset at this delay, I am ready to sacrifice myself.

With this I embrace you and I love you.

G. Sand

CXXXI. To George Sand 14 October, 1869

Dear master,

No! no sacrifices! so much the worse! If I did not look at Bouilhet's affairs as mine absolutely, I should have at once accepted your proposition. But: (1) it is my affair, (2) the dead must not hurt the living.

But I am angry at these gentlemen, I do not hide it from you, for not having said anything to us about Latour Saint-Ybars. For the aforesaid Latour was engaged a long time ago. Why did we not know anything about him?

In short, let Chilly write me the letter on which we agreed Wednesday, and let there be no more discussion about it.

It seems to me that your play can be given the 15th of December, if l'Affranchi begins about the 20th of November. Two and a half months are about fifty performances; if you go beyond that, Aisse will not be presented till next year.

Then, it is agreed, since we cannot suppress Latour Saint-Ybars; you shall go after him and Aisse next, if I think it suitable.

We shall meet Saturday at poor Sainte-Beuve's funeral. How the little band diminishes! How the few survivors of the Medusa's raft are disappearing!

A thousand affectionate greetings.

CXXXII. To Gustave Flaubert Paris, 20 or 21 October, 1869

Impossible, dear old beloved. Brebant is too far, I have so little time. And then I have made an engagement with Marchal and Berton at Magny's to say farewell. If you can come, I shall be very happy and on the other hand if it is going to make you ill, don't come, I know very well that you love me and shall not be angry with you about anything.

G. Sand

CXXXIII. To Gustave Flaubert, at Croisset Nohant,
15 Nov., 1869

What has become of you, my dear old beloved
troubadour? are you correcting proof like a galley slave, up to
the last minute? For the last two days they have been announcing
your book *for tomorrow.* I am looking for it with impatience, for
you are not going to forget me, are you? You will be praised and
condemned; you expect that. You are too truly superior not to
arouse envy and you don't care, do you? Nor I either for you.
You have the strength to be stimulated by what discourages
others. There will certainly be a rumpus; your subject will be
quite opportune in this time of *revolutionists.* The good
progressives, the true democrats will approve of you. The idiots
will be furious, and you will say: "Come weal, come woe!"

I am also correcting proof of Pierre qui roule and I have
half finished a new novel which will not make much of a stir;
that is all that I ask for at the moment. I work alternately on *my*
novel, the one that I like, and on the one that the Revue does not
dislike as much, but which I like very little. It is arranged that
way; I don't know if I am making a mistake. Perhaps those
which I like are the worst. But I have stopped worrying about
myself, so far as I have ever done so. Life has always taken me
out of myself, and so it will to the end. My heart is always
affected to the detriment of my head. At present it is my little
children who devour all my intellect; Aurore is a jewel, a nature
before which I bow in admiration; will it last like that?

You are going to spend the winter in Paris, and I, I don't
know when I shall go. The success of le Batard continues; but I

am not impatient, you have promised to come as soon as you are free, at Christmas at the very latest, to keep revel with us. I think only of that, and if you break your word we shall be in despair here. With this I embrace you with a full heart as I love you.

G. Sand

CXXXIV. To Gustave Flaubert, at Paris Nohant,
30 November, 1869

Dear friend of my heart, I wanted to reread your book;[29] my daughter-in-law has read it too, and some of my young people, all readers in earnest and of the first rank and not stupid at all. We are all of the same opinion, that it is a beautiful book, equal in strength to the best ones of Balzac and truer, that is to say more faithful to the truth from one end to the other.

One needs the great art, the exquisite form and the severity of your work to do without flowers of fancy. However, you throw poetry with a full hand on your picture, whether your characters understand it or not. Rosanette at Fontainebleau does not know on what grass she walks and nevertheless she is poetic.

All that issues from a master's hand, and your place is well won for always. Live then as calmly as possible in order to last a long time and to produce a great deal.

I have seen two short articles which did not seem to me to rebel against your success; but I hardly know what is going on, politics seems to me to absorb everything.

Keep me posted. If they did not do justice to you I should be angry and should say what I think. It is my right.

I don't know exactly when, but during the month, I shall go without doubt to embrace you and to get you, if I can pry you loose from Paris. My children still count on it, and all of us send you our praises and our affectionate greetings.

Yours, your old troubadour
G. Sand

---

[29] *l'Education sentimentale.*

CXXXV. To GEORGE SAND

Dear good master,

Your old troubadour is vehemently slandered by the papers. Read the *Constitutionnel* of last Monday, the Gaulois of this morning, it is blunt and plain. They call me idiotic and common. Barbey d'Aurevilly's article *(Constitutionnel)* is a model of this character, and the good Sarcey's, although less violent, is in no way behind it. These gentlemen object in the name of morality and the Ideal! I have also been annihilated in *le Figaro* and in Paris, by Cesana and Duranty. I most profoundly don't care a fig! but that does not make me any the less astonished by so much hatred and bad faith.

La Tribune, le Pays and l'Opinion nationale on the other hand have highly praised me...As for the friends, the persons who received a copy adorned by my hand, they have been afraid of compromising themselves and have talked to me of other things. The brave are few. The book is selling very well nevertheless, in spite of politics, and Levy appears satisfied.

I know that the bourgeois of Rouen are furious with me "because of pere Roque and the cancan at the Tuileries." They think that one ought to prevent the publication of books like that (textual), that I lend a hand to the Reds, that I am capable of inflaming revolutionary passions, etc., etc. In short, I have received very few laurels, up to now, and no rose leaf hurts me.

I told you, didn't I, that I was working over the fairy play? I am doing now a description of the races and I have cut out all that seemed to me hackneyed. Raphael Felix didn't seem to me eager to become acquainted with it. Problem!

All the papers cite as a proof of my depravity, the episode of the Turkish woman, which they misrepresent, naturally; and Sarcey compares me to Marquis de Sade, whom he confesses he has not read!

All that does not upset me at all. But I wonder what use there is in printing my book?

CXXXVI. To GEORGE SAND Tuesday, 4 o'clock,
7 December, 1869

Dear master,

Your old troubadour is being jumped on in an unheard of manner. Those people who have read my novel are afraid to talk to me of it lest they compromise themselves or out of pity for me. The more indulgent declare I have made only pictures and that both composition and plan are quite lacking.

Saint-Victor, who puffs the books of Arsene Houssaye, won't write articles on mine, finding it too bad. There you are. Theo is away, and no one, absolutely no one takes my defense.

Another story: yesterday Raphael and Michel Levy listened to the reading of the fairy play. Applause, enthusiasm. I saw the moment during the reading in which the contract was going to be signed. Raphael so well understood the play that he gave me two or three *excellent* criticisms. I found him in other ways a charming boy. He asked me until Saturday to give me a definite answer. Then a little while ago, a letter (very polite) from the aforesaid Raphael in which he declares that the fairy play would entail expenses that would be too much for him.

Ditched again. I must look elsewhere. Nothing new at the Odeon.

Sarcey has published a second article against me.

Barbey d'Aurevilly claims that I dirty a stream by washing myself in it (sic). All that does not bother me at all.

CXXXVII. To Gustave Flaubert
Thursday, two o'clock in the morning, December 9, 1869

My comrade, it is finished, the article shall go tomorrow. I address it to whom? Answer by telegram. I have a mind to send it to Girardin. But perhaps you have a better idea, I really don't know the importance and the credit of the various papers. Send me a suitable name and *address* by telegram; I have Girardin's.

I am not content with my prose, I have had the fever and a sort of sprain for two days. But we must make haste. I embrace you.

G. Sand

CXXXVIII. To George Sand
10 December, Friday, 10 o'clock in the evening, 1869

Dear master, good as good bread,

I have just sent you by telegraph this message: "To Girardin." La Liberte will publish your article, at once. What do you think of my friend Saint-Victor, who has refused to write an article about it because he finds "the book bad"? you have not such a conscience as that, have you?

I continue to be rolled in the mud. La Gironde calls me Prudhomme. That seems new to me.

How shall I thank you? I feel the need of saying affectionate things to you. I have so many in my heart that not one comes to the tips of my fingers. What a splendid woman you are and what a splendid man! To say nothing of all the other things!

CXXXIX. To Gustave Flaubert, Nohant,
Friday to Saturday during the night, 10 to 11 December, 1869

I have rewritten my article[30] today and this evening, I am better, it is clearer. I am expecting your telegram tomorrow. If you do not put your veto on it, I shall send the article to Ulbach, who begins his paper the 15th of this month; he wrote to me this morning to beg me urgently for any article I would send him. I think this first number will be widely read, and it would be good publicity. Michel Levy would be a better judge than we as to what is the best to do: consult him.

You seem astonished at the ill will. You are too simple. You do not know how original your book is, and how many personal feelings must be offended by the force it contains. You think you are doing things that will pass as a letter in the mail; ah! well, yes!

I have insisted on the *plan* of your book; that is what they understand the least and it is what is the most important. I tried to show the ordinary people how they should read; for it is the ordinary people who make successes. The clever ones don't like the successes of others. I don't pay attention to the malicious; it would honor them too much.

G. S.

My mother has your telegram and is sending her manuscript to Girardin.

4 o'clock in the afternoon.

Lina

---

[30] The article, *Sur l'Education sentimentale, de Flaubert,* was printed in the *Questions d'art et de litterature,* Calmann-Levy, p. 415.

CXL. To GUSTAVE FLAUBERT, in Paris Nohant,
14 December, 1869

I do not see my article coming out, but others are appearing which are bad and unjust. One's enemies are always better served than one's friends. And then, when one frog begins to croak, all the others follow suit. After a certain reverence has been violated every one tries to see who can best jump on the shoulders of the statue; it is always like that. You are undergoing the disadvantages of having a style that is not yet familiar through repetition, and all are making idiots of themselves so as not to see it.

Absolute impersonality is debatable, and I do not accept it *absolutely;* but I wonder that Saint-Victor who has preached it so much and has criticised my plays because they were not *impersonal,* should abandon you instead of defending you. Criticism is in a sad way; too much theory!

Don't be troubled by all that and keep straight on. Don't attempt a system, obey your inspiration.

What fine weather, at least with us, and we are getting ready for our Christmas festivals with the family at home. I told Plauchut to try to carry you off; we are expecting him. If you can't come with him, come at least for the Christmas Eve revels and to escape from Paris on New Year's day; it is so boring there then!

Lina charges me to say to you that you are authorized to wear your wrapper and slippers continually. There are no ladies, no strangers. In short you will make us very happy and you have promised for a long time.

I embrace you and I am still more angry than you at these attacks, but I am not overcome, and if I had you here we should stimulate each other so well that you would start off again at once on the other leg to write a new novel.

I embrace you.

Your old troubadour,

G. Sand

CXLI. To Gustave Flaubert, in Paris Nohant,
17 December, 1869

Plauchut writes us that *you promise* to come the 24th. Do come the 23d in the evening, so as to be rested for the night of the 24th to the 25th and join in our Christmas Eve revels. Otherwise you will arrive from Paris tired and sleepy and our follies will not amuse you. You are coming to the house of children, I warn you, and as you are kind and affectionate, you love children. Did Plauchut tell you to bring a wrapper and slippers, for we do not want to sentence you to dressing up? I add that I am counting on your bringing some manuscript.

The *Fairy Play* re-done, *Saint-Antoine,* whatever you have finished. I hope indeed that you are in the mood for work. Critics are a challenge that stimulates.

Poor Saint-Rene Taillandier is as asininely pedantic as the Revue. Aren't they prudish in that set? I am in a pet with Girardin. I know very well that I am not strong in letters; I am not sufficiently cultivated for these gentlemen; but the good public reads me and listens to me all the same.

If you did not come, we should be unhappy and you would be a big ingrate. Do you want me to send a carriage for you to Chateauroux on the 23d at four o'clock? I am afraid that you may be uncomfortable in that stage-coach which makes the run, and it is so easy to spare you two and a half hours of discomfort!

We embrace you full of hope. I am working like an ox so as to have my novel finished and not to have to think of it a minute when you are here.

G. Sand

CXLII. To GUSTAVE FLAUBERT Nohant, 19 December, 1869

So women are in it too? Come, forget that persecution here, at a hundred thousand leagues from Parisian and literary life, or rather come be glad of it, for these great slatings are the sure proof of great worth. Tell yourself indeed that those who have not gone through that are *good for the academy.*

Our letters crossed. I begged you and I beg you again not to come Christmas Eve, but the night before so as to join in the revels the next night, the Eve, that is to say, the 24th. This is the program: we dine promptly at six o'clock, we have the Christmas tree and the marionettes for the children, so, that they can go to bed at nine o'clock. After that we chatter, and sup at midnight. But the diligence gets here at the earliest at half past six, and we should not dine till seven o'clock, which would make impossible the great joy of our little ones who would be kept up too late. So you must start Thursday 23d at nine o'clock in the morning, so that everyone may be perfectly comfortable, so that everyone may have time to embrace everyone else, and so that no one may be interrupted in the joy of your arrival on account of the imperious and silly darlings.

You must stay with us a very long time, a very long time, we shall have some more follies for New Year's day, and for Twelfth Night. This is a crazy happy house and it is the time of holiday after work. I am finishing tonight my year's task.

Seeing you, dear old well-beloved friend, would be my recompense: do not refuse me.

G. Sand

Plauchut is hunting today with the prince, and perhaps will not return till Tuesday. I am writing him to wait for you till Thursday, you will be less bored on the way. I have just written to Girardin to complain.

CXLIII. To Gustave Flaubert 31 December, 1869

We hoped to have a word from you this morning. This sudden cold is so severe, I dreaded it for your trip. We know you got to Chateauroux all right. But did you find a compartment, and didn't you suffer on the way? Reassure us.

We were so happy to have you with us that we should be distressed if you had to suffer for this *winter* escapade. All goes well here and all of us adore one another. It is New Year's Eve. We send your share of the kisses that we are giving one another.

G. Sand

CXLIV. To GUSTAVE FLAUBERT, at Croissset Nohant,
9 January, 1870

I have had so much proof to correct that I am stupefied
with it. I needed that to console me for your departure,
troubadour of my heart, and for another departure also, that of
my drudge of a Plauchmar—and still another departure, that of
my grand-nephew Edme, my favorite, the one who played the
marionettes with Maurice. He has passed his examinations for
collector and goes to Pithiviers—unless by pull, we could get
him as substitute at La Chatre.

Do you know M. Roy, the head of the management of the
domains? If by chance the princess knew him and would be
willing to say a word to him in favor of young Simonnet? I
should be happy to owe her this joy for his family and this
economy for his mother who is poor. It appears that it is very
easy to obtain and that no rule opposes it. But one must *have
pull;* a word to the princess, a line from M. Roy and our tears
would change to joy.

That child is very dear to me. He is so loving and so
good! They had hard work to bring him up, he was always ill,
always dandled on the knees and always gentle and sweet. He
has a great deal of intelligence and he works well at La Chatre,
where his chief the collector adores him and mourns for him
also. Well, do what you can, if you can do anything at all.

They continue to damn your book. That doesn't prevent
it from being a fine and good book. Justice will come later,
justice is always done. Apparently it did not come at the right
moment, or rather it came too soon. It has demonstrated too well

the disorder that reigns in people's minds. It has rubbed the open wound, people recognize themselves too well in it.

Everyone adores you here and our consciences are too pure to be upset at the truth: we talk of you every day. Yesterday, Lina said to me that she admired very much all you do, but that she preferred *Salammbo* to your modern descriptions. If you had been in a corner, this is what you would have heard from her, from me, and from *the others:*

"He is taller and larger than the average person. His mind is like him, beyond ordinary proportions. In that he is like Victor Hugo, at least as much as like Balzac, but he has the taste and discernment that Hugo lacks, and he is an artist which Balzac was not.—Is he then more than both? *Chi lo sa?*—He hasn't let himself out yet. The enormous volume of his brain troubles him. He doesn't know if he is a poet or a realist; and the fact that he is both, hinders him.—He must get straightened out in his different lines of effort. He sees everything and wants to grasp everything at once.—He is not the cut of the public that wants to eat in little mouthfuls, whom large pieces choke. But the public will go to him, just the same, when it understands.—It will even go rather quickly if the author *condescends* to be willing to be quite understood.—For that, perhaps there will have to be asked some concessions to the indolence of its mind. One ought to reflect before daring to give this advice."

That sums up what we said. It is not useless to know the opinion of good people and of young people. The youngest say that *l'Education sentimentale* made them sad. They did not come across themselves in it, they who have not yet lived; but they have illusions and they say: "Why does this man, so good, so kind, so gay, so simple, so sympathetic, wish to discourage us from living?" What they say is poorly reasoned out, but as it is instinctive, perhaps it ought to be taken into account.

Aurore talks of you and still cradles her baby in her lap; Gabrielle calls Punch, *her little one,* and will not eat her dinner unless he is opposite her. They are our continual idols, these brats.

Yesterday, I received, after your letter of the day before, a letter from Berton, who thinks that they will not play l'Affranchi longer than the 18th or the 20th. Wait for me, since you can delay your departure a little. It is too bad weather to go to Croisset; it is always an effort for me to leave my dear nest to go to attend to my miserable profession; but the effort is less when I hope to find you in Paris.

I embrace you for myself and for all my brood.

G. Sand

CXLV. To GEORGE SAND Wednesday afternoon.

Dear master,

Your commission was done yesterday at one o'clock. The princess in my presence took some notes on what you wanted, in order to look after it at once. She seemed to me very glad to do you a service.

People talk of nothing but the death of Noir! The general sentiment is fear, nothing else!

Into what miserable ways we are plunged! There is so much imbecility in the air that one gets ferocious. I am less indignant than disgusted! What do you think of these gentlemen who come to confer armed with pistols and sword canes! And of this person, of this prince, who lives in the midst of an arsenal and makes use of it? Pretty! Pretty!

What a sweet letter you wrote me day before yesterday! But your friendship blinds you, dear good master. I do not belong to the tribe you mention. I am acquainted with myself, I know what I lack! And I am enormously lacking.

In losing my poor Bouilhet, I lost my midwife, it was he who saw into my thought more clearly than I did myself. His death has left a void that I notice more each day. What is the use of making concessions? Why force oneself? I am quite resolved, on the contrary, to write in future for my personal satisfaction, and without any constraint. Come what may!

CXLVI. To Gustave Flaubert Nohant, 15 January, 1870

L'Affranchi is for Tuesday. I am working hurriedly to finish my corrections and I leave Tuesday morning. Come to dine with me at Magny's at six o'clock. Can you? If not, am I to keep a seat for you in my box? A word during the day of Tuesday, to my lodgings. You won't be forced to swallow down the entire performance if it bores you.

I love you and I embrace you for myself and for my brood. Thank you for Edme.

G. Sand

CXLVII. To Gustave Flaubert Paris, 19 January, 1870

Dear friend of my heart, I did not see you in the theatre. The play applauded and hissed, more applauded than hissed. Barton very beautiful, Sarah very pretty, but no interest in the characters and too many second-rate actors, not good.—I do not think that it is a success.

I am better. Yet I am not bold enough to go to your house Saturday and to return from such a distance in this severe cold. I saw Theo this evening, I told him to come to dine with us both on Saturday at Magny's. Do say yes, it is I who invite you, and we shall have a quiet private room. After that we will smoke at my place.

Plauchut would not be able to go to you. He was invited to the prince's.

A word if it is *no*. Nothing if it is yes. So I don't want you to write to me. I saw Tourgueneff and I told him all that I think of him. He was as surprised as a child. We spoke ill of you.

Wednesday evening.

CXLVIII. To Gustave Flaubert
The 5th or the 6th February, 1870
(On the back of a letter from Edme Simonnet)

I don't see you, you come to the Odeon and when they tell me that you are there, I hurry and don't find you. Do set a day then when you will come to eat a chop with me. Your old exhausted troubadour who loves you.

CXLIX. To GUSTAVE FLAUBERT Paris, 15 February, 1870

My troubadour, we are two old rattle traps. As for me, I have had a bad attack of bronchitis and I am just out of bed. Now I am recovered but not yet out of my room. I hope to resume my work at the Odeon in a couple of days.

Do get well, don't go out, at least unless the thaw is not very bad. My play is for the 22d.[31] I hope very much to see you on that day. And meanwhile, I kiss you and I love you,

G. Sand

Tuesday evening

[31] This refers to L'Autre.

CL. To GUSTAVE FLAUBERT Sunday evening,
20th February, 1870

     I went out today for the first time, I am better without being well. I am anxious at not having news about that reading of the fairy play. Are you satisfied? Did they understand? L'Autre will take place on Thursday, or Friday at the latest.

     Will your nephew and niece go to the gallery or the balcony seats? Impossible to have a box. If yes, a word and I will send these seats out of my allotment—which, as usual, will not be grand.

     Your old troubadour.

CLI. To GUSTAVE FLAUBERT Paris, February, 1870

It is for Friday. Then I am disposing of the two seats that I intended for your niece.

If you have a moment free, and come to the Odeon that night, you will find me in the manager's box, proscenium, ground floor. I am heavy-hearted about all you tell me. Here you are again in gloom, sorrow and chagrin. Poor dear friend! Let us continue to hope that you will save your patient, but you are ill too, and I am very anxious about you, I was quite overwhelmed by it this evening, when I got your note, and I have no more heart for anything.

A word when you can, to give me news.

G. Sand

CLII. To GUSTAVE FLAUBERT Paris, 2d March, 1870

Poor dear friend, your troubles distress me, you have too many blows in quick succession, and I am going away Saturday morning leaving you in the midst of all these sorrows! Do you want to come to Nohant with me, for a change of air, even if only for two or three days? I have a compartment, we should be alone and my carriage is waiting for me at Chateauroux.

You could be sad without constraint at our house, we also have mourning in the family. A change of lodging, of faces, of habits, sometimes does physical good. One does not forget one's sorrow, but one forces one's body to endure it.

I embrace you with all my soul. A word and I expect you. Wednesday evening.

CLIII. To GUSTAVE FLAUBERT Nohant, 11 March, 1870

How are you, my poor child? I am glad to be here in the midst of my darling family, but I am unhappy all the same at having left you melancholy, ill and upset. Send me news, a word at least, and be assured that we all are unhappy over your troubles and sufferings.

G. Sand

CLIV. To George Sand 17 March, 1870

Dear master,

I received a telegram yesterday evening from Madame Cornu containing these words: "Come to me, urgent business." I therefore hurried to her today, and here is the story.

The Empress maintains that you made some very unkind allusions to her in the last number of the Revue! "What about me, whom all the world is attacking now! I should not have believed that! and I wanted to have her nominated for the Academy! But what have I done to her? etc., etc."

In short, she is distressed, and the Emperor too! He is not indignant but prostrated (sic).[32]

Madame Cornu explained to her that she was mistaken and that you had not intended to make any allusion to her.

Hereupon a theory of the manner in which novels are written.

—Oh well, then, let her write in the papers that she did not intend to wound me.

—But she will not do that, I answered.

—Write to her to tell you so.

—I will not allow myself to take that step.

—But I would like to know the truth, however! Do you know someone who...then Madame Cornu mentioned me.

—Oh, don't say that I spoke to you of it!

---

[32] Malgre tout, Calmann-Levy, 1870.

Such is the dialogue that Madame Cornu reported to me.

She wants you to write me a letter in which you tell me that the Empress was not used by you as a model. I shall send that letter to Madame Cornu who will have it given to the Empress.

I think that story stupid and those people are very sensitive! Much worse things than that are told to us.

Now dear master of the good God, you must do exactly what you please.

The Empress has always been very kind to me and I should not be sorry to do her a favor. I have read the famous passage.

I see nothing in it to hurt her. But women's brains are so queer!

I am very tired in mine (my brain) or rather it is very low for the moment! However hard I work, it doesn't go! Everything irritates me and hurts me; and since I restrain myself before people, I give way from time to time to floods of tears when it seems to me as if I should burst. At last I am experiencing an entirely new sensation: the approach of old age. The shadow invades me, as Victor Hugo would say.

Madame Cornu has spoken to me enthusiastically of a letter you wrote her on a method of teaching.

CLV. To GUSTAVE FLAUBERT, at Croissset Nohant,
17 March, 1870

I won't have it, you are not getting old. Not in the crabbed and *misanthropic* sense. On the contrary, when one is good, one becomes better, and, as you are already better than most others, you ought to become exquisite.

You are boasting, moreover, when you undertake to be angry against everyone and everything. You could not. You are weak before sorrow, like all affectionate people. The strong are those who do not love. You will never be strong, and that is so much the better. You must not live alone any more; when strength returns you must really live and not shut it up for yourself alone.

For my part, I am hoping that you will be reborn with the springtime. Today we have rain which relaxes, tomorrow we shall have the animating sun. We are all just getting over illnesses, our children had very bad colds, Maurice quite upset by lameness with a cold, I taken again by chills and anemia: I am very patient and I prevent the others as much as I can from being impatient, there is everything in that; impatience with evil always doubles the evil. When shall we be *wise* as the ancients understood it? That, in substance, meant being *patient,* nothing else. Come, dear troubadour, you must be a little patient, to begin with, and then you can get accustomed to it; if we do not work on ourselves, how can we hope to be always in shape to work on others?

Well, in the midst of all that, don't forget that we love you and that the hurt you give yourself hurts us too.

I shall go to see you and to shake you as soon as I have regained my feet and my will, which are both backward; I am waiting, I know that they will return.

Affectionate greetings from all our invalids. Punch has lost only his fiddle and he is still smiling and well gilded. Lolo's baby has had misfortunes, but its clothes dress other dolls.

As for me, I can flap only one wing, but I kiss you and I love you.

G. Sand

CLVI. To Gustave Flaubert, in Paris Nohant, 19 March, 1870

I know, my friend, that you are very devoted to her. I know that she[33] is very kind to unfortunates who have been recommended to her; that is all that I know of her private life. I have never had any revelation nor document about her, *not a word, not a deed,* which would authorize me to depict her. So I have drawn only a figure of fancy, I swear it, and those who pretended to recognize her in a satire would be, in any case, bad servants and bad friends.

But I don't write satires: I am ignorant even of the meaning of the word. I don't write *portraits* either; it is not my style. I invent. The public, who does not know in what invention consists, thinks it sees everywhere models. It is mistaken and it degrades art.

This is my *sincere* answer, I have only enough time to mail it.

G. Sand

---

[33] Letter written about the rumour current, that George Sand had meant to depict the Empress in one of the chief characters of her novel, Malgre tout; the letter was sent by Flaubert to Madame Cornu, god-child of Queen Hortense, and foster-sister of Napoleon III.

CLVII. To Madame Hortense Cornu

Your devotion was alarmed wrongly, dear madame, I was sure of it! Here is the answer that came to me by return mail.

People in society, I reiterate, see allusions where there are none. When I did *Madame Bovary* I was asked many times: "Is it Madame X. whom you meant to depict?" and I received letters from perfectly unknown people, among others one from a gentleman in Rheims who congratulated me on *having avenged him!* (against a faithless one).

Every pharmacist in Seine-Inferieure recognizing himself in Homais, wanted to come to my house to box my ears. But the best (I discovered it five years later) is that there was then in Africa the wife of an army doctor named Madame Bovaries who was like *Madame Bovary*, a name I had invented by altering that of Bouvaret.

The first sentence of our friend Maury in talking to me about *l'Education sentimentale* was this: "Did you know X, an Italian, a professor of mathematics? Your Senecal is his physical and moral portrait! Everything is exact even to the cut of his hair!"

Others assert that I meant to depict in Arnoux, Bernard Latte (the former editor), whom I have never seen, etc., etc.

All that is to tell you, dear madame, that the public is mistaken in attributing to us intentions which we do not have.

I was very sure that Madame Sand had not intended to make any portrait; (1) because of her loftiness of mind, her taste, her reverence for art, and (2) because of her character, her feeling for the conventions—and also *for justice.* I even think, between ourselves, that this accusation has hurt her a little. The papers roll us in the dirt every day without our ever answering them, we whose business it is, however, to wield the pen, and they think that in order to *make an effect,* to be applauded, we are going to attack such and such a one.

Oh! no! not so humble! our ambition is higher, and our courtesy greater.—When one thinks highly of one's mind one does not choose the necessary means to please the crowd. You understand me, don't you?

But enough of this. I shall come to see you one of these days. Looking forward to that with pleasure, dear madame, I kiss your hands and am entirely yours,

Gustave Flaubert

Sunday evening.

CLVIII. To GEORGE SAND March, 1870

Dear master,

I have just sent your letter (for which I thank you) to Madame Cornu, enclosing it in a letter from your troubadour, in which I permitted myself to give bluntly my conception of things.

The two letters will be placed under the eyes of the *lady* and will teach her a little about aesthetics.

I saw l'Autre last evening, and I wept several times. It did me good, really! How tender and exalting it is! What a charming work and how they love the author! I missed you. I wanted to give you a kiss like a little child. My oppressed heart is easier, thank you. I think that it will get better! There were a lot of people there. Berton and his son were recalled twice.

CLIX. To Gustave Flaubert Nohant, 3 April, 1870

Your old troubadour has passed through cruel anguish, Maurice has been seriously, dangerously ill.[34] Favre, *my own* doctor, the only one in whom I have confidence, hastened to us in time. After that Lolo had violent attacks of fever, other terrors! At last our savior went off this morning leaving us almost tranquil and our invalids went out to walk in the garden for the first time.—But they still want a great deal of care and oversight, and I shall not leave them for two or three weeks. If then you are awaiting me in Paris, and the sun calls you elsewhere, have no regret about it. I shall try to go to see you in Croisset from Paris between the dawn and the dusk sometime.

At least tell me how you are, what you are doing, if you are on your feet in every way.

My invalids and my well ones send you their affectionate regards, and I kiss you as I love you; it is not little.

G. Sand

My friend Favre has quite a *fancy* for you and wants to know you. He is not a physician who seeks practice, he only practices for his friends, and he is offended if they want to pay him. *your personality* interests him, that is all, and I have promised to present him to you, if you are willing. He is something more than a physician, I don't know what exactly, *a seeker*—after what?—*everything*. He is amusing, original and interesting to the utmost degree. You must tell me if you want to

---

[34] With diptheria.

see him, otherwise I shall manage for him not to think of it any more. Answer about this matter.

CLX. To GEORGE SAND Monday morning, 11 o'clock

I felt that something unpleasant had happened to you, because I had just written to you for news when your letter was brought to me this morning. I fished mine back from the porter; here is a second one.

Poor dear master! How uneasy you must have been and Madame Maurice also. You do not tell me what he had (Maurice). In a few days before the end of the week, write to confirm to me that everything has turned out well. The trouble lies, I think, with the abominable winter from which we are emerging! One hears of nothing but illnesses and funerals! My poor servant is still at the Dubois hospital, and I am distressed when I go to see him. For two months now he has been confined to his bed suffering horribly.

As for me, I am better. I have read prodigiously. I have overworked, but now I am almost on my feet again. The mass of gloom that I have in the depths of my heart is a little larger, that is all. But, in a little while, I hope that it will not be noticed. I spend my days in the library of the Institute. The Arsenal library lends me books that I read in the evening, and I begin again the next day. I shall return home to Croisset the first of May. But I shall see you before then. Everything will get right again with the sun.

The lovely lady in question made to me, for you, the most proper excuses, asserting to me that "she never had any intention of insulting genius."

Certainly, I shall be glad to meet M. Favre; since he is a friend of yours I shall like him.

CLXI. TO GEORGE SAND Tuesday morning

Dear master,

It is not staying in Paris that wears me out, but the series of misfortunes that I have had during the last eight months! I am not working too much, for what would become of me without work? However, it is very hard for me to be reasonable. I am overwhelmed by a black melancholy, which returns a propos of everything and nothing, many times a day. Then, it passes and it begins again. Perhaps it is because it is too long since I have written anything. Nervous reservoirs are exhausted. As soon as I am at Croisset, I shall begin the article about my poor Bouilhet, a painful and sad task which I am in a hurry to finish, so as to set to work at *Saint-Antoine*. As that is an extravagant subject, I hope it will divert me.

I have seen your physician, M. Favre, who seemed to me very strange and a little mad, between ourselves. He ought to like me for I let him talk all the time. There are high lights in his talk, things which sparkle for a moment, then one sees not a ray.

CLXII. To GEORGE SAND Paris, Thursday

M. X—— sent me news of you on Saturday: so now I know that everything is going well with you, and that you have no more uneasiness, dear master. But you, personally, how are you? The two weeks are almost up, and I do not see you coming.

My mood continues not to be sportive. I am still given up to abominable readings, but it is time that I stopped for I am beginning to be disgusted with my subject.

Are you reading Taine's powerful book? I have gobbled it down, the first volume with infinite pleasure. In fifty years perhaps that will be the philosophy that will be taught in the colleges.

And the preface to the Idees de M. Aubray?

How I long to see you and to jabber with you!

CLXIII. To Gustave Flaubert Nohant, 16 April, 1870

What ought I to say to Levy so that he will take the first steps? Tell me again how things are, for my memory is poor. You had sold him one volume for ten thousand;—there are two, he himself told me that that would be twenty thousand. What has he paid you up to now? What words did you exchange at the time of this payment?

Answer, and I act.

Things are going better and better here, the little ones well again, Maurice recovering nicely, I tired from having watched so much and from watching yet, for he has to drink and wash out his mouth during the night, and I am the only one in the house who has the faculty of keeping awake. But I am not ill, and I work a little now and then while loafing about. As soon as I can leave, I shall go to Paris. If you are still there, it will be *a piece of good luck,* but I do not dare to wish you to prolong your slavery there, for I can see that you are still ill and that you are working too hard.

Croisset will cure you if you consent to take care of yourself.

I embrace you tenderly for myself and for all the family which adores you.

G. Sand

CLXIV. To GUSTAVE FLAUBERT, at Croisset Nohant,
20 May, 1870

It is a very long time since I have had news of my old
troubadour. You must be in Croisset. If it is as warm there as it
is here, you must be suffering; here it is 34 degrees in the shade,
and in the night, 24. Maurice has had a bad relapse of sore
throat, without membranes this time, and without danger. But
the inflammation was so bad that for three days he could hardly
swallow even a little water and wine. Bouillon did not go down.
At last this excessive heat has cured him, it suits us all here, for
Lina went to Paris this morning vigorous and strong. Maurice
gardens all day. The children are gay and get prettier while you
look at them. As for me, I am not accomplishing anything; I
have too much to do taking care of and watching my boy, and
now that the little mother is away, the little children absorb me. I
work, however, planning and dreaming. That will be so much
done when I can scribble.

I am still *on my feet,* as Doctor Favre says. No old age
yet, or rather normal old age, the calmness ... *of virtue,* that thing
that people ridicule, and that I mention in mockery, but that
corresponds by an emphatic and silly word, to a condition of
forced inoffensiveness, without merit in consequence, but
agreeable and good to experience. It is a question of rendering it
useful to art when one believes in that, to the family and to
friendship when one cares for that; I don't dare to say how very
simple and primitive I am in this respect. It is the fashion to
ridicule it, but let them. I do not want to change.

There is my *spring* examination of my conscience, so as not to think all summer about anything except what is not myself.

Come, you, your health first? And this sadness, this discontent that Paris has left with you, is it forgotten? Are there no longer any painful external circumstances? You have been too much shaken also. Two of your dearest friends gone one after the other. There are periods in life when destiny is ferocious to us. You are too young to concentrate on the idea of *regaining* your affections in a better world, or in this world made better. So you must, at your age (and at mine I still try to), become more attached to what remains. You wrote that to me when I lost Rollinat, my double in this life, the veritable friend whose feeling for the differences between the sexes had never hurt our pure affection, even when we were young. He was my Bouilhet and more than that; for to my heart's intimacy was joined a religious reverence for a real type of moral courage, which had undergone all trials with a sublime *sweetness*. I have *owed* him everything that is good in me, I am trying to keep it for love of him. Is there not a heritage that our beloved dead leave us?

The despair that would make us abandon ourselves would be a treason to them and an ingratitude. Tell me that you are calm and soothed, that you are not working too much and that you are working well. I am not without some anxiety because I have not had a letter from you for a long time. I did not want to ask for one till I could tell you that Maurice was quite well again; he embraces you, and the children do not forget you. As for me, I love you.

G. Sand

CLXV. To George Sand

No, dear master! I am not ill, but I have been busy with moving from Paris and with getting settled in Croisset. Then my mother has been very much indisposed. She is well now; then I have had to set in order the rest of my poor Bouilhet's papers, on whom I have begun the article. I wrote this week nearly six pages, which was very good for me; this work is very painful in every way. The difficulty is in knowing what not to say. I shall console myself a little in blurting out two or three dogmatic opinions on the art of writing. It will be an opportunity to express what I think; a sweet thing and one I am always deprived of.

You say very lovely and also good things to me to restore my courage. I have hardly any, but I am acting as if I had, which perhaps comes to the same thing.

I feel no longer the need of writing, for I used to write especially for one person alone, who is no more. That is the truth! And yet I shall continue to write. But I have no more liking for it; the fascination is gone. There are so few people who like what I like, who are anxious about what I am interested in! Do you know in this Paris, which is so large, one SINGLE house where they talk about literature? And when it happens to be touched on incidentally, it is always on its subordinate and external sides, such as the question of success, of morality, of utility, of its timeliness, etc. It seems to me that I am becoming a fossil, a being unrelated to the surrounding world.

I would not ask anything better than to cast myself on some new affection. But how? Almost all my old friends are married officials, thinking of their little business the entire year, of the hunt during vacation and of whist after dinner. I don't know one of them who would be capable of passing an afternoon with me reading a poet. They have their business; I, I have none. Observe that I am in the same social position that I was at eighteen. My niece whom I love as my daughter, does not live with me, and my poor good simple mother has become so old that all conversation with her (except about her health) is impossible. All that makes an existence which is not diverting.

As for the ladies, "my little locality" furnishes none of them, and then,—even so! I have nevver been able to put Venus an Apollo in the same coop. It is one or the other, being a man of excess, a gentleman entirely given over to what he does.

I repeat to myself the phrase of Goethe: "Go forward beyond the tombs," and I hope to get used to the emptiness, but nothing more.

The more I know you, yourself, the more I admire you; how strong you are!

Aside from a little Spinoza and Plutarch, I have read nothing since my return, as I am quite occupied by my present work. It is a task that will take me up to the end of July. I am in a hurry to be through with it, so as to abandon myself to the extravagances of the good *Saint-Antoine,* but I am afraid of not being *sufficiently in the mood.*

That is a charming story, Mademoiselle Hauterive, isn't it? This suicide of lovers to escape misery ought to inspire fine moral phrases from Prudhomme. As for me, I understand it. What they did is not American, but how Latin and antique it is! They were not strong, but perhaps very sensitive.

CLXVI. To GEORGE SAND Sunday, 26 June, 1870

You forget your troubadour who has just buried another friend! From the seven that we used to be at the beginning of the dinners at Magny's, we are only three now! I am gorged with coffins like an old cemetery! I am having enough of them, frankly.

And in the midst of all that I keep on working! I finished yesterday, such as it is, the article on my poor Bouilhet. I am going to see if there is not some way of reviving one of his comedies in prose. After that I shall set to work on *Saint-Antoine*.

And you, dear master, what is happening to you and all your family? My niece is in the Pyrenees, and I am living alone with my mother, who is becoming deafer and deafer, so that my existence lacks diversion absolutely. I should like to go to sleep on a warm beach. But for that I lack time and money. So I must push on my scratches and grub as hard as possible.

I shall go to Paris at the beginning of August. Then I shall spend all the month of October there for the rehearsals of Aisse. My vacation will be confined to a week spent in Dieppe towards the end of August. There are my plans.

It was distressing, the funeral of Jules Goncourt. Theo wept buckets full.

CLXVII. To GUSTAVE FLAUBERT Nohant, 27 June, 1870

Another grief for you, my poor old friend. I too have a great one, I mourn for Barbes, one of my religions, one of those beings who make one reconciled with humanity. As for you, you miss poor Jules[35] and you pity the unhappy Edmond. You are perhaps in Paris, so as to try to console him. I have just written him, and I feel that you are struck again in your affections. What an age! Every one is dying, everything is dying, and the earth is dying also, eaten up by the sun and the wind. I don't know where I get the courage to keep on living in the midst of these ruins. Let us love each other to the end. You write me very little, I am worried about you.

G. Sand

---

[35] De Goncourt.

CLXVIII. To GEORGE SAND Saturday evening, 2 July, 1870

Dear good master,

Barbes' death has saddened me because of you. We, both of us, have our mourning. What a succession of deaths during a year! I am as dazed by them as if I had been hit on the head with a stick. What troubles me (for we refer everything to ourselves), is the terrible solitude in which I live. I have no longer anyone, I mean anyone with whom to converse, "who is interested today in eloquence and style."

Aside from you and Tourgueneff, I don't know a living being to whom to pour out my soul about those things which I have most at heart; and you live far away from me, both of you!

However, I continue to write. I have resolved to start at my *Saint-Antoine* tomorrow or the day after. But to begin a protracted effort I need a certain lightness which I lack just now. I hope, however, that this extravagant work is going to get hold of me. Oh! how I would like not to think any more of my poor Moi, of my miserable carcass! It is getting on very well, my carcass. I sleep tremendously! "The coffer is good," as the bourgeois say.

I have read lately some amazing theological things, which I have intermingled with a little of Plutarch and Spinoza. I have nothing more to say to you.

Poor Edmond de Goncourt is in Champagne at his relatives'. He has promised to come here the end of this month. I don't think that the hope of seeing his brother again in a better world consoles him for having lost him in this one.

One juggles with empty words on this question of immortality, for the question is to know if the moi persists. The affirmative seems to me a presumption of our pride, a protest of our weakness against the eternal order. Has death perhaps no more secrets to reveal to us than life has?

What a year of evil! I feel as if I were lost in the desert, and I assure you, dear master, that I am brave, however, and that I am making prodigious efforts to be stoical. But my poor brain is enfeebled at moments. I need only one thing (and that is not given me), it is to have some kind of enthusiasm!

Your last letter but one was very sad. You also, heroic being, you feel worn out! What then will become of us!

I have just reread the conversations between Goethe and Eckermann. There was a man, that Goethe! But then he had everything on his side, that man.

CLXIX. To Gustave Flaubert, at Croissset Nohant,
29 June, 1870

Our letters are always crossing, and I have now the feeling that if I write to you in the evening I shall receive a letter from you the next morning; we could say to each other:

"You appeared to me in my sleep, looking a little sad."

What preoccupies me most about poor Jules' (de Goncourt) death, is the survivor. I am sure that the dead are well off, that perhaps they are resting before living again, and that in all cases they fall back into the crucible so as to reappear with what good they previously had and more besides. Barbes only suffered all his life. There he is now, sleeping deeply. Soon he will awaken; but we, poor beasts of survivors, we see them no longer. A little while before he died, Duveyrier, who seemed to have recovered, said to me: "Which one of us will go first?" We were exactly the same age. He complained that those who went first could not let those who were left know that they were happy, and that they remembered their friends. I said, *who knows?* Then we promised each other that the first one to die should appear to the survivor, and should at least try to speak to him.

He did not come, I have waited for him, he has said nothing to me. He had one of the tenderest hearts, and a sincere good will. He was not able to; it was not permitted, or perhaps, it was I; I did not hear or understand.

It is, I say, this poor Edmond who is on my mind. That life lived together, quite ended. I cannot think why the bond was broken, unless he too believes that one does not really die.

I would indeed like to go to see you; apparently you have *cool weather* in Croisset since you want to sleep *on a warm beach*. Come here, you will not have a beach, but 36 degrees in the shade and a stream cold as ice, is not to be despised. I go there to dabble in it every day after my work; for I must work, Buloz advances me too much money. Here I am *doing my business,* as Aurore says, and not being able to budge till autumn. I was too lazy after my fatigues as sick-nurse. Little Buloz recently came to stir me up again. Now here I am hard at it.

Since you are to be in Paris in August, you must come to spend several days with us. You did laugh here anyhow; we will try to distract you and to shake you up a bit. You will see the little girls grown and prettier; the little one is beginning to talk. Aurore chatters and argues. She calls Plauchut, *old bachelor.* And a propos, accept the best regards of that fine and splendid boy along with all the affectionate greetings of the family.

As for me, I embrace you tenderly and beg you to keep well.

G. Sand

CLXX. To GEORGE SAND Croisset, Wednesday evening...1870

What has become of you, dear master, of you and yours? As for me, I am disheartened, distressed by the folly of my compatriots. The hopeless barbarism of humanity fills me with a black melancholy. That enthusiasm which has no intelligent motive makes me want to die, so as not to see it any longer.

The good Frenchman wants to fight: (1) because he thinks he is provoked to it by Prussia; (2) because the natural condition of man is savagery; (3) because war in itself contains a mystic element which enraptures crowds.

Have we returned to the wars of races? I fear so. The terrible butchery which is being prepared has not even a pretext. It is the desire to fight for the sake of fighting.

I bewail the destroyed bridges, the staved-in tunnels, all this human labor lost, in short a negation so radical.

The Congress of Peace is wrong at present. Civilization seems to me far off. Hobbes was right: Homo homini lupus.

I have begun *Saint-Antoine,* and it would go perhaps rather well, if I did not think of the war. And you?

The bourgeois here cannot contain himself. He thinks Prussia was too insolent and wants to "avenge himself." Did you see that a gentleman has proposed in the Chamber the pillage of the duchy of Baden! Ah! why can't I live among the Bedouins!

CLXXI. TO GUSTAVE FLAUBERT, at Croisset Nohant,
26 July, 1870

I think this war is infamous; that authorized Marseillaise,
a sacrilege. Men are ferocious and conceited brutes; we are in
the *half as much* of Pascal; when will come the *more than ever!*

It is between 40 and 45 degrees *in the shade* here. They
are burning the forests; another barbarous stupidity! The wolves
come and walk into our court, and we chase them away at night,
Maurice with a revolver and I with a lantern. The trees are losing
their leaves and perhaps their lives. Water for drinking is
becoming scarce; the harvests are almost nothing; but we have
war, what luck!

Farming is going to nought, famine threatens, poverty is
lurking about while waiting to transform itself into Jacquerie;
but we shall fight with the Prussians. Malbrough s'en va-t-en
guerre!

You said rightly that in order to work, a certain lightness
was needed; where is it to be found in these accursed times?

Happily, we have no one ill at our house. When I see
Maurice and Lina acting, Aurore and Gabrielle playing, I do not
dare to complain for fear of losing all.

I love you, my dear old friend, we all love you.

Your troubadour,

G. Sand

CLXXII. To GEORGE SAND Croisset, Wednesday,
3 August, 1870

What! dear master, you too are demoralized, sad? What will become of the weak souls?

As for me, my heart is oppressed in a way that astonishes me, and I wallow in a bottomless melancholy, in spite of work, in spite of the good *Saint-Antoine* who ought to distract me. Is it the consequence of my repeated afflictions? Perhaps. But the war is a good deal responsible for it. I think that we are getting into the dark.

Behold then, the *natural man*. Make theories now! Boast the progress, the enlightenment and the good sense of the masses, and the gentleness of the French people! I assure you that anyone here who ventured to preach peace would get himself murdered. Whatever happens, we have been set back for a long time to come.

Are the wars between races perhaps going to begin again? One will see, before a century passes, several millions of men kill one another in one engagement. All the East against all Europe, the old world against the new! Why not? Great united works like the Suez Canal are, perhaps, under another form, outlines and preparations for these monstrous conflicts of which we have no idea.

Is Prussia perhaps going to have a great drubbing which entered into the schemes of Providence for reestablishing European equilibrium? That country was tending to be hypertrophied like France under Louis XIV and Napoleon. The other organs are inconvenienced by it. Thence universal trouble. Would formidable bleedings be useful?

Ah! we intellectuals! Humanity is far from our ideal! and our immense error, our fatal error, is to think it like us and to want to treat it accordingly.

The reverence, the fetichism, that they have for universal suffrage revolts me more than the infallibility of the pope (which has just delightfully missed its point, by the way). Do you think that if France, instead of being governed on the whole by the crowd, were in the power of the mandarins, we should be where we are now? If, instead of having wished to enlighten the lower classes, we had busied ourselves with instructing the higher, we should not have seen M. de Keratry proposing the pillage of the duchy of Baden, a measure that the public finds very proper!

Are you studying Prudhomme now? He is gigantic! He admires Musset's Rhin, and asks if Musset has done anything else. Here you have Musset accepted as the national poet and ousting Beranger! What immense buffoonery is...everything! But a not at all gay buffoonery.

Misery is very evident. Everyone is in want, beginning with myself! But perhaps we were too accustomed to comfort and tranquillity. We buried ourselves in material things. We must return to the great tradition, hold no longer to life, to happiness, to money nor to anything; be what our grandfathers were, light, effervescing people.

Once men passed their life in starving. The same prospect is on the horizon. What you tell me about poor Nohant is terrible. The country has suffered less here than with you.

CLXXIII. To GUSTAVE FLAUBERT, at Croisset. Nohant,
8 August, 1870

Are you in Paris in the midst of all this torment? What a
lesson the people are getting who want absolute masters! France
and Prussia are cutting each other's throats for reasons that they
don't understand! Here we are in the midst of great disasters,
and what tears at the end of it all, even should we be the victors!
One sees nothing but poor peasants mourning for their children
who are leaving.

The mobilization takes away those who were left with us
and how they are being treated to begin with! What disorder,
what disarray in that military administration, which absorbed
everything and had to swallow up everything! Is this horrible
experience going to prove to the world that warfare ought to be
suppressed or that civilization has to perish?

We have reached the point this evening of knowing that
we are beaten. Perhaps tomorrow we shall know that we have
beaten, and what will there be good or useful from one or the
other?

It has rained here at last, a horrible storm which
destroyed everything.

The peasant is working and ploughing his fields; digging
hard always, sad or gay. He is imbecile, people say; no, he is a
child in prosperity, a man in disaster, more of a man than we
who complain; he says nothing, and while people are killing, he
is sowing, repairing continually on one side what they are
destroying from the other. We are going to try to do as he, and to
hunt a bubbling spring fifty or a hundred yards below ground.

The engineer is here, and Maurice is explaining to him the geology of the soil.

We are trying to dig into the bowels of the earth to forget all that is going on above it. But we cannot distract ourselves from this terror!

Write me where you are; I am sending this to you on the day agreed upon to rue Murillo. We love you, and we all embrace you.

G. Sand

Nohant, Sunday evening.

CLXXIV. To George Sand. Croisset, Wednesday, 1870

I got to Paris on Monday, and I left it again on Wednesday. Now I know the Parisian to the very bottom, and I have excused in my heart those most ferocious politics of 1793. Now, I understand them! What imbecility! what ignorance! what presumption! My compatriots make me want to vomit. They are fit to be put in the same sack with Isidore!

This people deserves to be chastised, and I fear that it will be.

It is impossible for me to read anything whatever, still more so to write anything. I spend my time like everyone else in waiting for news. Ah! if I did not have my mother, I would already be gone!

CLXXV. To Gustave Flaubert, at Croisset. Nohant, 15 August, 1870

I wrote to you to Paris according to your instructions the 8th. Weren't you there then? Probably so: in the midst of all this confusion, to publish Bouilhet, a poet! this is not the moment. As for me, my courage is weak. There is always a woman under the skin of the old troubadour. This human butchery tears my poor heart to pieces. I tremble too for all my children and friends, who perhaps are to be hacked to pieces.

And *yet,* in the midst of all that, my soul exults and has ecstasies of faith; these terrific lessons which are necessary for us to understand our imbecility, must be of use to us. We are perhaps making our last return to the ways of the old world. There are sharp and clear principles for everyone today that ought to extricate them from this torment. Nothing is useless in the material order of the universe. The moral order cannot escape the law. Bad engenders good. I tell you that we are in the *half as much* of Pascal, so as to get *to the more than ever!* That is all the mathematics that I understand.

I have finished a novel in the midst of this torment, hurrying up so as not to be worn out before the end. I am as tired as if I had fought with our poor soldiers.

I embrace you. Tell me where you are, what you are thinking.

We all love you.

What a fine St. Napoleon we have!

G. Sand

CLXXVI. To GEORGE SAND. Saturday, 1870

Dear master,

Here we are in the depths of the abyss! A shameful peace will perhaps not be accepted! The Prussians intend to destroy Paris! That is their dream.

I don't think the siege of Paris is very imminent. But in order to force Paris to yield, they are going to (1) terrify her by the sight of cannon, and (2) ravage the surrounding country.

We expect the visit of these gentlemen at Rouen, and as I have been (since Sunday) lieutenant of my company, I drill my men and I am going to Rouen to take lessons in military tactics.

The most deplorable thing is that opinions are divided, some for defence to the utmost, and others for peace at any price.

I am dying of humiliation. What a house mine is! Fourteen persons who sigh and unnerve me! I curse women! It is because of them that we perish.

I expect that Paris will have the fate of Warsaw, and you distress me, you with your enthusiasm for the Republic. At the moment when we are overcome by the plainest positivism, how can you still believe in phantoms? Whatever happens, the people who are now in power will be sacrificed, and the Republic will follow their fate. Observe that I defend that poor Republic; but I do not believe in it.

That is all that I have to say to you. Now I should have many more things to say, but my head is not clear. It is as if cataracts, floods, oceans of sadness, were breaking over me. It is not possible to suffer more. Sometimes I am afraid of going mad. The face of my mother, when I turn my eyes toward her, takes away all my strength.

This is where our passion for not wanting to see the truth has taken us! Love of pretence and of flap-doodle. We are going to become a Poland, then a Spain. Then it will be the turn of Prussia who will be devoured by Russia.

As for me, I consider myself a man whose career is ended. My brain is not going to recover. One can write no longer when one does not think well of oneself. I demand only one thing, that is to die, so to be at rest.

CLXXVII. To GEORGE SAND Sunday evening

I am still alive, dear master, but I am hardly any better, for I am so sad! I didn't write you any sooner, for I was waiting, for news from you. I didn't know where you were.

Here it is six weeks that we have been expecting the coming of the Prussians from day to day. We strain our ears, thinking we can hear the sound of the cannon from a distance. They are surrounding Seine-Inferieure in a radius of from fourteen to twenty leagues. They are even nearer, since they are occupying Vexin, which they have completely destroyed. What horrors! It makes one blush for being a man!

If we have had a success on the Loire, their appearance will be delayed. But shall we have it? When the hope comes to me, I try to repel it, and yet, in the very depths of myself, in spite of all, I cannot keep myself from hoping a little, a very little bit.

I don't think that there is in all France a sadder man than I am! (It all depends on the sensitiveness of people.) I am dying of grief. That is the truth, and consolations irritate me. What distresses me is: (1) the ferocity of men; (2) the conviction that we are going to enter upon a stupid era. People will be utilitarian, military, American and Catholic! Very Catholic! You will see! The Prussian War ends the French Revolution and destroys it.

But supposing we were conquerors? you will say to me. That hypothesis is contrary to all historical precedents. Where did you ever see the south conquer the north, and the Catholics dominate the Protestants? The Latin race is agonizing. France is going to follow Spain and Italy, and boorishness (pignouflism) begins!

What a cataclysm! What a collapse! What misery! What abominations! Can one believe in progress and in civilization in the face of all that is going on? What use, pray, is science, since this people abounding in scholars commits abominations worthy of the Huns and worse than theirs, because they are systematic, cold-blooded, voluntary, and have for an excuse, neither passion nor hunger?

Why do they abhor us so fiercely? Don't you feel overwhelmed by the hatred of forty millions of men? This immense infernal chasm makes me giddy.

Ready-made phrases are not wanting: France will rise again! One must not despair! It is a salutary punishment! We were really too immoral! etc. Oh! eternal poppycock! No! one does not recover from such a blow! As for me, I feel myself struck to my very marrow!

If I were twenty years younger, I should perhaps not think all that, and if I were twenty years older I should be resigned.

Poor Paris! I think it is heroic. But if we do find it again, it will not be our Paris any more! All the friends that I had there are dead or have disappeared. I have no longer any center. Literature seems to me to be a vain and useless thing! Shall I ever be in a condition to write again?

Oh! if I could flee into a country where one does not see uniforms, where one does not hear the drum, where one does not talk of massacres, where one is not obliged to be a citizen! But the earth is no longer habitable for the poor mandarins.

CLXXVIII. To GEORGE SAND Wednesday

I am sad no longer. I took up my *Saint-Antoine* yesterday. So much the worse, one has to get accustomed to it! One must accustom oneself to what is the natural condition of man, that is to say, to evil.

The Greeks at the time of Pericles made art without knowing if they should have anything to eat the next day. Let us be Greeks. I shall confess to you, however, dear master, that I feel rather a savage. The blood of my ancestors, the Natchez or the Hurons, boils in my educated veins, and I seriously, like a beast, like an animal, want to fight!

Explain that to me! The idea of making peace now exasperates me, and I would rather that Paris were burned (like Moscow), than see the Prussians enter it. But we have not gotten to that; I think the wind is turning.

I have read some soldiers' letters, which are models. One can't swallow up a country where people write like that. France is a resourceful jade, and will be up again.

Whatever happens, another world is going to begin, and I feel that I am very old to adapt myself to new customs.

Oh! how I miss you, how I want to see you!

We have decided here to all march on Paris if the compatriots of Hegel lay siege to it. Try to get your Berrichons to buck up. Call to them: "Come to help me prevent the enemy from drinking and eating in a country which is foreign to them!"

The war (I hope) will make a home thrust at the "authorities."

The individual, disowned, overwhelmed by the modern world, will he regain his importance? Let us hope so!

CLXXIX. To George Sand. Tuesday, 11 October, 1870

Dear master,

Are you still living? Where are you, Maurice, and the others?

I don't know how it is that I am not dead, I have suffered so atrociously for six weeks.

My mother has fled to Rouen. My niece is in London. My brother is busy with town affairs, and, as for me, I am alone here, eaten up with impatience and chagrin! I assure you that I have wanted to do right; what misery! I have had at my door today two hundred and seventy-one poor people, and they were all given something. What will this winter be?

The Prussians are now twelve hours from Rouen, and we have no commands, no orders, no discipline, nothing, nothing! They hold out false hopes to us continually with the army of the Loire. Where is it? Do you know anything about it? What are they doing in the middle of France? Paris will end by being starved, and no one is taking her any aid!

The imbecilities of the Republic surpass those of the Empire. Are they playing under all this some abominable comedy? Why such inaction?

Ah! how sad I am. I feel that the world is going by.

CLXXX. To Gustave Flaubert, at Croisset. Le Chatre, 14 October, 1870

We are living at Le Chatre. Nohant is ravaged by smallpox with complications, horrible. We had to take our little ones into the Creuse, to friends who came to get us, and we spent three weeks there, looking in vain for quarters where a family could stay for three months. We were asked to go south and were offered hospitality; but we did not want to leave the country where, from one day to another, one can be useful, although one hardly knows yet in what way to go at it.

So we have come back to the friends who lived the nearest to our abandoned hearth; and we are awaiting events. To speak of all the peril and trouble there is in establishing the Republic in the interior of our provinces would be quite useless. There can be no illusion: everything is at stake, and the end will perhaps be *Orleanism.* But we are pushed into the unforeseen to such an extent that it seems to me puerile to have anticipations; the thing to do is to escape the next catastrophe.

Don't let's say that it is impossible; don't let's think it. Don't let's despair about France. She is going through expiation for her madness, she will be reborn no matter what happens. We shall perhaps be carried away, the rest of us. To die of pneumonia or of a bullet is dying just the same. Let's die without cursing our race!

We still love you, and we all embrace you.

G. Sand

CLXXXI. To GUSTAVE FLAUBERT, at Croisset. Nohant,
4 February, 1871.

Don't you receive my letters, then? Write to me I beg
you, one word only: *I am well.* We are so worried!

They are all well in Paris.

We embrace you.

G. Sand

CLXXXII. To Gustave Flaubert. Nohant, 22 February, 1871

I received your letter of the 15th this morning; what a cruel thorn it takes from my heart! One gets frantic with anxiety now when one does not receive answers. Let us hope that we can talk soon and tell all about our *absence* from each other. I too have had the good fortune not to lose any of my friends, young or old. That is all the good one can say. I do not regret this Republic, it has been the greatest failure of all! the most unfortunate for Paris, the most unsuitable in the provinces. Besides, if I had loved it, I should not regret anything; if only this odious war might end! We love you and we embrace you affectionately. I shall not hurry to go to Paris. It will be pestilential for some time to come.

Yours.

CLXXXIII. To GEORGE SAND. Dieppe, 11 March, 1871

When shall we meet? Paris does not seem amusing to me. Ah! into what sort of a world are we going to enter! Paganism, Christianity, idiotism, there are the three great evolutions of humanity! It is sad to find ourselves at the beginning of the third.

I shall not tell you all I have suffered since September. Why didn't I die from it? That is what surprises me! No one was more desperate than I was. Why? I have had bad moments in my life, I have gone through great losses. I have wept a great deal. I have undergone much anguish. Well! all these pangs accumulated together, are nothing in comparison to that. And I cannot get over them! I am not consoled! I have no hope!

Yet I did not see myself as a progressivist and a humanitarian. That doesn't matter. I had some illusions! What barbarity! What a slump! I am wrathful at my contemporaries for having given me the feelings of a brute of the twelfth century! *I'm stifling in gall!* These officers who break mirrors with white gloves on, who know Sanskrit and who fling themselves on the champagne, who steal your watch and then send you their visiting card, this war for money, these civilized savages give me more horror than cannibals. And all the world is going to imitate them, is going to be a soldier! Russia has now four millions of them. All Europe will wear a uniform. If we take our revenge, it will be ultra-ferocious, and observe that one is going to think only of that, of avenging oneself on Germany! The government, whatever it is, can support itself only by speculating on that passion. Wholesale murder is going to be the end of all our efforts, the ideal of France!

I cherish the following dream: of going to live in the sun in a tranquil country!

Let us look for new hypocrisies: declamations on virtue, diatribes on corruption, austerity of habits, etc. Last degree of pedantry!

I have now at Croisset twelve Prussians. As soon as my poor dwelling (of which I have a horror now) is emptied and cleaned, I shall return there; then I shall go doubtless to Paris, despite its unhealthfulness! But I don't care a hang for that.

CLXXXIV. To GUSTAVE FLAUBERT, at Croisset. Nohant, 17 March, 1871

I received your letter of the 11th yesterday.

We have all suffered in spirit more than at any other time of our lives, and we shall always suffer from that wound. It is evident that the savage instinct tends to take the upper hand; but I fear something worse; it is the egoistic and cowardly instinct; it is the ignoble corruption of false patriots, of ultra-republicans who cry out for vengeance, and who hide themselves; a good pretext for the bourgeois who want a *strong* reaction. I fear lest we shall not even be vindictive,—all that bragging, coupled with poltroonery, will so disgust us and so impel us to live from day to day as under the Restoration, submitting to everything and only asking to be let alone.

There will be an awakening later. I shall not be here then, and you, you will be old! Go to live in the sun in a tranquil country! Where? What country is going to be tranquil in this struggle of barbarity against civilization, a struggle which is going to be universal? Is not the sun itself a myth? Either he hides himself or he burns you up, and it is thus with everything on this unhappy planet. Let us love it just the same, and accustom ourselves to suffering on it.

I have written day by day my impressions and my reflections during the crisis. The *Revue des Deux Mondes* is publishing this diary. If you read it, you will see that everywhere life has been torn from its very foundations, even in the country where the war has not penetrated.

You will see too, that I have not swallowed, although very greedy, party humbugs. But I don't know if you are of my opinion, that full and entire liberty would save us from these disasters and restore us to the path of possible progress again. The abuses of liberty give me no anxiety of themselves; but those whom they frighten always incline towards the abuse of power. Just now M. Thiers seems to understand it; but can he and will he know how to preserve the principle by which he has become the arbiter of this great problem?

Whatever happens, let us love each other, and do not keep me in ignorance of what concerns you. My heart is full to bursting and the remembrance of you eases it a little from its perpetual disquiet. I am afraid lest these barbarous guests devastate Croisset; for they continue in spite of peace to make themselves odious and disgusting everywhere. Ah! how I should like to have five billions in order to chase them away! I should not ask to get them back again.

Now, do come to us, we are so quiet here; materially, we have been so always. We force ourselves to take up our work again, we resign ourselves; what is there better to do? You are beloved here, we live here in a continual state of loving one another; we are holding on to our Lamberts, whom we shall keep as long as possible. All our children have come out of the war safe and sound. You would live here in peace and be able to work; for that must be, whether one is in the mood or not! The season is going to be lovely. Paris will calm itself during that time. You are looking for a peaceful spot. It is under your nose, with hearts which love you!

I embrace you a thousand times for myself and for all my brood. The little girls are splendid. The Lamberts' little boy is charming.

CLXXXV. To GEORGE SAND. Neuville near Dieppe,
Friday, 31 March, 1871

Dear master,

Tomorrow, at last, I resign myself to re-enter Croisset! It is hard! But I must! I am going to try to make up again my poor *Saint-Antoine* and to forget France.

My mother stays here with her grandchild, till one knows where to go without fear of the Prussians or of a riot.

Some days ago I went from here with Dumas to Brussels from where I thought to go direct to Paris. But "the new Athens" seems to me to surpass Dahomey in ferocity and imbecility. Has the end come to the *humbugs?* Will they have finished with hollow metaphysics and conventional ideas? All the evil comes from our gigantic ignorance. What ought to be studied is believed without discussion. Instead of investigating, people make assertions.

The French Revolution must cease to be a dogma, and it must become once more a part of science, like the rest of human things. If people had known more, they would not have believed that a mystical formula is capable of making armies, and that the word "Republic" is enough to conquer a million of well disciplined men. They would have left Badinguet on the throne *expressly* to make peace, ready to put him in the galleys afterward. If they had known more, they would have known what the volunteers of '92 were and the retreat of Brunswick gained by bribery through Danton and Westermann. But no! always the same old story! always poppycock! There is now the

Commune of Paris which is returning to the real Middle Ages! That's flat! The question of leases especially, is splendid! The government interferes in natural rights now, it intervenes in contracts between individuals. The Commune asserts that we do not owe what we owe, and that one service is not paid for by another. It is an enormity of absurdity and injustice.

Many conservatives who, from love of order, wanted to preserve the Republic, are going to regret Badinguet and in their hearts recall the Prussians. The people of the Hotel de Ville have changed the object of our hatred. That is why I am angry with them. It seems to me that we have never been lower.

We oscillate between the society of Saint-Vincent de Paul and the International. But this latter commits too many imbecilities to have a long life. I admit that it may overcome the troops at Versailles and overturn the government, the Prussians will enter Paris, and "order will reign" at Warsaw. If, on the contrary, it is conquered, the reaction will be furious and all liberty will be strangled.

What can one say of the socialists who imitate the proceedings of Badinguet and of William: requisitions, suppressions of newspapers, executions without trial, etc.? Ah! what an immoral beast is the crowd! and how humiliating it is to be a man!

I embrace you!

CLXXXVI. To GEORGE SAND. Croisset,
Monday evening, two o'clock.

Dear master,

Why no letters? Haven't you received mine sent from Dieppe? Are you ill? Are you still alive? What does it mean? I hope very much that neither you (nor any of yours) are in Paris, capital of arts, cornerstone of civilization, center of fine manners and of urbanity?

Do you know the worst of all that? *It is that we get accustomed to it.* Yes! one does. One becomes accustomed to getting along without Paris, to worrying about it no longer, and almost to thinking that it exists no longer.

As for me, I am not like the bourgeois; I consider that after the invasion there are no more misfortunes. The war with Prussia gave me the effect of a great upheaval of nature, one of those cataclysms that happen every six thousand years; while the insurrection in Paris is, to my eyes, a very clear and almost simple thing.

What retrogressions! What savages! How they resemble the people of the League and the men in armor! Poor France, who will never free herself from the Middle Ages! who labors along in the Gothic idea of the Commune, which is nothing else than the Roman municipality. Oh! I assure you that my heart is heavy over it!

And the little reaction that we are going to have after that? How the good ecclesiastics are going to flourish again!

I have started at *Saint-Antoine* once more, and I am working tremendously.

CLXXXVII. To GUSTAVE FLAUBERT, at Croisset. Nohant,
28 April, 1871

No, certainly I do not forget you! I am sad, sad, that is to
say, that I am stunned, that I watch the spring, that I am busy,
that I talk as if there were nothing; but I have not been able to be
alone an instant since that horrible occurrence without falling
into a bitter despair. I make great efforts to prevent it; I do not
want to be discouraged; I do not want to deny the past and dread
the future; but it is my will, it is my reason that struggles against
a profound impression unsurmountable up to the present
moment.

That is why I did not want to write to you before feeling
better, not that I am ashamed to have crises of depression, but
because I did not want to increase your sadness already so
profound, by adding the weight of mine to it. For me, the ignoble
experiment that Paris is attempting or is undergoing, proves
nothing against the laws of the eternal progression of men and
things, and, if I have gained any principles in my mind, good or
bad, they are neither shattered nor changed by it. For a long time
I have accepted patience as one accepts the sort of weather there
is, the length of winter, old age, lack of success in all its forms.
But I think that partisans (sincere) ought to change their
formulas or find out perhaps the emptiness of every a priori
formula.

It is not that which makes me sad. When a tree is dead,
one should plant two others. My unhappiness comes from pure
weakness of heart that I don't know how to overcome. I cannot
sleep over the suffering and even over the ignominy of others. I

pity those who do the evil! while I recognize that they are not at all interesting, their moral state distresses me. One pities a little bird that has fallen from its nest; why not pity a heap of consciences fallen in the mud? One suffered less during the Prussian siege. One loved Paris unhappy in spite of itself, one pities it so much the more now that one can no longer love it. Those who never loved get satisfaction by mortally hating it. What shall we answer? Perhaps we should not answer at all. The scorn of France is perhaps the necessary punishment of the remarkable cowardice with which the Parisians have submitted to the riot and its adventurers. It is a consequence of the acceptance of the adventurers of the Empire; other felons but the same cowardice.

But I did not want to talk to you of that, you *roar* about it enough as it is! one ought to be distracted; for if one thinks too much about it, one becomes separated from one's own limbs and lets oneself undergo amputation with too much stoicism.

You don't tell me in what state you found your charming nest at Croisset. The Prussians occupied it; did they ruin it, dirty it, rob it? Your books, your bibelots, did you find them all? Did they respect your name, your workshop? If you can work again there, peace will come to your spirit. As for me, I am waiting till mine gets well, and I know that I shall have to help myself to my own cure by a certain faith often shaken, but of which I make a duty.

Tell me whether the tulip tree froze this winter, and if the poppies are pretty.

I often take the journey in spirit; I see again your garden and its surroundings. How far away that is! How many things have happened since! One hardly knows whether one is a hundred years old or not!

My little girls bring me back to the notion of time; they are growing, they are amusing and affectionate; it is through them and the two beings who gave them to me that I feel myself still of the world; it is through you too, dear friend, whose kind and loving heart I always feel to be good and alive. How I should like to see you! But I have no longer a way of going and coming.

We embrace you, all of us, and we love you.

G. Sand

CLXXXVIII. To George Sand

I am answering at once your questions that concern me personally. No! the Prussians did not loot my house. They *hooked* some little things of no importance, a dressing case, a bandbox, some pipes; but on the whole they did no harm. As for my study, it was respected. I had buried a large box full of letters and hidden my voluminous notes on *Saint-Antoine*. I found all that intact.

The worst of the invasion for me is that it has aged my poor, dear, old mother by ten years! What a change! She can no longer walk alone, and is distressingly weak! How sad it is to see those whom one loves deteriorate little by little!

In order to think no longer on the public miseries or on my own, I have plunged again with fury into *Saint-Antoine,* and if nothing disturbs me and I continue at this pace, I shall have finished it next winter. I am very eager to read to you the sixty pages which are done. When we can circulate about again on the railroad, do come to see me for a little while. Your old troubadour has waited for you for such a long time! Your letter of this morning has saddened me. What a proud fellow you are and what immense courage you have!

I am not like a lot of people whom I hear bemoaning the war of Paris. For my part, I find it more tolerable than the invasion, there is no more despair possible, and that is what proves once more our abasement. "Ah! God be thanked, the Prussians are there!" is the universal cry of the bourgeois. I put messieurs the workmen into the same pack, and would have them all thrust together into the river! Moreover they are on the way there, and then calm will return. We are going to become a great, flat industrial country like Belgium. The disappearance of Paris (as center of the government) will render France colorless and dull. She will no longer have a heart, a center, nor, I think, a spirit.

As for the Commune, which is about to die out, it is the last manifestation of the Middle Ages. The very last, let us hope!

I hate democracy (at least the kind that is understood in France), that is to say, the exaltation of mercy to the detriment of justice, the negation of right, in a word, antisociability.

The Commune rehabilitates murderers, quite as Jesus pardoned thieves, and they pillage the residences of the rich, because they have been taught to curse Lazarus, who was not a bad rich man, but simply a rich man. "The Republic is above every criticism" is equivalent to that belief: "The pope is infallible!" Always formulas! Always gods!

The god before the last, which was universal suffrage, has just shown his adherents a terrible farce by nominating "the murderers of Versailles." What shall we believe in, then? In nothing! That is the beginning of wisdom. It was time to have done with "principles" and to take up science, and investigation. The only reasonable thing (I always come back to that) is a government by mandarins, provided the mandarins know something and even that they know many things. The people is an eternal infant, and it will be (in the hierarchy of social elements) always in the last row, since it is number, mass, the unlimited. It is of little matter whether many peasants know how to read and listen no longer to their cure, but it is of great matter that many men like Renan or Littre should be able to live and be listened to! Our safety is now only in a *legitimate aristocracy,* I mean by that, a majority that is composed of more than mere numbers.

If they had been more enlightened, if there had been in Paris more people acquainted with history, we should not have had to endure Gambetta, nor Prussia, nor the Commune. What did the Catholics do to meet a great danger? They crossed themselves while consigning themselves to God and to the saints. We, however, who are advanced, we are going to cry out, "Long live the Republic!" while recalling what happened in '92; and there was no doubt of its success, observe that. The Prussian existed no longer, they embraced one another with joy and restrained themselves from running to the defiles of the Argonne where there are defiles no longer; never mind, that is according to tradition. I have a friend in Rouen who proposed to a club the manufacture of lances to fight against the breech-loaders!

Ah! it would have been more practical to keep Badinguet, in order to send him to the galleys once peace was made! Austria did not have a revolution after Sadowa, nor Italy after Novara, nor Russia after Sebastopol! But the good French hasten to demolish their house as soon as the chimney has caught fire.

Well, I must tell you an atrocious idea; I am *afraid* that the destruction of the Vendome column is sowing the seeds of a third Empire! Who knows if in twenty or in forty years, a grandson of Jerome will not be our master?

For the moment Paris is completely epileptic. A result of the congestion caused by the siege. France, on the whole, has lived for several years in an extraordinary mental state. The success of la Lanterne and Troppman have been very evident symptoms of it. That folly is the result of too great imbecility, and that imbecility comes from too much bluffing, for because of lying they had become idiotic. They had lost all notion of right and wrong, of beautiful and ugly. Recall the criticism of recent years. What difference did it make between the sublime and the ridiculous? What lack of respect; what ignorance! what a mess! "Boiled or roasted, same thing!" and at the same time, what servility for the opinion of the day, the dish of the fashion!

All was false! False realism, false army, false credit, and even false harlots. They were called "marquises," while the great ladies called themselves familiarly "cochonnettes." Those girls who were of the tradition of Sophie Arnould, like Lagier, roused horror. You have not seen the reverence of Saint-Victor for la Paiva. And this falseness (which is perhaps a consequence of romanticism, predominance of passion over form, and of inspiration over rule) was applied especially in the manner of judging. They extolled an actress not as an actress, but as a good mother of a family! They asked art to be moral, philosophy to be clear, vice to be decent, and science to be within the range of the people.

But this is a very long letter. When I start abusing my contemporaries, I never get through with it.

CLXXXIX. To GEORGE SAND Croisset,
Sunday evening, 10 June, 1871

Dear master,

I never had a greater desire or a greater need to see you than now. I have just come from Paris and I don't know to whom to talk. I am choking. I am overcome, or rather, absolutely disheartened.

The odor of corpses disgusts me less than the miasmas of egotism that exhale from every mouth. The sight of the ruins is as nothing in comparison with the great Parisian inanity. With a very few exceptions it seemed to me that everybody ought to be tied up.

Half the population wants to strangle the other half, and *vice versa*. This is clearly to be seen in the eyes of the passers-by.

And the Prussians exist no longer! People excuse them and admire them. The "reasonable people" want to be naturalized Germans. I assure you it is enough to make one despair of the human race.

I was in Versailles on Thursday. The excesses of the Right inspire fear. The vote about the Orleans is a concession made to it, so as not to irritate it, and so as to have the time to prepare against it.

I except from the general folly, Renan who, on the contrary, seemed to me very philosophical, and the good Soulie who charged me to give you a thousand affectionate messages.

I have collected a mass of horrible and unpublished details which I spare you.

My little trip to Paris has troubled me extremely, and I am going to have a hard time in getting down to work again.

What do you think of my friend Maury, who kept the tricolor over the Archives all during the Commune? I think few men are capable of such pluck.

When history clears up the burning of Paris, it will find several elements among which are, without any doubt: (1) the Prussians, and (2) the people of Badinguet; they have *no longer any* written proof against the Empire, and Haussman is going to present himself boldly to the elections of Paris.

Have you read, among the documents found in the Tuileries last September, a plot of a novel by Isidore? What a scenario!

CXC. To GUSTAVE FLAUBERT, at Paris[36] Nohant, 23 July, 1871

No, I am not ill, my dear old troubadour, in spite of the sorrow which is the daily bread of France; I have an iron constitution and an exceptional old age, abnormal even, for my strength increases at the age when it ought to diminish. The day that I resolutely buried my youth, I grew twenty years younger. You will tell me that the bark undergoes none the less the ravages of time. I don't care for that, the heart of the tree is very good and the sap still runs as in the old apple trees in my garden, which bear fruit all the better the more gnarly they are. Thank you for having worried over the illness which the papers have bestowed upon me. Maurice thanks you also and embraces you. He is still mingling with his scientific, literary, and agricultural studies, beautiful marionette shows. He thinks of you every time and says that he would like to have you here to note his progress, for he continually improves.

In what condition are we, according to your opinion?

In Rouen, you no longer have any Prussians at your back, that's something, and one would say that the bourgeois Republic wants to impose itself. It will be foolish. You foretold that, and I don't doubt it; but after the inevitable rule of the Philistines, life will extend and spread on all sides. The filth of the Commune shows us dangers which were not sufficiently foreseen and which enforce a new political life on everybody, carrying on one's affairs oneself and forcing the charming proletariat created by the Empire to know what is possible and what is not.

---

[36] Evidently an answer to a lost letter.

Education does not teach honesty and disinterestedness overnight. The vote is immediate education. They have appointed Raoul Rigault and company. They know how much people like that cost now by the yard; let them go on and they will die of hunger. There is no other way to make them understand in a short time.

Are you working? Is *Saint-Antoine* going well? Tell me what you are doing in Paris, what you are seeing, what you are thinking. I have not the courage to go there. Do come to see me before you return to Croisset. I am blue from not seeing you, it is a sort of death.

G. Sand

CXCI. To George Sand 25 July, 1871

I find Paris a little less mad than in June, at least on the surface. They are beginning to hate Prussia in a natural manner, that is to say, they are getting back into French tradition. They no longer make phrases in praise of her civilizations. As for the Commune, they expect to see it rise again later, and the "established order" does absolutely nothing to prevent its return. They are applying old remedies to new woes, remedies that have never cured (nor prevented) the least ill. The reestablishment of credit seems to me colossally absurd. One of my friends made a good speech against it; the godson of your friend Michel de Bourges, Bardoux, mayor of Clermont-Ferrand.

I think, like you, that the bourgeois republic can be established. Its lack of elevation is perhaps a guarantee of stability. It will be the first time that we have lived under a government without principles. The era of positivism in politics is about to begin.

The immense disgust which my contemporaries give me throws me back on the past, and I am working on my good *Saint-Antoine* with all my might. I came to Paris only for it, for it is impossible for me to get in Rouen the books that I need now; I am lost in the religions of Persia. I am trying to get a clear idea of the God Horn, and it isn't easy. I spent all the month of June in studying Buddhism, on which I already had many notes. But I wanted to get to the bottom of the subject as soon as possible. And I also did a little Buddha that I consider charming. Don't I want to read you that book (mine)!

I am not going to Nohant, for I don't care to go further I away from my mother now. Her society afflicts me and unnerves me, my niece Caroline takes turns with me in carrying on the dear and painful burden.

In a fortnight I shall be back in Croisset. Between the 15th and the 20th of August I am expecting the good Tourgueneff there. It would be very kind of you to come after him, dear master. I say come after, for we have only one decent room since the visit of the Prussians. Come, make a good effort. Come in September.

Have you any news of the Odeon? I can't get any response whatsoever from de Chilly. I have been to his house several times and I have written three letters to him: not a word! Those gay blades behave towards one like great lords, which is charming.

I don't know if he is still director, or if the management has been given to the Berton, Laurent, Bernard company, do you?

Berton wrote to me to recommend him (and them) to d'Osmoy, deputy and president of the dramatic commission, but since then I have not heard anything mentioned.

CXCII. To GUSTAVE FLAUBERT, at Croissset Nohant,
August, 1871

You want to see me, and you need me, and you don't
come see me! That is not nice; for I too, and all of us here, sigh
for you. We parted so gaily eighteen months ago, and so many
atrocious things have happened in the meantime! Seeing each
other would be the consolation *due* us. For my part, I cannot stir,
I have not a penny, and I have to work like a negro. And then I
have not seen a single Prussian, and I would like to keep my
eyes pure from that stain. Ah! my friend, what years we are
going through! We cannot go back again, for hope departs with
the rest.

What will be the reaction from the infamous Commune?
Isidore or Henry V. or the kingdom of incendiaries restored by
anarchy? I who have had so much patience with my species and
who have so long looked on the bright side, now see nothing but
darkness. I judge others by myself. I had improved my real
character, I had extinguished useless and dangerous enthusiasms,
I had sowed grass and flowers that grew well on my volcanoes,
and I imagined that all the world could become enlightened,
could correct itself, or restrain itself; that the years passed over
me and over my contemporaries could not be lost to reason and
experience: and now I awaken from a dream to find a generation
divided between idiocy and delirium tremens! Everything is
possible at present.

However, it is bad to despair. I shall make a great effort,
and perhaps I shall become just and patient again; but today I
cannot. I am as troubled as you, and I don't dare to talk, nor to

think, nor to write, I have such a fear of touching the wounds open in every soul.

I have indeed received your other letter, and I was waiting for courage to answer it; I would like to do only good to those I love, especially to you, who feel so keenly. I am no good at this moment. I am filled with a devouring indignation and a disgust which is killing me.

I love you, that is all I know. My children say the same. Embrace your good little mother for me.

G. Sand

CXCIII. To Gustave Flaubert Nohant, 6 September, 1871

Where are you, my dear old troubadour?

I don't write to you, I am quite troubled in the depths of my soul. But that will pass, I hope; but I am ill with the illness of my nation and my race. I cannot isolate myself in my reason and in my own *irreproachability*. I feel the great bonds loosened and, as it were, broken. It seems to me that we are all going off, I don't know where. Have you more courage than I have? Give me some of it?

I am sending you the pretty faces of our little girls. They remember you, and tell me I must send you their pictures. Alas! they are girls, we raise them with love like precious plants. What men will they meet to protect them and continue our work? It seems to me that in twenty years there will be only hypocrites and blackguards!

Give me news of yourself, tell me of your poor mother, your family, of Croisset. Love us still, as we love you.

G. Sand

CXCIV. To GEORGE SAND Croisset, Wednesday, 6 September

Well, dear master, it seems to me that you are forgetting your troubadour, aren't you? Are you then quite overwhelmed with work! How long a time it is since I saw your good firm writing! How long it is since we have talked together! What a pity that we should live so far from each other! I need you very much.

I don't dare to leave my poor mother! When I am obliged to be away, Caroline comes to take my place. If it were not for that, I should go to Nohant. Shall you stay there indefinitely? Must we wait till the middle of the winter to embrace each other?

I should like very much to read you *Saint-Antoine,* which is half done, then to stretch myself and to roar at your side.

Some one who knows that I love you and who admires you brought me a copy of le Gaulois in which there were parts of an article by you on the workmen, published in *le Temps.* How true it is! How just and well said! Sad! Sad! Poor France! And they accuse me of being skeptical.

But what do you think of Mademoiselle Papevoine, the incendiary, who, in the midst of a barricade, submitted to the assaults of eighteen citizens! That surpasses the end of *l'Education sentimentale* where they limit themselves to offering flowers.

But what goes beyond everything now, is the conservative party, which is not even going to vote, and which is still in a panic! You cannot imagine the alarm of the Parisians.

"In six months, sir, the Commune will be established everywhere" is the answer or rather the universal groan.

I do not look forward to an imminent cataclysm because nothing that is foreseen happens. The International will perhaps triumph in the end, but not as it hopes, not as they dread. Ah! how tired I am of the ignoble workmen, the incompetent bourgeois, the stupid peasant and the odious ecclesiastic!

That is why I lose myself as much as I can in antiquity. Just now I am making all the gods talk in a state of agony. The subtitle of my book could be The Height of Insanity. And the printing of it withdraws further and further into my mind. Why publish? Who pray is bothering about art nowadays? I make literature for myself as a bourgeois turns napkin rings in his garret. You will tell me that I had better be useful. But how? How can I make people listen to me?

Tourgueneff has written me that he is going to stay in Paris all winter beginning with October. That will be some one to talk to. For I can't talk of anything whatever with anyone whatever.

I have been looking after the grave of my poor Bouilhet today; so tonight I have a twofold bitterness.

CXCV. To GEORGE SAND Croisset, 8 September, 1871

Ah! how sweet they are! What darlings! What fine little heads so serious and sweet! My mother was quite touched by it, and so was I. That is what I call a delicate attention, dear master, and I thank you very much for it. I envy Maurice, his existence is not arid as mine is.

Our two letters crossed again. That proves beyond a doubt that we feel the same things at the same time in the same degree.

Why are you so sad?

Humanity offers nothing new.

Its irremediable misery has filled me with sadness ever since my youth. And in addition I now have no disillusions. I believe that the crowd, the common herd will always be hateful. The only important thing is a little group of minds—always the same—which passed the torch from one to another.

As long as we do not bow to mandarins, as long as the Academy of Sciences does not replace the pope, politics as a whole and society, down to its very roots, will be nothing but collection of disheartening humbugs. We are floundering in the after-birth of the Revolution, which was an abortion, a failure, a misfire, "whatever they say." And the reason is that it proceeded from the Middle Ages and Christianity. The idea of equality (which is all the modern democracy) is an essentially Christian idea and opposed to that of justice. Observe how mercy predominates now. Sentiment is everything, justice is nothing. People are now not even indignant against murderers, and the people who set fire to Paris are less punished than the calumniator of M. Favre.

In order for France to rise again, she must pass from inspiration to science, she must abandon all metaphysics, she must enter into criticism, that is to say into the examination of things.

I am persuaded that we shall seem extremely imbecile to posterity. The words republic and monarchy will make them laugh, as we on our part, laughed, at realism and nominalism. For I defy anyone to show me an essential difference between those two terms. A modern republic and a constitutional monarchy are identical. Never mind! They are squabbling about that, they are shouting, they are fighting!

As for the good people, "free and compulsory" education will do it. When every one is able to read le Petit Journal and *le Figaro*, they won't read anything else, because the bourgeois and the rich man read only these. The press is a school of demoralization, because it dispenses with thinking. Say that, you will be brave, and if you prevail, you will have rendered a fine service.

The first remedy will be to finish up with universal suffrage, the shame of the human mind. As it is constituted, one single element prevails to the detriment of all the others: numbers dominate over mind, education, race and even money, which is worth more than numbers.

But society (which always needs a good God, a Saviour), isn't it perhaps capable of taking care of itself? The conservative party has not even the instinct of the brute (for the brute at least knows how to fight for its lair and its living). It will be divided by the Internationals, the Jesuits of the future. But those of the past, who had neither country nor justice, have not succeeded and the International will founder because it is in the wrong. No ideas, nothing but greed!

Ah! dear, good master, if you only could hate! That is what you lack, hate. In spite of your great Sphinx eyes, you have seen the world through a golden color. That comes from the sun in your heart; but so many shadows have arisen that now you are not recognizing things any more. Come now! Cry out! Thunder! Take your great lyre and touch the brazen string: the monsters will flee. Bedew us with the drops of the blood of wounded Themis.

Why do you feel "the great bonds broken?" What is broken? Your bonds are indestructible, your sympathy can attach itself only to the Eternal.

Our ignorance of history makes us slander our own times. Man has always been like that. Several years of quiet deceived us. That is all. I too, I used to believe in the amelioration of manners. One must wipe out that mistake and think of oneself no more highly than they did in the time of Pericles or of Shakespeare, atrocious epochs in which fine things were done. Tell me that you are lifting your head and that you are thinking of your old troubadour, who cherishes you.

CXCVI. To GUSTAVE FLAUBERT, at Croisset Nohant,
8 September, 1871

As usual our letters have crossed; you should receive today the portraits of my little grandchildren, not pretty at this period of their growth, but with such beautiful eyes that they can never be ugly.

You see that I am as disheartened as you are and indignant, alas! without being able to hate either the human race or our poor, dear country. But one feels too much one's helplessness to pluck up one's heart and spirit. One works all the same, even if only turning napkin rings, as you say: and, as for me, while serving the public, I think about it as little as possible. *Le Temps* has done me the service of making me rummage in my waste basket. I find there the prophecies that the conscience of each of us has inspired in him, and these little returns to the past ought to give us courage; but it is not at all so. The lessons of experience are of no use until too late.

I think that without subvention, the Odeon will be in no condition to put on well a literary play such as Aisse, and that you should not let them murder it. You had better wait and see what happens. As for the Berton company, I have no news of it; it is touring the provinces, and those who compose it will not be reengaged by Chilly, who is furious with them.

The Odeon has let Reynard go, an artist of the first rank, whom Montigny had the wit to engage. There really is no one left at the Odeon, as far as I know. Why don't you consider the Theatre Francais?

Where is the Princess Mathilde? At Enghien, or in Paris, or in England? I am sending you a note which you must enclose in the first letter that you have occasion to write to her.

I cannot go to see you, dear old man, and yet I had earned one of those happy vacations; but I cannot leave the *home,* for all sorts of reasons too long to tell and of no interest, but inflexible. I do not know even if I shall go to Paris this winter. Here am I so old! I imagine that I can only bore others and that people cannot endure me anywhere except at home. You absolutely must come to see me with Tourgueneff, since you are planning to go away this winter; prepare him for this abduction. I embrace you, as I love, and my world does too.

G. Sand

CXCVII. To GUSTAVE FLAUBERT 14 September, 1871, Nohant[37]

And what, you want me to stop loving? You want me to say that I have been mistaken all my life, that humanity is contemptible, hateful, that it has always been and always will be so? And you chide my anguish as a weakness, and puerile regret for a lost illusion? You assert that the people has always been ferocious, the priest always hypocritical, the bourgeois always cowardly, the soldier always brigand, the peasant always stupid? You say that you have known all that ever since your youth and you rejoice that you never have doubted it, because maturity has not brought you any disappointment; have you not been young then? Ah! We are entirely different, for I have never ceased to be young, if being young is always loving.

What, then, do you want me to do, so as to isolate myself from my kind, from my compatriots, from my race, from the great family in whose bosom my own family is only one ear of corn in the terrestrial field? And if only this ear could ripen in a sure place, if only one could, as you say, live for certain privileged persons and withdraw from all the others!

But it is impossible, and your steady reason puts up with the most unrealizable of Utopias. In what Eden, in what fantastic Eldorado will you hide your family, your little group of friends, your intimate happiness, so that the lacerations of the social state and the disasters of the country shall not reach them? If you want to be happy through certain people—those certain people,

---

[37] Appeared in le Temps, 3 October, 1871, under the title, Reponse a un ami, and published in Impressions et Souvenirs, p. 53.

the favorites of your heart, must be happy in themselves. Can they be? Can you assure them the least security?

Will you find me a refuge in my old age which is drawing near to death? And what difference now does death or life make to me for myself? Let us suppose that we die absolutely, or that love does not follow into the other life, are we not up to our last breath tormented by the desire, by the imperious need of assuring those whom we leave behind all the happiness possible? Can we go peacefully to sleep when we feel the shaken earth ready to swallow up all those for whom we have lived? A continuous happy life with one's family in spite of all, is without doubt relatively a great good, the only consolation that one could and that one would enjoy. But even supposing external evil does not penetrate into our house, which is impossible, you know very well, I could not approve of acquiescing in indifference to what causes public unhappiness.

All that was foreseen. ... Yes, certainly, I had foreseen it as well as anyone! I saw the storm rising. I was aware, like all those who do not live without thinking, of the evident approach of the cataclysm. When one sees the patient writhing in agony is there any consolation in understanding his illness thoroughly? When lightning strikes, are we calm because we have heard the thunder rumble a long time before?

No, no, people do not isolate themselves, the ties of blood are not broken, people do not curse or scorn their kind. Humanity is not a vain word. Our life is composed of love, and not to love is to cease to live.

The people, you say! The people is yourself and myself. It would be useless to deny it. There are not two races, the distinction of classes only establishes relative and for the most part illusory inequalities. I do not know if your ancestors were high up in the bourgeoisie; for my part, on my mother's side my roots spring directly from the people, and I feel them continually alive in the depth of my being. We all have them, even if the origin is more or less effaced; the first men were hunters and shepherds, then farmers and soldiers. Brigandage crowned with success gave birth to the first social distinctions. There is perhaps not a title that was not acquired through the blood of men. We certainly have to endure our ancestors when we have any, but these first trophies of hatred and of violence, are they a glory in which a mind ever so little inclined to be philosophical, finds grounds for pride? *The people always ferocious,* you say? As for me, I say, the nobility always savage!

And certainly, together with the peasants, the nobility is the class most hostile to progress, the least civilized in consequence. Thinkers should congratulate themselves on not being of it, but if we are bourgeois, if we have come from the serf, and from the class liable to forced labor, can we bend with love and respect before the sons of the oppressors of our fathers? Whoever denies the people cheapens himself, and gives to the world the shameful spectacle of apostasy. Bourgeoisie, if we want to raise ourselves again and become once more a class, we have only one thing to do, and that is to proclaim ourselves the people, and to fight to the death against those who claim to be our superiors by divine right. On account of having failed in the dignity of our revolutionary mandate, of having aped the nobility, of having usurped its insignia, of having taken possession of its playthings, of having been shamefully ridiculous and cowardly, we count for nothing; we are nothing any more: the people, which ought to unite with us, denies us, abandons us and seeks to oppress us.

The people ferocious? No, it is not imbecile either, its real trouble is in being ignorant and foolish. It is not the people of Paris that has massacred the prisoners, destroyed the monuments, and tried to burn the town. The people of Paris is all who stayed in Paris after the siege, since whoever had any means hastened to breathe the air of the provinces and to embrace their absent families after the physical and moral sufferings of the siege. Those who stayed in Paris were the merchant and the workman, those two agents of labor and of exchange, without whom Paris would exist no longer. Those are what constitutes positively the people of Paris; it is one and the same family, whose political blunders cannot restore their relationship and solidarity. It is now recognized that the oppressors of that torment were in the minority. Then the people of Paris was not disposed to fury, since the majority gave evidence only of weakness and fear. The movement was organized by men already enrolled in the ranks of the bourgeoisie, who belong no longer to the habits and needs of the proletariat. These men were moved by hatred, disappointed ambition, mistaken patriotism, fanaticism without an ideal, sentimental folly or natural maliciousness—there was all that in them—and even certain doctrinaire points of honor, unwilling to withdraw in the face of danger. They certainly did not lean on the middle class, which trembled, fled or hid itself. They were forced to put in action the real proletariat which had nothing to lose. Well, the proletariat even escaped them to a great degree, divided as it was by various shades of opinion, some wanting disorder to profit by it, others dreading the consequences of being drawn in, the most of them not reasoning at all, because the evil had become extreme and the lack of work forced them to go to war at thirty sous a day.

Why should you maintain that this proletariat which was shut up in Paris, and was at most eighty thousand soldiers of hunger and despair, represented the people of France? They do not even represent the people of Paris, unless you desire to maintain the distinction between the producer and the trader, which I reject.

But I want to follow you up and ask on what this distinction rests. Is it on more or less education? The limit is incomprehensible if you see at the top of the bourgeoisie, cultivated and learned people, if you see at the bottom of the proletariat, savages and brutes, you have none the less the crowd of intermediaries which will show to you, here intelligent and wise proletarians, there bourgeois who are neither wise nor intelligent. The great number of civilized citizens dates from yesterday and many of those who know how to read and write, have parents still living who can hardly sign their names.

Would it then be only more or less wealth that would classify men into two distinct parties? The question then is where the people begins and where it ends, for each day competencies shift, ruin lowers one, and fortune raises another; roles change, he who was a bourgeois this morning is going to become again a proletarian this evening, and the proletarian of just now, may turn into a bourgeois in a day, if he finds a purse, or inherits from an uncle.

You can well see that these denominations have become idle and that the work of classifying, whatever method one desired to use, would be impracticable.

Men are only over or under one another because of more or less reason or morality. Instruction which develops only egoistic sensuality is not as good as the ignorance of the proletarian, honest by instinct or by custom. This compulsory education which we all desire through respect for human rights, is not, however, a panacea whose miracles need to be exaggerated. Evil natures will find there only more ingenious and more hidden means to do evil. It will be as in all the things that man uses and abuses, both the poison and the antidote. It is an illusion that one can find an infallible remedy for our woes. We have to seek from day to day, all the means immediately possible, we must think of nothing else in practical life except the amelioration of habits and the reconciliation of interests. France is agonizing, that is certain; we are all sick, all corrupt, all ignorant, all discouraged: to say that it was *written,* that it had to be so, that it has always been and will always be, is to begin again the fable of the pedagogue and the child who is drowning. You might as well say at once.

It is all the same to me; but if you add: That does not concern me, you are wrong. The deluge comes and death captures us. In vain you are prudent and withdraw, your refuge will be invaded in its turn, and in perishing with human civilization you will be no greater a philosopher for not having loved, than those who threw themselves into the flood to save some debris of humanity. The debris is not worth the effort, very good! They will perish none the less, that is possible. We shall perish with them, that is certain, but we shall die while in the fulness of life. I prefer that to a hibernation in the ice, to an anticipated death. And anyway, I could not do otherwise. Love does not reason. If I asked why you have the passion for study, you would not explain it to me any better than those who have a passion for idleness can explain their indolence.

Then you think me upset, since you preach detachment to me? You tell me that you have read in the papers some extracts from my articles which indicate a change of ideas, and these papers which quote me with good will, endeavor to believe that I am illuminated with a new light, while others which do not quote me believe that perhaps I am deserting the cause of the future. Let the politicians think and say what they want to. Let us leave them to their critical appreciations. I do not have to protest, I do not have to answer, the public has other interests to discuss than those of my personality. I wield a pen, I have an honorable position of free discussion in a great paper; if I have been wrongly interpreted, it is for me to explain myself better when the occasion presents itself. I am reluctant to seize this opportunity of talking of myself as an isolated individual; but if you judge me converted to false notions, I must say to you and to others who are interested in me: read me as a whole, and do not judge me by detached fragments; a spirit which is independent of party exactions, sees necessarily the pros and cons, and the sincere writer tells both without busying himself about the blame or the approbation of partizan readers. But every being who is not mad maintains a certain consistency, and I do not think that I have departed from mine. Reason and sentiment are always in accord in me to make me repulse whatever attempts to make me revert to childhood in politics, in religion, in philosophy, in art. My sentiment and my reason combat more than ever the idea of factitious distinctions, the inequality of conditions imposed as a right acquired by some, as a loss deserved by others. More than ever I feel the need of raising what is low, and of lifting again what has fallen. Until my heart is worn out it will be open to pity, it will take the part of the weak, it will rehabilitate the slandered. If today it is the people that is under foot, I shall hold out my hand to the people—if it is the oppressor and executioner, I shall tell it that it is cowardly and odious. What do I care for this or that group of men, these names which have become standards, these personalities which have become catchwords? I know only wise and foolish, innocent and guilty. I do not have to ask myself where are my friends or my enemies. They are where torment has thrown them. Those who have deserved my love, and who do not see through my eyes, are none the less dear to me. The thoughtless blame of those who leave me does not make me consider them as enemies. All friendship unjustly withdrawn remains intact in the heart that has not merited the outrage. That heart is above self-love, it knows how to wait for the awakening of justice and affection.

Such is the correct and easy role of a conscience that is not engaged in the party interests through any personal interest. Those who cannot say that of themselves will certainly have success in their environment, if they have the talent to avoid all that can displease them, and the more they have of this talent, the more they will find the means to satisfy their passions. But do not summon them in history to witness the absolute truth. From the moment that they make a business of their opinion, their opinion has no value.

I know sweet, generous and timorous souls, who in this terrible moment of our history, reproach themselves for having loved and served the cause of the weak. They see only one point in space, they believe that the people whom they have loved and served exist no longer, because in their place a horde of bandits followed by a little army of bewildered men has occupied momentarily the theatre of the struggle.

These good souls have to make an effort to say to themselves that what good there was in the poor and what interest there was in the disinherited still exists, only it is no longer in evidence and the political disturbance has sidetracked it from the stage. When such dramas take place, those who rush in light-heartedly are the vain or the greedy members of the family, those who allow themselves to be pulled in are the idiots.

There is no doubt that there are greedy souls, idiots, and vain persons by the thousands in France; but there are as many and perhaps more in the other states. Let an opportunity present itself similar to too frequent opportunities which put our evil passions in play, and you will see whether other nations are any better than we are. Wait till the Germanic race gets to work, the race whose disciplinary aptitudes we admire, the race whose armies have just shown us brutal appetites in all their barbarous simplicity, and you will see what will be its license! The people of Paris will seem sober and virtuous by comparison.

That ought not to be what is called a crumb of comfort, we shall have to pity the German nation for its victories as much as ourselves for our defeats, because this is the first act of its moral dissolution. The drama of its degradation has begun, and as this is being worked out by its own hands it will move very quickly. All these great material organizations in which right, justice, and the respect for humanity are not recognized, are colossi of clay, as we have found to our cost. Well! the moral abasement of Germany is not the future safety of France, and if we are called upon to return to her the evil that has been done us, her collapse will not give us back our life. It is not in blood that races are re-invigorated and rejuvenated. Vital exhalations can issue still from the corpse of France, that of Germany will be the focus of the pestilence of Europe. A nation that has lost its ideals does not survive itself. Its death fertilizes nothing and those who breathe its fetid emanations are struck by the ill that killed it.

Poor Germany! the cup of the wrath of the Eternal is poured out on you quite as much as on us, and while you rejoice and become intoxicated, the philosophic spirit is weeping over you and prepares your epitaph. This pale and bleeding, wounded thing that is called France, holds still in its tense hands, a fold of the starry mantle of the future, and you drape yourself in a soiled flag, which will be your winding sheet. Past grandeurs have no longer a place to take in the history of men. It is all over with kings who exploit the peoples; it is all over with exploited peoples who have consented to their own abasement.

That is why we are so sick and why my heart is broken.

But it is not in scorn of our misery that I regard the extent of it. I do not want to believe that this holy country, that this cherished race, all of whose chords I feel vibrate in me, both harmonious and discordant,—whose qualities and whose defects I love in spite of everything, all of whose good or bad responsibilities I consent to accept rather than to detach myself from them through disdain; no, I do not want to believe that my country and my race are struck to death, I feel it in my suffering, in my mourning, in my hours of pure dejection even, I love, therefore I live; let us love and live.

Frenchmen, let us love one another, my God! my God! let us love one another or we are lost. Let us destroy, let us deny, let us annihilate politics, since it divides us and arms us against one another; let us ask from no one what he was and what he wanted yesterday. Yesterday all the world was mistaken, let us know what we want today. If it is not liberty for all and fraternity towards all, do not let us attempt to solve the problem of humanity, we are not worthy of defining it, we are not capable of comprehending it. Equality is a thing that does not impose itself, it is a free plant that grows only on fertile lands, in salubrious air. It does not take root on barricades, we know that now! It is immediately trodden under the foot of the conqueror, whoever he may be. Let us desire to establish it in our customs, let us be eager to consecrate it in our ideas. Let us give it for a starting point, patriotic charity, love! It is the part of a madman to think that one issues from a battle with respect for human rights. All civil war has brought forth and will bring forth great crime....

Unfortunate International, is it true that you believe in the lie that strength is superior to right? If you are as numerous, as powerful as one fancies, is it possible that you profess destruction and hatred as a duty? No, your power is a phantom of death. A great number of men of every nationality would not, could not, deliberate and act in favor of an iniquitous principle. If you are the ferocious party of the European people, something like the Anabaptists of Munster, like them you will destroy yourself with your own hands. If, on the contrary, you are a great and legitimate fraternal association, your duty is to enlighten your adherents and to deny those who cheapen and compromise your principles. I hope still that you include in your bosom, humane and hard-working men in great numbers, and that they suffer and blush at seeing bandits take shelter under your name. In this case your silence is inept and cowardly. Have you not a single member capable of protesting against ignoble attacks, against idiotic principles, against furious madness? Your chosen chiefs, your governors, your inspirers, are they all brigands and idiots? No, it is impossible; there are no groups, there is no club, there are no crossroads where a voice of truth could not make itself heard. Speak then, justify yourself, proclaim your gospel. Dissolve yourself in order to make yourself over if the discord is in your own midst. Make an appeal to the future if you are not an ancient invasion of Barbarians. Tell those who still love the people what they ought to do for them, and if you have nothing to say, if you cannot speak a word of life, if the iniquities of your mysteries are sealed by fear, renounce noble sympathies, live on the scorn of honest folk, and struggle between the jailer and the police.

All France has heard the word of your destiny which might have been the word of hers. She has waited for it in vain. I too, simple, I waited. While blaming the means I did not want to prejudice the end. There has always been one in revolutions, and the revolutions that fail are not always those with the weakest basis. A patriotic fanaticism seems to have been the first sentiment of this struggle. These lost children of the democratic army were going perhaps to subscribe to an inevitable peace that they judged shameful: Paris had sworn to bury herself under her ruins.

The democratic people were going to force the bourgeois to keep their word. They took possession of the cannon, they were going to turn them on the Prussians, it was mad, but it was grand.... Not at all. The first act of the Commune is to consent to the peace, and in all the course of its management, it does not have an insult, not a threat for the enemy, it conceives and commits the remarkable cowardice of overturning under the eyes of the enemy the column that recalls his defeats and our victories. It is angry against the powers emanating from universal suffrage, and yet it invokes this suffrage in Paris to constitute itself. It is true that this was not favorable to it; it dispenses with the appearance of legality that it intended to give itself and functions by brute force, without invoking any other right than that of hate and scorn for all that is not itself. It proclaims *positive social science* of which it calls itself the sole depository, but about which it does not let a word escape in its deliberations and in its decrees.

It declares that it is going to free man from his shackles and his prejudices, and at that very instant, it exercises a power without control and threatens with death whoever is not convinced of its infallibility. At the same time it pretends to take up the tradition of the Jacobins, it usurps the papal social authority and assumes the dictatorship. What sort of a republic is that? I see nothing vital in it, nothing rational, nothing constituted, nothing constitutable. It is an orgy of false reformers who have not one idea, not one principle, not the least serious organization, not the least solidarity with the nation, not the least outlook towards the future. Ignorance, cynicism and brutality, that is all that emanates from this false social revolution. Liberation of the lowest instincts, impotence of bold ambitions, scandal of shameless usurpations. That is the spectacle which we have just seen. Moreover, this Commune has inspired the most deadly disgust in the most ardent political men, men most devoted to the democracy. After useless essays, they have understood that there was no reconciliation possible where there were no principles; they withdrew from it with consternation, with sorrow, and, the next day, the Commune declared them traitors, and decreed their arrest. They would have been shot if they had remained in its hands.

And you, friend, you want me to see these things with a stoic indifference? You want me to say: man is made thus, crime is his expression, infamy is his nature?

No, a hundred times no. Humanity is outraged in me and with me. We must not dissimulate nor try to forget this indignation which is one of the most passionate forms of love. We must make great efforts in behalf of brotherhood to repair the ravages of hate. We must put an end to the scourge, wipe out infamy with scorn, and inaugurate by faith the resurrection of the country.

G. Sand

CXCVIII. To GUSTAVE FLAUBERT Nohant, 16 September, 1871

Dear old friend,

I answered you day before yesterday, and my letter took such proportions that I sent it as an article to *le Temps* for my next fortnightly contribution; for I have promised to give them two articles a month. The letter a un ami does not indicate you by even an initial, for I do not want to argue against you in public. I tell you again in it my reasons for suffering and for hoping still. I shall send it to you and that will be talking with you again. You will see that my chagrin is a part of me, and that believing progress to be a dream does not depend on me. Without this hope no one is good for anything. The mandarins do not need knowledge and even the education of a limited number of people has no longer reason for existing unless there is hope of influence on the masses; philosophers have only to keep silent and those great minds on whom the need of your soul leans, Shakespeare, Moliere, Voltaire, etc. have no reason for existing and for expressing themselves.

Come, let me suffer! That is worth more than viewing *injustice with a serene countenance,* as Shakespeare says. When I have drained my cup of bitterness, I shall feel better. I am a woman, I have affections, sympathies, and wrath. I shall never be a sage, nor a scholar.

I received a kind little note from the Princess Mathilde. Is she then again settled in Paris? Has she anything to live on from the effects of M. Demidoff, her late and I think unworthy husband? On the whole it is brave and good of her to return near to her friends, at the risk of new upsets.

I am glad that these little faces of children pleased you. I embrace you very much, you are so kind, I was sure of it. Although you are a mandarin, I do not think that you are like a Chinaman at all, and I love you with a full heart.

I am working like a convict.

G. Sand

CXCIX. To George Sand

Dear master, I received your article yesterday, and I should answer it at length if I were not in the midst of preparations for my departure for Paris. I am going to try to finish up with Aisse.

The middle of your letter made me *shed a tear,* without converting me, of course. I was moved, that was all, without being persuaded.

I look vainly in your article for one word: "justice," and all our ill comes from forgetting absolutely that first notion of morality, which to my way of thinking composes all morality. Humanitarianism, sentiment, the ideal, have played us sufficiently mean tricks for us to try righteousness and science.

If France does not pass in a short time to the crisis, I believe that she will be irrevocably lost. Free compulsory education will do nothing but augment the number of imbeciles. Renan has said that very well in the preface to his Questions contemporaines. What we need most of all, is a natural, that is to say, a legitimate aristocracy. No one can do anything without a head, and universal suffrage as it exists is more stupid than divine right. You will see remarkable things if they let it keep on! The masses, the numbers, are always idiotic. I have few convictions, but I have that one strongly. But the masses must be respected, however inept they may be, because they contain the germs of an incalculable fecundity. Give it liberty but not power.

I believe no more than you do in class distinction. Castes belong to archeology. But I believe that the poor hate the rich, and that the rich are afraid of the poor. It will be so forever. It is as useless to preach love to the one as to the other. The most important thing is to instruct the rich, who, on the whole, are the strongest. Enlighten the bourgeois first, for he knows nothing, absolutely nothing. The whole dream of democracy is to elevate the proletarian to the level of the imbecility of the bourgeois. The dream is partly accomplished. He reads the same papers and has the same passions.

The three degrees of education have shown within the last year what they can accomplish: (1) higher education made Prussia win; (2) secondary education, bourgeois, produced the men of the 4th of September; (3) primary education gave us the Commune. Its minister of public instruction was the great Valles, who boasted that he scorned Homer!

In three years every Frenchman can know how to read. Do you think that we shall be the better off? Imagine on the other hand that in each commune, there was *one* bourgeois, only one, who had read Bastiat, and that this bourgeois was respected, things would change.

However I am not discouraged as you are, and the present government pleases me, because it has no principle, no metaphysics, no humbug. I express myself very badly. Moreover you deserve a different response, but I am much hurried.

I hear today that the mass of the Parisians regrets Badinguet. A plebiscite would declare for him, I do not doubt it, universal suffrage is such a fine thing.

CC.   To Gustave Flaubert Nohant, 10 October, 1871

I am answering your *post scriptum,* if I had answered Flaubert I should not have ... *answered,* knowing well that your heart does not always agree with your mind, a discordance into which we all moreover are continually compelled to fall. I answered a part of a letter of some friend whom no one knows, no one can recognize, since I address myself to a part of your reasoning that is not you entirely.

You are a troubadour all the same, and if I had to write to you *publicly* the character would be what it ought to be. But our real discussions ought to remain between ourselves, like caresses between lovers, and even sweeter, since friendship also has its mysteries without the storms of personality.

That letter that you wrote me in haste, is full of well expressed truths against which I do not protest. But the connection and agreement between your truths of reason and my truths of sentiment must be found. France, alas! is neither on your side nor my side; she is on the side of blindness, ignorance and folly. Oh! that I do not deny, it is exactly that over which I despair.

Is this a time to put on Aisse? You told me it was a thing of distinction, delicate like all that *he* did, and I hear that the public of the theatres is more *thickheaded* than ever. You would do well to see two or three plays, no matter which, in order to appreciate the literary condition of the Parisian. The provinces will contribute less than in the past. The little fortunes are too much cut down to permit frequent trips to Paris.

If Paris offered, as in my youth, an intelligent and influential nucleus, a good play would perhaps not have a hundred performances, but a bad play would not have three hundred. But this nucleus has become imperceptible and its influence is swamped. Who then will fill the theatres? The shopkeepers of Paris, without a guide, and without good criticism? Well, you are not the master in the matter of Aisse. There is an heir who is impatient, probably.—They write me that Chilly is very; seriously ill, and that Pierre Berton is reengaged.

You must be very busy; I will not write a long letter to you.

I embrace you affectionately, my children love you and ask to be remembered to you.

G. Sand

CCI. To George Sand

Never, dear good master, have you given such a proof of your inconceivable candor! Now, seriously, you think that you have offended me! The first page is almost like excuses! It made me laugh heartily! Besides, you can always say everything to me, to me! everything! Your blows will be caresses to me.

Now let us talk again! I continually repeat my insistence on justice! Do you see how they are denying it everywhere? Has not modern criticism abandoned art for history? The intrinsic value of a book is nothing in the school of Sainte-Beuve and Taine. They take everything into consideration there except talent. Thence, in the petty journals, the abuse of personality, the biographies, the diatribes. Conclusion: lack of respect on the part of the public.

In the theatre, the same thing. They don't bother about the play, but the lesson to be preached. Our friend Dumas dreams the glory of Lacordaire, or rather of Ravignan! To prevent the tucking up of petticoats has become with him obsession. We cannot have progressed very far since all morality consists for women, in not committing adultery, and for men in abstaining from theft! In short, the first injustice is practised by literature; it has no interest in esthetics, which is only a higher justice. The romantics will have a fine account to render with their immoral sentimentality. Do you recall a bit of Victor Hugo in la Legende des siecles, where a sultan is saved because he had pity on a pig? it is always the story of the penitent thief blessed because he has repented! To repent is good, but not to do evil is better. The school of rehabilitations has led us to see no difference between a rascal and an honest man. I became enraged once before witnesses, against Sainte-Beuve, while begging him to have as much indulgence for Balzac as he had for Jules Lecomte. He answered me, calling me a dolt! That is where *breadth of view* leads you.

They have so lost all sense of proportion, that the war council at Versailles treats Pipe-en-Bois more harshly than M. Courbet, Maroteau is condemned to death like Rossel! It is madness! These gentlemen, however, interest me very little. I think that they should have condemned to the galleys all the Commune, and have forced these bloody imbeciles to clear up the ruins of Paris, with a chain on their necks, like ordinary convicts. But that would have wounded *humanity*. They are kind to the mad dogs, and not at all to the people whom the dogs have bitten.

That will not change so long as universal suffrage is what it is. Every man (as I think), no matter how low he is, has a right to *one* voice, his own, but he is not the equal of his neighbor, who may be worth a hundred times more. In an industrial enterprise (Societe anonyme), each holder votes according to the value of his contribution. It ought to be so in the government of a nation. I am worth fully twenty electors of Croisset. Money, mind, and even race ought to be reckoned, in short every resource. But up to the present I only see one! numbers! Ah! dear master, you who have so authority, you ought to take the lead. Your articles in *le Temps*, which have had a great success, are widely read and who knows? You would perhaps do France a great service?

Aisse keeps me very busy, or rather provokes me. I have not seen Chilly, I have had to do with Duquesnel. They are depriving me definitely of the senior Berton and proposing his son. He is very nice, but he is not at all the type conceived by the author. The Theatre Francais perhaps would ask nothing better than to take Aisse! I am very perplexed, and it is going to be necessary for me to decide. As for waiting till a literary wind arises, as it will never arise in my lifetime, it is better to risk the thing at once.

These theatrical affairs disturb me greatly, for I was in great form. For the last month I was even in an exaltation bordering on madness!

I have met the unavoidable Harrisse, a man who knows everyone, and who is a judge of everything, theatre, novels, finances, politics, etc. What a race is that of enlightened men!!! I have seen Plessy, charming and always beautiful. She asked me to send you a thousand friendly messages.

For my part, I send you a hundred thousand affectionate greetings.

Your old friend

CCII. To GEORGE SAND 14 November, 1871

Ouf! I have just finished *my gods,* that is to say the mythological part of my *Saint-Antoine,* on which I have been working since the beginning of June. How I want to read it to you, dear master of the good God!

Why did you resist your good impulse? Why didn't you come this autumn? You should not stay so long without seeing Paris. I shall be there day after tomorrow, and I shall have no amusement there at all this winter, what with Aisse, a volume of verse to be printed (I should like to show you the preface), and Heaven knows what else. A lot of things that are not at all diverting.

I did not receive the second article that was announced. Your old troubadour has an aching head. My longest nights these three months have not exceeded five hours. I have been grubbing in a frantic manner. Furthermore, I think I have brought my book to a pretty degree of insanity. The idea of the foolish things that it will make the bourgeois utter sustains me, or rather I don't need to be sustained, as such a situation pleases me naturally.

The good bourgeois is becoming more and more stupid! He does not even go to vote! The brute beasts surpass him in their instinct for self-preservation. Poor France! Poor us!

What do you think I am reading now to distract myself? Bichat and Cabanis, who amuse me enormously. They knew how to write books then. Ah! how far our doctors of today are from those men!

We suffer from one thing only: Absurdity. But it is formidable and universal. When they talk of the brutishness of the plebe, they are saying an unjust, incomplete thing. Conclusion: the enlightened classes must be enlightened. Begin by the head, which is the sickest, the rest will follow.

You are not like me! You are full of compassion. There are days when I choke with wrath, I would like to drown my contemporaries in latrines, or at least deluge their cockscombs with torrents of abuse, cataracts of invectives. Why? I wonder myself.

What sort of archeology is Maurice busy with? Embrace your little girls warmly for me.

Your old friend

CCIII. To GUSTAVE FLAUBERT Nohant, 23 November, 1871

I hear from Plauchut that you won't let yourself be abducted for our Christmas Eve *revels*. You say you have too much to do. That is so much the worse for us, who would have had such pleasure in seeing you.—You were at Ch. Edmond's successful play, you are well, you have a great deal to do, you still detest the silly bourgeois; and with all that, is *Saint-Antoine* finished and shall we read it soon?

I am giving you an easy commission to do, this is it: I have had to aid a respectable and interesting person[38] to whom the Prussians have left for a bed and chair, only an old garden bench. I sent her 300 francs, she needed 600. I begged from kind souls. They sent me what was necessary, all except the Princess Mathilde, from whom I asked 200 francs. She answered me the 19th of this month: *How shall I send this to you?*

I replied the same day; simply by mail. But I have received nothing. I do not insist, but I fear that the money may have been stolen or lost, and I am asking you to clear up the affair as quickly as possible.

With this, I embrace you, and Lolo, *Aurore embraces you too*[39] and all the family which loves you.

G. Sand

---

[38] Mademoiselle de Flaugergues.
[39] The words 'Aurore embraces you too' were written by the little girl herself.

CCIV. To George Sand, 1 December

Your letter which I have just found again, makes me remorseful, for I have not yet done your errand to the princess. I was several days without knowing where the princess was. She was to have come to get settled in Paris, and send me word of her arrival. Today at last I learn that she is at Saint-Gratien where I shall go on Sunday evening probably. Anyway your commission shall be done next week.

You must forgive me, for I have not had for the last two weeks ten minutes of freedom. The revival of Ruy Blas which was going to be put ahead of Aisse had to be *put off* (it was a hard job). Well, the rehearsals are to begin on Monday next. I read the play to the actors today, and the roles are to be verified tomorrow. I think it will go well. I have had Bouilhet's volume of verse printed, the preface of which I re-wrote. In short I am worn out! and sad! sad enough to croak. When I have to get into action I throw myself into it head first. But my heart is breaking in disgust. That is the truth.

I have seen none of our friends except Tourgueneff, whom I have found more charming than ever. Give a good kiss to Aurore for her sweet message, and let her kiss you for me.

Your old friend

CCV. To GUSTAVE FLAUBERT Nohant, 7 December, 1871

The money was stolen, I did not receive it, and it cannot be claimed, for the sender would be liable to a suit. Thank the princess just the same for me, and for poor Mademoiselle de Flaugergues whom by the way, the minister is aiding with 200 francs. Her pension is 800.

You are in the midst of rehearsals, I pity you, and yet I imagine that in working for a friend one puts more heart in it, more confidence and much more patience. Patience, there is everything in that, and that is acquired.

I love you and I embrace you, how I would like to have you at Christmas! You cannot, so much the worse for us. We shall drink you a toast and many speaches [sic].

G. Sand

CCVI. To GUSTAVE FLAUBERT Nohant, 4 January, 1872

I want to embrace you at the first of the year and tell you that I love my old troubadour now and always, but I don't want you to answer me, you are in the thick of theatrical things, and you have not the time and the calmness to write. Here we called you at the stroke of midnight on Christmas, we called your name three times, did you hear it at all?

We are all getting on well, our little girls are growing, we speak of you often; my children embrace you also. May our affection bring you good luck!

G. Sand

CCVII. To GEORGE SAND Sunday, January, 1872

At last I have a moment of quiet and I can write to you. But I have so many things to chat with you about, that I hardly know where to begin: (1) Your little letter of the 4th of January, which came the very morning of the premiere of Aisse, moved me to tears, dear well-beloved master. You are the only one who shows such delicacies of feeling.

The premiere was splendid, and then, that is all. The next night the theatre was almost empty. The press, in general, was stupid and base. They accused me of having wanted to advertise by *inserting* an incendiary tirade! I pass for a Red (sic). You see where we are!

The management of the Odeon has done nothing for the play! On the contrary. The day of the premiere it was I who brought with my own hands the properties for the first act! And on the third performance I led the supernumeraries.

Throughout the rehearsals they advertised in the papers the revival of Ruy Blas, etc., etc. They made me strangle la Baronne quite as Ruy Blas will strangle Aisse. In short, Bouilhet's heir will get very little money. Honor is saved, that is all.

I have had Dernieres Chansons printed. You will receive this volume at the same time as Aisse and a letter of mine to the Conseil municipal de Rouen. This little production seemed too violent to le Nouvelliste de Rouen, which did not dare to print it; but it will appear on Wednesday in *le Temps,* then at Rouen, as a pamphlet.

What a foolish life I have been leading for two and a half months! How is it that I have not croaked with it? My longest nights have not been over five hours. What running about! What letters! and what anger!—repressed—unfortunately! At last, for three days I have slept all I wanted to, and I am stupefied by it.

I was present with Dumas at the premiere of Roi Carotte. You cannot imagine such rot! It is sillier and emptier than the worst of the fairy plays of Clairville. The public agreed with me absolutely.

The good Offenbach has had another failure at the Opera-Comique with Fantasio. Shall one ever get to hating piffle? That would be a fine step on the right path.

Tourgueneff has been in Paris since the first of December. Every week we have an engagement to read *Saint-Antoine* and to dine together. But something always prevents and we never meet. I am harassed more than ever by life and am disgusted with everything, which does not prevent me from being in better health than ever. Explain that to me.

CCVIII. To GUSTAVE FLAUBERT Nohant, 18 January, 1872

You must not be sick, you must not be a grumbler, my dear old troubadour. You must cough, blow your nose, get well, say that France is mad, humanity silly, and that we are crude animals; and you must love yourself, your kind, and your friends above all. I have some very sad hours. I look at *my flowers,* these two little ones who are always smiling, their charming mother and my wise hardworking son whom the end of the world will find hunting, cataloguing, doing his daily task, and gay withal *as punch,* in the *rare* moments when he is resting.

He said to me this morning: "Tell Flaubert to come, I will take a vacation at once. I will play the marionettes for him, I will make him laugh."

Life in a crowd forbids reflection. You are too much alone. Come quickly to our house and let us love you.

G. Sand

CCIX. TO GUSTAVE FLAUBERT Friday, 19 January, 1872

I did not know about all that affair at Rouen and I now understand your anger. But you are too angry, that is to say too good, and too good for them. With a *bitter* and vindictive man these louts would be less spiteful and less bold. You have always called them brutes, you and Bouilhet, now they are avenging themselves on the dead and on the living. Ah! well, it is indeed that and nothing else.

Yesterday I was preaching the calmness of disdain to you. I see that this is not the moment, but you are not wicked, strong men are not cruel! With a bad mob at their heels, these fine men of Rouen would not have dared what they have dared!

I have the Chansons, tomorrow I shall read your preface, from beginning to end.

I embrace you.

CCX. To George Sand

You will receive very soon: Dernieres Chansons, Aisse and my Lettre au Conseil municipal de Rouen, which is to appear tomorrow in *le Temps* before appearing as a pamphlet.

I have forgotten to tell you something, dear master. I have used your name. I have *compromised* you in citing you among the illustrious people who have subscribed to the monument for Bouilhet. I found that it looked well in the sentence. An effect of style being a sacred thing with me, don't disavow it.

Today I am starting again my metaphysical readings for *Saint-Antoine*. Next Saturday, I shall read a hundred and thirty pages of it, all that is finished, to Tourgueneff. Why won't you be there!

I embrace you.

Your old friend

CCXI. To GUSTAVE FLAUBERT Nohant, 25 January, 1872

You were quite right to put me down and I want to *contribute* too. Put me down for the sum you would like and tell me so that I may have it sent to you.

I have read your preface in *le Temps*: the end of it is very beautiful and touching. But I see that this poor friend was, like you, one who *did not get over his anger,* and at your age I should like to see you less irritated, less worried with the folly of others. For me, it is lost time, like complaining about being bored with the rain and the flies. The public which is accused often of being silly, gets angry and only becomes sillier; for angry or irritated, one becomes sublime if one is intelligent, idiotic if one is silly.

After all, perhaps this chronic indignation is a need of your constitution; it would kill me. I have a great need to be calm so as to reflect and to think things over. At this moment I am doing *the useful* at the risk of your anathemas. I am trying to simplify a child's approach to culture, being persuaded that the first study makes its impression on all the others and that pedagogy teaches us to look for knots in bulrushes. In short, I am working over *a primer,* do not *eat me alive.*

I have *only one* regret about Paris: it is not to be a third with Tourgueneff when you read your *Saint-Antoine.* For all the rest, Paris does not call me at all; my heart has affections there that I do not wish to hurt, by disagreement with their ideas. It is impossible not to be tired of this spirit of party or of sect which makes people no longer French, nor men, nor themselves. They have no country, they belong to a church. They do what they disapprove of, so as not to disobey the discipline of the school. I prefer to keep silent. They would find me cold or stupid; one might as well stay at home.

You don't tell me of your mother; is she in Paris with her grandchild? I hope that your silence means that they are well. Everything has gone wonderfully here this winter; the children are excellent and give us nothing but joy. After the dismal winter of '70 to '71, one ought to complain of nothing.

Can one live peaceably, you say, when the human race is so absurd? I submit, while saying to myself that perhaps I am as absurd as every one else and that it is time to turn my mind to correcting myself.

I embrace you for myself and for all mine.

G. Sand

CCXII. To George Sand

No! dear master! it is not true. Bouilhet never injured the bourgeois of Rouen; no one was gentler to them, I add even more cowardly, to tell the truth. As for me, I kept apart from them, that is all my crime.

I find by chance just today in Nadar's Memoirs du Geant, a paragraph on me and the people of Rouen which is absolutely exact. Since you own this book, look at page 100.

If I had kept silent they would have accused me of being a coward. I protested naively, that is to say brutally. And I did well.

I think that one ought never begin the attack; but when one answers, one must try to kill cleanly one's enemy. Such is my system. Frankness is part of loyalty; why should it be less perfect in blame than in praise?

We are perishing from indulgence, from clemency, from *cowishness* and (I return to my eternal refrain) from lack of *justice!*

Besides, I have never insulted any one, I have kept to generalities,—as for M. Decorde, my intentions are for open warfare;—but enough of that! I spent yesterday, a fine day, with Tourgueneff to whom I read the hundred and fifteen pages of *Saint-Antoine* that are finished. After which, I read to him almost half of the Dernieres Chansons. What a listener! What a critic! He dazzled me by the depth and the clearness of his judgment. Ah! if all those who attempt to judge books had been able to hear, what a lesson! Nothing escapes him. At the end of a passage of a hundred lines, he remembers a weak epithet! he gave me two or three suggestions of exquisite detail for *Saint-Antoine*.

Do you think me very silly since you believe I am going to blame you for your primer? I have enough philosophic spirit to know that such a thing is very serious work.

Method is the highest thing in criticism, since it gives the means of creating.

CCXIII. To GUSTAVE FLAUBERT Nohant, 28 January, 1872

Your preface is splendid and the book[40] is divine! Mercy! I have made a line of poetry without realizing it, God forgive me. Yes, you are right, he was not second rank, and ranks are not given by decree, above all in an age when criticism undoes everything and does nothing. All your heart is in this simple and discreet tale of his life. I see very well now, why he died so young; he died from having lived too extensively in the mind. I beg of you not to absorb yourself so much in literature and learning. Change your home, move about, have mistresses or wives, whichever you like, and during these phases, must change the end that one lights.

At my advanced age I throw myself into torrents of far niente; the most infantile amusements, the silliest, are enough for me and I return more lucid from my attacks of imbecility.

It was a great loss to art, that premature death. In ten years there will not be one single poet. Your preface is beautiful and well done. Some pages are models, and it is very true that the bourgeois will read that and find nothing remarkable in it. Ah! if one did not have the little sanctuary, the interior little shrine, where, without saying anything to anyone, one takes refuge to contemplate and to dream the beautiful and the true, one would have to say: "What is the use?"

I embrace you warmly.

Your old troubadour.

---

[40] Dernieres Chansons, by Louis Bouilhet.

CCXIV. To George Sand

Dear good master,

Can you, for *le Temps,* write on Dernieres Chansons? It would oblige me greatly. Now you have it.

I was ill all last week. My throat was in a frightful state. But I have slept a great deal and I am again afloat. I have begun anew my reading for *Saint-Antoine.*

It seems to me that Dernieres Chansons could lend itself to a beautiful article, to a funeral oration on poetry. Poetry will not perish, but its eclipse will be long and we are entering into the shades.

Consider if you have a mind for it and answer by a line.

CCXV. TO GUSTAVE FLAUBERT, in Paris Nohant, 17 February

My troubadour, I am thinking of what you asked me to do and I will do it; but this week I must rest. I played the fool too much at the carnival with my grandchildren and my great-nephews.

I embrace you for myself and for all my brood.

G. Sand

CCXVI. To George Sand

What a long time it is since I have written to you, dear master. I have so many things to say to you that I don't know where to begin. Oh! how horrid it is to live so separated when we love each other.

Have you given Paris an eternal adieu? Am I never to see you again there? Are you coming to Croisset this summer to hear *Saint-Antoine?*

As for me, I cannot go to Nohant, because my time, considering my straitened purse, is all counted; but I have still I a full month of readings and researches in Paris. After that I am going away with my mother: we are in search of a companion for her. It is not easy to find one. Then, towards Easter I shall be back at Croisset, and shall start to work again at the manuscript. I am beginning to want to write.

Just now, I am reading in the evening, Kant's Critique de la raison pure, translated by Barni, and I am freshening up my Spinoza. During the day I amuse myself by looking over bestiaries of the middle ages; looking up in the "authorities" all the most baroque animals. I am in the midst of fantastic monsters.

When I have almost exhausted the material I shall go to the Museum to muse before real monsters, and then the researches for the good *Saint-Antoine* will be finished.

In your letter before the last one you showed anxiety about my health; reassure yourself! I have never been more convinced that it was robust. The life that I have led this winter was enough to kill three rhinoceroses, but nevertheless I am well. The scabbard must be solid, for the blade is well sharpened; but everything is converted into sadness! Any action whatever disgusts me with life! I have followed your counsels, I have sought distractions! But that amuses me very little. Decidedly nothing but sacrosanct literature interests me.

My preface to the Dernieres Chansons has aroused in Madame Colet a pindaric fury. I have received an anonymous letter from her, in verse, in which she represents me as a charlatan who beats the drum on the tomb of his friend, a vulgar wretch who debases himself before criticism, after having "flattered Caesar"! "Sad example of the passions," as Prudhomme would say.

A propos of Caesar, I cannot believe, no matter what they say, in his near return. In spite of my pessimism, we have not come to that! However, if one consulted the God called Universal Suffrage, who knows?...Ah! we are very low, very low!

I saw Ruy Blas badly played except for Sarah. Melingue is a sleep-walking drain-man, and the others are as tiresome. As Victor Hugo had complained in a friendly way that I had not paid him a call, I thought I ought to do so and I found him ...charming! I repeat the word, not at all "the great man," not at all a pontiff! This discovery greatly surprised me and did me worlds of good. For I have the bump of veneration and I like to love what I admire. That is a personal allusion to you, dear, kind master.

I have met Madame Viardot whom I found a very curious temperament. It was Tourgueneff who took me to her house.

CCXVII. To GUSTAVE FLAUBERT,
at Croissset Nohant, from the 28 to the 29 February 1872.
Night of Wednesday to Thursday, three o'clock in the morning.

Ah! my dear old friend, what a dreadful twelve days I have spent! Maurice has been very ill. Continually these terrible sore throats, which in the beginning seem nothing, but which are complicated with abscesses and tend to become membranous. He has not been in danger, but always *in danger of danger,* and he has had cruel suffering, loss of voice, he could not swallow; every anguish attached to the violent sore throat that you know well, since you have just had one. With him, this trouble continually tends to get worse, and his mucous membrane has been so often the seat of the same illness that it lacks energy to react. With that, little or no fever, almost always on his feet, and the moral depression of a man used to continual exercise of body and mind, whom the mind and body forbids to exercise. We have looked after him so well that he is now, I think, out of the woods, although, this morning, I was afraid again and sent for Doctor Favre, our *usual* savior.

Throughout the day I have been talking to him, to distract him, about your researches on monsters; he had his papers brought so as to hunt among them for what might be useful you; but he has found only the pure fantasies of his own invention. I found them so original and so funny that I have encouraged him to send them to you. They will be of no use to you except to make you burst out laughing in your hours recreation.

I hope that we are going to come to life again without new relapses. He is the soul and the life of the house. When he is depressed we are dead; mother, wife, and children. Aurore says that she would like to be very ill in her father's place We love each other passionately, we five, and the *sacrosanct literature* as you call it, is only secondary in my life. I have always loved some one more than it and my family more than that some one.

Pray why is your poor little mother so irritable and desperate, in the very midst of an old age that when I last saw her was still so green and so gracious? Is her deafness sudden? Did she entirely lack philosophy and patience before these infirmities? I suffer with you because I understand what you are suffering.

Another old age which is worse, since it is becoming malicious, is that of Madame Colet. I used to think that all her hatred was directed against me, and that seemed to me a bit of madness; for I had never done or said anything against her, even after that vile book in which she poured out all her fury *without* cause. What has she against you now that passion has become ancient history? Strange! strange! And, a propos of Bouilhet, she hated him then, him too this poor poet? She is mad.

You may well think that I was not able to write an iota for these twelve days. I am going, I hope, to start at work as soon as I have finished my novel which has remained with one foot in the air at the last pages. It is on the point of being published but has not yet been finished. I am up every night till dawn; but I have not had a sufficiently tranquil mind to be distracted from my patient.

Good night, dear good friend of my heart.

Heavens! don't work nor sit up too much, as you also have sore throats. They are terrible and treacherous illnesses. We all love you, and we embrace you. Aurore is charming; she learns all that we want her to, we don't know how, without seeming to notice it.

What kind of a woman do you want as a companion for your mother? Perhaps I know of such a one. Must she converse and read aloud? It seems to me that the deafness is a barrier to that. Isn't it a question of material care and continual diligence? What are the stipulations and what is the compensation?

Tell me how and why father Hugo did not have one single visit after Ruy Blas? Did Gautier, Saint-Victor, his faithful ones, neglect him? Have they quarreled about politics?

CCXVIII. To GEORGE SAND March, 1872

Dear master,

I have received the fantastic drawings, which have diverted me. Is there perhaps profound symbolism hidden in Maurice's work? But I did not find it.... Revery!

There are two very pretty monsters: (1) an embryo in the form of a balloon on four feet; (2) a death's head emanating from an intestinal worm.

We have not found a companion yet. It seems difficult to me, we must have someone who can read aloud and who is very gentle; we should also give her some charge of the household. She would not have much bodily care to give, as my mother would keep her maid.

We must have someone who is kind above all, and perfectly honest. Religious principles are not objected to! The rest is left to your perspicacity, dear master! That is all.

I am uneasy about Theo. I think that he is getting strangely old. He must be very ill, doubtless with heart trouble, don't you think so? Still another who is preparing to leave me.

No! literature is not what I love most in the world, I explained myself badly (in my last letter). I spoke to you of distractions and of nothing more. I am not such a pedant as to prefer phrases to living beings. The further I go the more my sensibility is exasperated. But the basis is solid and the thing goes on. And then, after the Prussian war there is no further great annoyance possible.

And the Critique de la raison pure of the previously mentioned Kant, translated by Barni, is heavier reading than the Vie Parisienne of Marcelin; never mind! I shall end by understanding it.

I have almost finished the scenario of the last part of Saint Antoine. I am in a hurry to start writing. It is too long since I have written. I am bored with style!

And tell me more about you, dear master! Give me at once news of Maurice, and tell me if you think that the lady you know would suit us.

And thereupon I embrace you with both arms.

Your old troubadour always agitated, always as wrathful as Saint Polycarp.

CCXIX. To Gustave Flaubert 17 March, 1872

No, dear friend, Maurice is almost well again but I have been tired, worn out with *urgent* work: finishing my novel, and correcting a mass of proof from the beginning. And then unanswered letters, business, no time to breathe! That is why I have not been able to write the article on Bouilhet, and as Nanon has begun, as they are publishing five numbers a week in *le Temps,* I don't see where I shall publish that article very soon.

In the *Revue des Deux Mondes,* they don't want me to write criticism; whoever is not, or was not of their circle, has no talent, and they do not give me the right to say the contrary.

There is, to be sure, a new review wide open to me, which is published by very fine people, but it is more widely read in other countries than in France, and you will find perhaps that an article in that would not excite comment. It is the Revue universelle directed by Amedee Marteau. Discuss that with Charles Edmond. Ask him if, in spite of the fact that Nanon is being published, he could find me a little corner in the body of the paper.

As for the companion, you may rest assured that I am looking for her. The one whom I had in view is not suitable, for she could not read aloud, and I am not sure enough of the others to propose them. I thought that your poor mother was too deaf to listen to reading, and to converse, and that it would be enough for her to have some one very gentle, and charming, to care for her, and to stay with her.

That is all, my dear old friend, it is not my fault, I embrace you with all my heart. For the moment that is the only thing that is functioning. My brain is too stupefied.

G. Sand

CCXX. To GEORGE SAND Croisset

Here I am, back again here, dear master, and not very happy; my mother worries me. Her decline increases from day to day, and almost from hour to hour. She wanted me to come home although the painters have not finished their work, and we are very inconveniently housed. At the end of next week, she will have a companion who will relieve me in this foolish business of housekeeping.

As for me, I have quite decided not to make the presses groan for many years, solely not to have "business" to look after, to avoid all connection with publishers, editors and papers, and above all not to hear of money.

My incapacity, in that direction, has developed to frightful proportions. Why should the sight of a bill put me in a rage? It verges on madness. Aisse has not made money. Dernieres Chansons has almost gotten me into a lawsuit. The story of la Fontaine is not ended. I am tired, profoundly tired, of everything.

If only I do not make a failure also of *Saint-Antoine*. I am going to start working on it again in a week, when I have finished with Kant and Hegel. These two great men are helping to stupefy me, and when I leave them I fall with eagerness upon my old and thrice great Spinoza. What genius, how fine a work the Ethics is!

CCXXI. To GUSTAVE FLAUBERT, at Croissset 9 April, 1872

I am with you all day and all night, and at every instant, my poor dear friend. I am thinking of all the sorrow that you are in the midst of. I would like to be near you. The misfortune of being tied here distresses me. I would like a word so as to know if you have the courage that you need. The end of that noble and dear life has been sad and long; for from the day that she became feeble, she declined and you could not distract her and console her. Now, alas! the incessant and cruel task is ended, as the things of this world end, anguish after struggle! What a bitter achievement of rest! and you are going to miss this anxiety, I am sure of that. I know the sort of dismay that follows the combat with death.

In short, my poor child, I can only open a maternal heart to you which will replace nothing, but which is suffering with yours, and very keenly in each one of your troubles.

G. Sand

CCXXII. To GUSTAVE FLAUBERT Nohant, 14 April, 1872

My daughter-in-law has been staying several days with our friends, at Nimes, to stop a bad case of *whooping-cough* that Gabrielle was suffering with, to separate her from Aurore, from fear of contagion, and to recuperate, for she has not been well for some time. As for me, I am well again. That little illness and this departure suddenly resolved upon and accomplished, have upset my plans somewhat. I had to look after Aurore so that she might be reconciled to it, and I have not had a moment to answer you. I am wondering too if you don't like it better to be left to yourself these first few days. But I beguile the need I feel of being near you at this sad time, by telling you over and over again, my poor, dear friend, how much I love you. Perhaps, too, your family has taken you to Rouen or to Dieppe, so as not to let you go back at once into that sad house. I don't know anything about your plans, in case those which you made to absorb yourself in work are changed. If you have any inclination to travel, and the sinews of war are lacking, I have ready for you a few sous that I have just earned, and I put them at your disposal. Don't feel constrained with me any more than I would with you, dear child. They are going to pay me for my novel in five or six days at the office of *le Temps;* you need only to write me a line and I shall see that you get it in Paris. A word when you can, I embrace you, and so does Maurice, very tenderly.

CCXXIII. To GEORGE SAND Tuesday, 16 April, 1872

Dear good master,

I should have answered at once your first, very kind letter.

But I was too sad. I lacked physical strength.

At last, today, I am beginning to hear the birds singing and to see the leaves growing green. The sun irritates me no longer, which is a good sign. If I could feel like working again I should be all right.

Your second letter (that of yesterday) moved me to tears! You are so good! What a splendid creature you are! I do not need money now, thank you. But if I did need any, I should certainly ask you for it.

My mother has left Croisset to Caroline with the condition that I should keep my apartments there. So, until the estate is completely settled, I stay here. Before deciding on the future, I must know what I have to live on, after that we shall see.

Shall I have the strength to live absolutely alone in solitude?

I doubt it, I am growing old. Caroline cannot live here now. She has two dwellings already, and the house at Croisset is expensive. I think I shall give up my Paris lodging. Nothing calls me to Paris any longer. All my friends are dead, and the last one, poor Theo, is not for long, I fear. Ah! it is hard to grow a new skin at fifty years of age!

I realized, during the last two weeks, that my poor dear, good mother was the being that I have loved the most! It is as if someone had torn out a part of my vitals.

CCXXIV. To GUSTAVE FLAUBERT Nohant, 28 April, 1872

I hold my poor Aurore, who has a terrible case of whooping-cough, day and night in my arms. I have an important piece of work that I must finish, and which I shall finish in spite of everything. If I have not already done the article on Bouilhet, rest assured it is because it is *impossible.* I shall do it at the same time as that on l'Annee terrible. I shall go to Paris between the 20th and 25th of May, at the latest. Perhaps sooner, if Maurice takes Aurore to Nimes where Lina and the littlest one are. I shall write to you, you must come to see me in Paris, or I will go to see you.

I thirst too to embrace you, to console you—no, but to tell you that your sorrows are mine. Good-bye till then, a line to tell me if your affairs are getting settled, and if you are coming out on top.

Your old G. Sand

CCXXV. To George Sand

What good news, dear master! In a month and even before a month, I shall see you at last!

Try not to be too hurried in Paris, so that we may have the time to talk. What would be very nice, would be, if you came back here with me to spend several days. We should be quieter than there; "my poor old mother" loved you very much, would be sweet to see you in her house, when she has been gone only such a short time.

I have started work again, for existence is only tolerable when one forgets one's miserable self.

It will be a long time before I know what I have to live on. For all the fortune that is left to us is in meadowland, and in order to divide it, we have to sell it all.

Whatever happens, I shall keep my apartments at Croisset. That will be my refuge, and perhaps even my only habitation. Paris hardly attracts me any longer. In a little while I shall have no more friends there. The human being (the eternal feminine included) amuses me less and less.

Do you know that my poor Theo is very ill? He is dying from boredom and misery. No one speaks his language anymore! We are like fossils who subsist astray in a new world.

CCXXVI. To GUSTAVE FLAUBERT Nohant, 18 May, 1872

Dear friend of my heart, your inability does not disturb me at all, on the contrary. I have the grippe and the prostration that follows it. I cannot go to Paris for a week yet, and shall be there during the first part of June. My little ones are both in the sheepfold. I have taken good care of and cured the eldest, who is strong. The other is very tired, and the trip did not prevent the whooping-cough. For my part, I have worked very hard in caring for my dear one, and as soon as my task was over, as soon as I saw my dear world reunited and well again, I collapsed. It will be nothing, but I have not the strength to write. I embrace you, and I count on seeing you soon.

G. Sand

CCXXVII. To Gustave Flaubert
Paris, Monday, 3 June, 1872, Rue Gay Lussac, 5

I am in Paris, and for all this week, in the horror of personal business. But next week will you come? I should like to go to see you in Croisset, but I do not know if I can. I have taken Aurore's whooping-cough, and, at my age, it is severe. I am, however, better, but hardly able to go about. Write me a line, so I can reserve the hours that you can give me. I embrace you, as I love you, with a full heart.

G. Sand

CCXXVIII. To GEORGE SAND 1872

The hours that I could give you, dear Master! Why, all the hours, now, by and by, and forever.

I am planning to go to Paris at the end of next week, the 14th or the 16th. Shall you be there still? If not, I shall go earlier.

But I should like it much better if you came here. We should be quieter, without callers or intruders! More than ever, I should like to have you now in my poor Croisset.

It seems to me that we have enough to talk about without stopping for twenty-four hours. Then I would read you *Saint-Antoine,* which lacks only about fifteen pages of being finished. However, don't come if your cough continues. I should be afraid that the dampness would hurt you.

The mayor of Vendome has asked me "to honor with my presence" the dedication of the statue of Ronsard, which occurs the 23rd of this month: I shall go. And I should even like to deliver an address there which would be a protest against the universal modern flap-doodle. The occasion is good. But for the production of a really appropriate little gem, I lack the snap and vivacity.

Hoping to see you soon, dear master, your old troubadour who embraces you.

CCXXIX. TO GUSTAVE FLAUBERT 7 June, 1872

Dear friend,

Your old troubadour has such a bad cough that a little bit more would be the last straw. On the other hand, they cannot get on without me at our house, and I cannot stay longer than next week, that is to say, the 15th or the 16th. If you could come next Thursday, the 13th, I should reserve the 13th, the 14th, even the 15th, to be with you at my house for the day for dinner, for the evening, in short, just as if we were in the country, where we could read and converse. I would be supposed to have gone away.

A word at once, I embrace you as I love you.

G. Sand

CCXXX. To George Sand

Dear master,

Have you promised your support to the candidacy of Duquesnel? if not, I should like to beg you to use to the utmost your influence to support my friend, Raymond Deslandes, as if he were
Your old troubadour,
G. Flaubert
Thursday, three o'clock, 13 June, 1872.
Answer me categorically, so that we may know what you will do.

CCXXXI. To GUSTAVE FLAUBERT, at Croisset. Nohant, 5 July, 1872

I must write to you today. Sixty-eight years old. Perfect health in spite of the cough, which lets me sleep now that I am plunging daily in a furious little torrent, cold as ice. It boils around the stones, the flowers, the great grasses in a delicious shade. It is an ideal place to bathe.

We have had some terrible storms: lightning struck in our garden; and our stream, the Indre, has become like a torrent in the Pyrenees. It is not unpleasant. What a fine summer! The grain is seven feet high, the wheat fields are sheets of flowers. The peasant thinks that there are too many; but I let him talk, it is so lovely! I go on foot to the stream, I jump, all boiling hot, into the icy water. The doctor says that is madness. I let him talk, too; I am curing myself while his patients look after themselves and croak. I am like the grass of the fields: water and sun, that is all I need.

Are you off for the Pyrenees? Ah! I envy you, I love them so! I have taken frantic trips there; but I don't know Luchon. Is it lovely, too? You won't go there without seeing the Cirque of Gavarnie, and the road that leads there, will you? And Cauterets and the lake of Gaube? And the route of Saint-Sauveur? Heavens! How lucky one is to travel and to see the mountains, the flowers, the cliffs! Does all that bore you?

Do you remember the editors, the theatrical managers, the readers and the public when you are running about the country! As for me, I forget everything as I do when Pauline Viardot is singing.

The other day we discovered, about three leagues from here, a wilderness, an absolute wilderness of woods in a great expanse of country, where not one hut could be seen, not a human being, not a sheep, not a fowl, nothing but flowers, butterflies and birds all day. But where will my letter find you? I shall wait to send it to you till you give me an address!

CCXXXII. To George Sand Bagneres de Luchon,
12th July, 1872

I have been here since Sunday evening, dear master, and
no happier than at Croisset, even a little less so, for I am very
idle. They make so much noise in the house where we are that it
is impossible to work. Moreover, the sight of the bourgeois who
surround us is unendurable. I am not made for travelling. The
least inconvenience disturbs me. Your old troubadour is very
old, decidedly! Doctor Lambron, the physician of this place,
attributes my nervous tendencies to the excessive use of tobacco.
To be agreeable I am going to smoke less; but I doubt very much
if my virtue will cure me!

I have just read Dickens's *Pickwick*. Do you know that?
There are superb passages in it; but what defective composition!

All English writers are the same; Walter Scott excepted,
all lack a plot. That is unendurable for us Latins.

Mister —— is certainly nominated, as it seems. All the
people who have had to do with the Odeon, beginning with you,
dear master, will repent of the support that they have given him.
As for me, who, thank Heaven, have no more connection with
that establishment, I don't give a whoop.

As I am going to begin a book which will exact much
reading, and since I don't want to ruin myself in books, do you
know of any dealer in Paris who would rent me all the books that
I designated?

What are you doing now? We saw each other so little and
so inconveniently the last time.

This letter is stupid. But they are making such a noise over my head that it is not clear (my head).

In the midst of my bewilderment, I embrace you and yours also. Your old blockhead who loves you.

CCXXXIII. To GUSTAVE FLAUBERT Nohant, 19 July, 1872

Dear old troubadour,

We too are going away, but without knowing yet where we are going; it doesn't make any difference to me. I wanted to take my brood to Switzerland; they would rather go in the opposite direction, to the Ocean; the Ocean will do! If only we travel and bathe, I shall be out of my mind with joy.

Decidedly our two old troubadourships are two opposites. What bores you, amuses me; I love movement and noise, and even the tiresome things about travelling find favor in my eyes, provided they are a part of travelling. I am much more sensible to what disturbs the calm of sedentary life, than to that which is a normal and necessary disturbance in the life of motion.

I am absolutely like my grandchildren, who are intoxicated beforehand without knowing why. But it is curious to see how children, while loving the change, want to take with them their surroundings, their accustomed playthings, when they go out into the world. Aurore is packing her dolls' trunk, and Gabrielle, who likes animals better, intends to take her rabbits, her little dog, and a little pig that she is taking care of until she eats it. *Such is life* [sic].

I believe that, in spite of your bad temper, this trip will do you good. It will make you rest your brain, and if you have to smoke less, so much the better! Health above all. I hope that your niece will make you move around a bit; she is your child;

she ought to have some authority over you, or the world would be turned upside down.

I cannot refer you to the bookshop that you need for borrowing books. I send for such things to Mario Proth, and I don't know where he finds them. When you get back to Paris, tell him from me to inform you. He is a devoted fellow, as obliging as possible. He lives at 2 rue Visconti. It occurs to me that Charles Edmond, too, might give you very good information; Troubat,[41] also.

You are surprised that spoken words are not contracts; you are very simple; in business nothing holds except written documents. We are Don Quixotes, my old troubadour; we must resign ourselves to being trimmed by the innkeepers. Life is like that, and he who does not want to be deceived must go to live in a desert. It is not living to keep away from all the evil of this nether-world. One must swallow the bitter with the sweet.

As to your *Saint-Antoine,* if you let me, I shall see about finding you a publisher or a review on my next trip to Paris, but we ought to talk about it together and you ought to read it to me. Why shouldn't you come to us in September? I shall be at home until winter.

You ask me what I am doing now: I have done, since I left Paris, an article on Mademoiselle de Flaugergues, which will appear in *l'Opinion nationale* with a work by her; an article for *le Temps* on Victor Hugo, Bouilhet, Leconte de Lisle and Pauline Viardot. I hope that you will be pleased with what I said about your friend; I have done a second fantastic tale for the *Revue des Deux Mondes,* a tale for children. I have written about a hundred letters, for the most part to make up for the folly or to soften the misery of imbeciles of my acquaintance. Idleness is the plague of this age, and life is passed in working for those who do not work. I do not complain. I am well! every day I plunge into the Indre and into its icy cascades, my sixty-eight

---

[41] Sainte-Beuve's secretary.

years and my whooping-cough. When I am no longer useful nor agreeable to others, I want to go away quietly without saying OUF! or at least, not saying anything except that against poor mankind, which is not worth much, but of which I am part, not being worth perhaps very much myself.

I love you and I embrace you. My family does too, Plauchut included. He is going to travel with us.

When we are *somewhere for several days* I shall write to you for news.

G. Sand

CCXXXIV. To GEORGE SAND Croisset, Thursday

Dear master,

In the letter I received from you at Luchon a month ago, you told me that you were packing up, and then that was all. No more news! I have permitted myself to assume, as the good Brantome would say, that you were at Cabourg! When do you return? Where do you go then? To Paris or to Nohant? A question.

As for me, I am not leaving Croisset. From the 1st to the 20th or 25th of September I shall have to go about a bit on business. I shall go to Paris. Write then to rue Murillo.

I should like very much to see you: (1) to see you; (2) to read you *Saint-Antoine,* then to talk to you about another more important book, etc., and to talk about a hundred other things privately.

CCXXXV. To Gustave Flaubert Nohant, 31 August, 1872

My old troubadour,

Here we are back again at home, after a month passed, just as you said, at Cabourg, where chance more than intention placed us. We all took wonderful sea baths, Plauchut, too. We often talked of you with Madame Pasca who was our neighbor at table, and had the room next us. We have returned in splendid health, and we are glad to see our old Nohant again, after having been glad to leave it for a little change of air.

I have resumed my usual work, and I continue my river baths, but no one will accompany me, it is too cold. As for me, I found fault with the sea for being too warm. Who would think that, with my appearance and my tranquil old age, I would still love *excess?* My dominant passion on the whole is my Aurore. My life depends on hers. She was so lovely on the trip, so gay, so appreciative of the amusements that we gave her, so attentive to what she saw, and curious about everything with so much intelligence, that she is real and sympathetic company at every hour. Ah! how *unliterary* I am! Scorn me but still love me.

I don't know if I shall find you in Paris when I go there for my play. I have not arranged with the Odeon for the date of its performance. I am waiting for Duquesnel for the final reading.—And then I expect Pauline Viardot about the 20th of September, and I hope Tourgueneff too, won't you come also? it would be so nice and so complete!

In this hope which I will not give up, I love you and I embrace you with all my soul, and my children join me in loving you and summoning you.

G. Sand

CCXXXVI. To GUSTAVE FLAUBERT, at Paris Nohant,
25 October, 1872

Your letters fall on me like a rain that refreshes, and develops at once all that is germinating in the soil; they make me want to answer your reasons, because your reasons are powerful and inspire a reply.

I do not assume that my replies will be strong too; they are sincere, they issue from the roots of my being, like the plants aforesaid. That is why I have just written a paper on the subject that you raise, addressing myself this time *to a woman friend,* who has written me also in your vein, but less well than you, of course, and a little from an aristocratically intellectual point of view, to which she has not *all the rights she desires.*

My roots, one can't extirpate them, and I am astonished that you ask me to make tulips come from them when they can answer you by producing only potatoes. Since the beginning of my intellectual blooming, when, studying quite alone at the bedside of my paralyzed grandmother, or in the fields at the times when I entrusted her to Deschartres, I asked myself the most elementary questions about society; I was no more advanced at seventeen than a child of six, not as much! thanks to Deschartres, my father's teacher, who was a contradiction from his head to his feet, much learning and little sense; thanks to the convent, into which they stuck me, God knows why, as they believed in nothing; thanks also to a purely Restoration surrounding in which my grandmother, a philosopher, but dying, breathed her last without resisting further the monarchical current.

Then I read Chateaubriand, and Rousseau; I passed from the Gospels to the Contrat social. I read the history of the Revolution written by the pious, the history of France, written by philosophers; and, one fine day, I made all that agree like light proceeding from two lamps, and I had *principles*. Don't laugh, very candid, childish principles which have remained with me through all, through Lelia and the romantic epoch, through love and doubt, enthusiasm and disenchantments. To love, to make sacrifices, only to reconsider when the sacrifice is harmful to those who are the object of it, and to sacrifice oneself again in the hope of serving a real cause, love.

I am not speaking here of personal passion, but of love of race, of the widening sentiment of self-love, of the horror of *the isolated moi*. And that ideal of *justice* of which you speak, I have never seen it apart from love, since the first law on which the existence of a natural society depends, is that we shall serve each other mutually, like the bees and the ants. This concurrence of all to the same end, we have agreed to call instinct among beasts, and it does not matter, but among men, the instinct is love; he who withdraws himself from love, withdraws himself from truth, from justice.

I have experienced revolutions, and I have seen the principal actors near to; I have seen the depth of their souls, I should say the bottom of their bag: *no principles!* and no real intelligence, no force, nor endurance. Nothing but means and a personal end. Only one had principles, not all of them good, but in comparison with their integrity, he counted his personality for nothing: Barbes.

Among artists and literary men, I have found no depth. You are the only one with whom I have been able to exchange other ideas than those of the profession. I don't know if you were at Magny's one day when I said to them that they were all *gentlemen*. They said that one should not write for ignoramuses. They spurned me because I wanted to write only for them, as they are the only ones who need anything. The masters are provided for, are rich, satisfied. Imbeciles lack everything, I am sorry for them. Loving and pitying are not to be separated. And there you have the uncomplicated mechanism of my thought.

I have the passion for goodness and not at all for prejudiced sentimentality. I spit with all my might upon him who pretends to hold my principles and acts contrary to them. I do not pity the incendiary and the assassin who fall under the hand of the law; I do pity profoundly the class which a brutal, degenerate life without upward trend and without aid, brings to the point of producing such monsters. I pity humanity, I wish it were good, because I cannot separate myself from it; because it is myself; because the evil it does strikes me to the heart; because its shame makes me blush; because its crimes gnaw at my vitals, because I cannot understand paradise in heaven nor on earth for myself alone.

You ought to understand me, you who are goodness from head to foot.

Are you still in Paris? It has been such fine weather that I have been tempted to go there to embrace you, but I don't dare to spend the money, however little it may be, when there is so much poverty. I am miserly because I know that I am extravagant when I forget, and I continually forget. And then I have so much to do!...I don't know anything and I don't learn anything, for I am always forced to learn it over again. I do very much need, however, to see you again, for a little bit; it is a part of myself which I miss.

My Aurore keeps me very busy. She understands too quickly and we have to take her at a hard gallop. To understand fascinates her, to know repels her. She is as lazy as monsieur, her father, was. He has gotten over it so well that I am not impatient. She promises me to write you a letter soon. You see that she does not forget you. Titite's Punch has lost his head, literally, because he has been so embraced and caressed. He is loved as much without his head; what an example of fidelity in misfortune! His stomach has become a receptacle where playthings are put.

Maurice is deep in his archeological studies, Lina is always adorable, and all goes well except that the maids are not clean. What a road the creatures have still to travel who do not keep themselves clean!

I embrace you. Tell me how you are getting on with Aisse, the Odeon and all that stuff you are busy about. I love you; that is the end of all my discourses.

G. Sand

CCXXXVII. To George Sand

Dear master,

In your last letter, among the nice things that you say to me, you praise me for not being "haughty"; one is not haughty with what is high. Therefore, in this aspect, you cannot know me. I object.

Although I consider myself a good man, I am not always an agreeable gentleman, witness what happened to me Thursday last. After having lunched with a lady whom I had called "imbecile," I went to call on another whom I had said was "ninny"; such is my ancient French gallantry. The first one had bored me to death with her spiritualistic discourses and her pretensions to ideality; the second outraged me by telling me that Renan was a rascal. Observe that she confessed to me that she had not read his books. There are some subjects about which I lose patience, and, when a friend is slandered before my very face, the savage in my blood returns, I see red. Nothing more foolish! for it serves no purpose and hurts me frightfully.

This vice, by the way, *betraying one's friends in public,* seems to me to be taking gigantic proportions!

CCXXXVIII. To GUSTAVE FLAUBERT Nohant, 26 October, 1872

Dear friend,

Here is another chagrin for you; a sorrow foreseen, but none the less distressing. Poor Theo! I pity him deeply, not because he is dead, but because he has not been really living for twenty years; and if he had consented to live, to exist, to act, to forget a bit his intellectual personality so as to conserve his material personality, he could have lived a long time yet, and have renewed his resources which he was too much inclined to make a sterile treasure. They say that he suffered greatly from hardship during the siege. I understand it, but afterward? why and how?

I am worried at not having had news from you for a long time. Are you at Croisset? You must have been in Paris for the funeral of this poor friend. What cruel and repeated separations! I am angry with you for becoming savage and discontented with life. It seems to me that you regard happiness too much as a possible thing, and that the absence of happiness which is our chronic state, angers you and astonishes you too much. You shun friends, you plunge into work, and reckon ass lost the time you might employ in loving or in being loved. Why didn't you come to us with Madame Viardot and Tourgueneff? You like them, you admire them, you know that you are adored here, and you run away to be alone. Well, how about getting married? Being alone is odious, it is deadly, and it is cruel also for those who love you. All your letters are unhappy and grip my heart. Haven't you any woman whom you love or by whom you would be loved with pleasure? Take her to live with you. Isn't there anywhere a little urchin whose father you can believe you are? Bring him up. Make yourself his slave, forget yourself in him.

What do I know? To live in oneself is bad. There is intellectual pleasure only in the possibility of returning to it when one has been out for a long time; but to live always in this Moi which is the most tyrannical, the most exacting, the most fantastic of companions, no, one must not.—I beg you, listen to me! You are shutting up an exuberant nature in a jail, you are making out of a tender and indulgent heart, a deliberate misanthrope,—and you will not make a success of it. In short, I am worried about you, and I am saying perhaps some foolishness to you; but we live in cruel times and we must not undergo them with curses. We must rise above them with pity. That's it! I love you, write to me.

I shall not go to Paris until after a month's time to put on *Mademoiselle La Quintinie*. Where shall you be?

CCXXXIX. To GEORGE SAND Monday night, 28 October, 1872

You have guessed rightly, dear master, that I had an increase of sorrow, and you have written me a very tender, good letter, thanks; I embrace you even more warmly than usual.

Although expected, the death of poor Theo has distressed me. He is the last of my intimates to go. He closes the list. Whom shall I see now when I go to Paris? With whom shall I talk of what interests me? I know some thinkers (at least people who are called so), but an artist, where is there any? For my part, I tell you he died from the "putrescence of modern times." That is his word, and he repeated it to me this winter several times: "I am dying of the Commune," etc.

The 4th of September has inaugurated an order of things in which people like him have nothing more in the world to do. One must not demand apples of orange trees. Artisans in luxury are useless in a society dominated by plebeians. How I regret him! He and Bouilhet have left an absolute void in me, and nothing can take their place. Besides he was always so good, and no matter what they say, so simple. People will recognize later (if they ever return seriously to literature), that he was a great poet. Meanwhile he is an absolutely unknown author. So indeed is Pierre Corneille.

He hated two things: the hate of the Philistines in his youth, that gave him his talent; the hate of the blackguards in his riper years, this last killed him. He died of suppressed fury, of wrath at not being able to say what he thought. He was *oppressed* by Girardin, by Fould, by Dalloz, and by the first Republic. I tell you that, because *I have seen* abominable things and I am the only man perhaps to whom he made absolute confidences. He lacked what was the most important thing in life for him and for others: *character.* That he failed of the Academy was to him a dreadful chagrin. What weakness! and how little he must have esteemed himself! To seek an honor no matter what, seems to me, besides, an act of incomprehensible modesty.

I was not at his funeral owing to the mistake of Catulle Mendes, who sent me a telegram too late. There was a crowd. A lot of scoundrels and buffoons came to advertise themselves as usual, and today, Monday, the day of the theatrical paper, there must be bits in the bulletins, *that will make copy.* To resume, I do not pity him, *i envy him.* For, frankly, life is not amusing.

No, I don't think that *happiness is possible,* but certainly tranquillity. That is why I get away from what irritates me. A trip to Paris is for me now, a great business. As soon as I shake the vessel, the dregs mount and permeate all. The least conversation with anyone at all exasperates me because I find everyone idiotic. My feeling of justice is continually revolted. They talk *only* of politics and in what a fashion! Where is there a sign of an idea? What can one get hold of? What shall one get excited about?

I don't think, however, that I am a monster of egoism. My Moi scatters itself in books so that I pass whole days without noticing it. I have bad moments, it is true, but I pull myself together by this reflection: "No one at least bothers me." After that, I regain my balance. So I think that I am going on in my natural path; am I right?

As for living with a woman, marrying as you advise me to do that is a prospect that I find fantastic. Why? I don't know. But it is so. Explain the riddle. The feminine being has never been included in my life; and then, I am not rich enough, and then, and then—...I am too old, and too decent to inflict forever my person on another. There is in me an element of the ecclesiastical that people don't know. We shall talk about that better than we can write of it.

I shall see you in Paris in December, but in Paris one is disturbed by others. I wish you three hundred performances for *Mademoiselle La Quintinie*. But you will have a lot of bother with the Odeon. It is an institution where I suffered horribly last winter. Every time that I attempted to do anything they dished me. So, enough! enough! "Hide thy life," maxim of Epictetus. My whole ambition now is to flee from bother, and I am sure by that means never to cause any to others, that is much.

I am working like a madman, I am reading medicine, metaphysics, politics, everything. For I have undertaken a work of great scope, which will require a lot of time, a prospect that pleases me.

Ever since a month ago, I have been expecting Tourgueneff from week to week. The gout is delaying him still.

CCXL. TO GUSTAVE FLAUBERT, at Croissset Nohant,
22 November, 1872

I don't think that I shall go to Paris before February. My play is postponed on account of the difficulty of finding the chief actor. I am content about it, for the idea of leaving Nohant, my occupations, and the walks that are so lovely in this weather, didn't look good to me at all; what a warm autumn and how good for old people! Two hours distant from here, we have a real wilderness, where, the next day after a rain, it is as dry as in a room, and where there are still flowers for me, and insects for Maurice. The little children run like rabbits in the heather which is higher than they are. Heavens! how good it is to be alive when all one loves is living and scurrying around one. You are the only *black spot* in my heart-life, because you are sad and don't want to look at the sun. As for those about whom I don't care, I don't care either about the evils or the follies they can commit against me or against themselves. They will pass as the rain passes. The eternal thing is the feeling of beauty in a good heart. You have both, confound it! you have no right not to be happy.—Perhaps you ought to have had in your life the *inclusion of the feminine sentiment* which you say you have defied.—I know that the feminine is worth nothing; but, perhaps, in order to be happy, one must have been unhappy.

I have been, and I know enough about it; but I forget so well. Well, sad or gay, I love you and I am still waiting for you, although you never speak of coming to see us, and you cast aside the opportunity emphatically; we love you here just the same, we are not literary enough for you here, I know that, but we love, and that gives life occupation.

Is *Saint-Antoine* finished, that you are talking of a work of great scope? or is it *Saint-Antoine* that is going to spread its wings over the entire universe? It could, the subject is immense.

I embrace you, shall I say again, my old troubadour, since you have resolved to turn into an old Benedictine? I shall remain a troubadour, naturally.

G. Sand

I am sending you two novels for your collection of my writings: you are not *obliged* to read them immediately, if you are deep in serious things.

CCXLI. To George Sand
Monday evening, eleven o'clock, 25 November, 1872

The postman just now, at five o'clock, has brought your two volumes to me. I am going to begin Nanon at once, for I am very curious about it.

Don't worry any more about your old troubadour (who is becoming a silly animal, frankly), but I hope to recover. I have gone through, several times, melancholy periods, and I have come out all right. Everything wears out, boredom with the rest.

I expressed myself badly: I did not mean that I scorned "the feminine sentiment." But that woman, materially speaking, had never been one of my habits, which is quite different. I have *loved* more than anyone, a presumptuous phrase which means "quite like others," and perhaps even more than average person. Every affection is known to me, "the storms of the heart" have "poured out their rain" on me. And then chance, force of circumstances, causes solitude to increase little by little around me, and now I am alone, absolutely alone.

I have not sufficient income to take unto myself a wife, nor even to live in Paris for six months of the year: so it is impossible for me to change my way of living.

Do you mean to say that I did not tell you that *Saint-Antoine* had been finished since last June? What I am dreaming of just now, is something of greater scope, which will aim to be comic. It would take too long to explain to you with a pen. We shall talk of it when we meet.

Adieu, dear good, adorable master, yours with his best affection,

Your old friend.

Always as indignant as Saint Polycarp.

Do you know, in all history, including that of the Botocudos, anything more imbecile than the Right of the National Assembly? These gentlemen who do not want the simple and frivolous word Republic, who find Thiers too advanced!!! O profoundness! problem, revery!

CCXLII. To Gustave Flaubert Nohant, 27 November, 1872

Maurice is quite happy and very proud of the letter you wrote him; there is no one who could give him as much pleasure and whose encouragement counts more with him. I thank you too, for my part; for I agree with him.

What! you have finished *Saint-Antoine?* Well, should I find a publisher, since you are not doing so? You cannot keep it in your portfolio. You don't like Levy, but there are others; say the word, and I will act as if it were for myself.

You promise me to get well later, but in the mean time you don't want to do anything to jolt yourself. Come, then, to read *Saint-Antoine* to me, and we will talk of publishing it. What is coming here from Croisset, for a man? If you won't come when we are gay and having a holiday, come while it is quiet and I am alone. All the family embraces you.

Your old troubadour G. Sand

CCXLIII. To George Sand

Dear master,

Here it is a night and a day that I have spent with you. I had finished Nanon at four o'clock in the morning, and Francia at three o'clock in the afternoon. All of it is still dancing around in my head. I am going to try to gather my ideas together to talk about these excellent books to you. They have done me good. So thank you, dear, good master. Yes, they were like a great whiff of air, and, after having been moved, I feel refreshed.

In Nanon, in the first place I was charmed with the style, with a thousand simple and strong things which are included in the web of the work, and which make it what it is; for instance: "as the burden seemed to me enormous, the beast seemed to me beautiful." But I did not pay any attention to any thing, I was carried away, like the commonest reader. (I don't think that the common reader could admire it as much as I do.) The life of the monks, the first relations between Emilien and Nanon, the fear caused by the brigands and the imprisonment of Pere Fructueux which could be commonplace and which it is not at all. What a fine page is 113! and how difficult it was to stay within bounds! "Beginning with this day, I felt happiness in everything, and, as it were, a joy to be in the world."

La Roche aux Fades is an exquisite idyll. One would like to share the life of those three fine people.

I think that the interest slackens a little when Nanon gets the idea of becoming rich. She becomes too strongminded, too intelligent! I don't like the episode of the robbers either. The reappearance of Emilien with his arm cut off, stirred me again, and I shed a tear at the last page over the portrait of the Marquise de Francqueville in her old age.

I submit to you the following queries: Emilien seems to me very much up in political philosophy; at that period did people see as far ahead as he? The same objection applies to the prior, whom I think otherwise charming, in the middle of the book especially. But how well all that is brought in, how well sustained, how fascinating, how charming! What a creature you are! What power you have!

I give you on your two cheeks, two little nurse's kisses, and I pass to Francia! Quite another style, but none the less good. And in the first place I admire enormously your Dodore. This is the first time that anyone has made a Paris gamin real; he is not too generous, nor too intemperate, nor too much of a vaudevillist. The dialogue with his sister, when he consents to her becoming a kept woman, is a feat. Your Madame de Thievre, with her shawl which she slips up and down over her fat shoulders, isn't she decidedly of the Restoration! And the uncle who wants to confiscate his nephew's grisette! And Antoine, the good fat tinsmith so polite at the theatre! The Russian is a simple-minded, natural man, a character that is not easy to do.

When I saw Francia plunge the poignard into his heart, I frowned first, fearing that it might be a classic vengeance that would spoil the charming character of that good girl. But not at all! I was mistaken, that unconscious murder completed your heroine.

What strikes me the most in the book is that it is very intelligent and exact. One is completely in the period.

I thank you from the bottom of my heart for this twofold reading. It has relaxed me. Everything then is not dead. There is still something beautiful and good in the world.

CCXLIV. To GUSTAVE FLAUBERT Nohant, 29 November, 1872

You spoil me! I did not dare to send you the novels, which were wrapped up addressed to you for a week. I was afraid of interrupting your train of thought and of boring you. You stopped everything to read Maurice first, and then me. We should be remorseful if we were not egoists, very happy to have a reader who is worth ten thousand others! That helps a great deal; for Maurice and I work in a desert, never knowing, except from each other, if a thing is a success or a mess, exchanging our criticisms, and never having relations with accredited *judges.*

Michel never tells us until after a year or two if a book has *sold.* As for Buloz, if it is with him we have to do, he tells us invariably that the thing is bad or poor. It is only Charles Edmond who encourages us by asking us for copy. We write without consideration for the public; that is perhaps not a bad idea, but we carry it too far. And praise from you gives us the courage which does not depart from us, but which is often a sad courage, while you make it sparkling and gay, and healthful for us to breathe.

I was right then in not throwing Nanon into the fire, as I was ready to do, when Charles Edmond came to tell me that it was very well done, and that he wanted it for his paper. I thank you then, and I send you back your good kisses, for Francia especially, which Buloz only put in with a sour face and for lack of something better: you see that I am not spoiled, but I never get angry at all that and I don't talk about it. That is how it is, and it is very simple. As soon as literature is a merchandise, the salesman who exploits it, appreciates only the client who buys it, and if the client depreciates the object, the salesman declares to the author that his merchandise is not pleasing. The republic of letters is only a market in which one sells books. Not making concession to the publisher is our only virtue; let us keep that and let us live in peace, even with him when he is peevish, and let us recognize, too, that he is not the guilty one. He would have taste if the public had it.

Now I've emptied my bag, and don't let us talk of it again except to advise about *Saint-Antoine,* meanwhile telling ourselves that the editors will be brutes. Levy, however, is not, but you are angry with him. I should like to talk of all that with you; will you come? or wait until my trip to Paris? But when shall I go? I don't know.

I am a little afraid of bronchitis in the winter, and I do not leave home unless I absolutely have to for business reasons.

I don't think that they will play *Mademoiselle La Quintinie.* The censors have declared that it is a *masterpiece of the most elevated and healthiest morality,* but that they could not *take upon themselves* to authorize the performance. *It will have to be taken to higher authorities,* that is to say, to the minister who will send it to General Ladmirault; it is enough to make you die laughing. But I don't agree to all that, and I prefer to keep quiet till the new administration. If the *new* administration is the clerical monarchy, we shall see strange things. As for me, I don't care if they stand in my way, but how about the future of our generation?...

CCXLV. To GEORGE SAND Wednesday, 4th December, 1872

Dear master,

I notice a phrase in your last letter: "The publisher would have taste if the public had it...or if the public forced him to have it." But that is asking the impossible. They have *literary ideas,* rest assured, and so have messieurs the managers of the theatre. Both insist that they are *judges in that respect,* and their estheticism mingling with their commercialism makes a pretty result.

According to the publishers, one's last book is always inferior to the preceding one. May I be hung if that is not true. Why does Levy admire Ponsard and Octave Feuillet more than father Dumas and you? Levy is academic. I have made more money for him than Cuvillier-Fleury has, haven't I? Well, draw a parallel between us two, and you will see how you will be received. You know that he did not want to sell more than 1200 copies of the Dernieres Chansons, and the 800 which were left over, are in my niece's garret, rue de Clichy! That is very narrow of me, I agree to that; but I confess that the proceeding has simply enraged me. It seems to me that my prose might have been more respected by a man for whom I have turned a penny or two.

Why publish, in these abominable times? Is it to get money? What mockery! As if money were the recompense for work, or could be! That will be when one has destroyed speculation, till then, no! And then how measure work, how estimate the effort? The commercial value of the work remains.

For that one would be obliged to suppress all intermediaries between the producer and the purchaser, and even then, that question in itself permits of no solution. For I write (I speak of an author who respects himself) not for the reader of today, but for all the readers who can present themselves as long as the language lives. My merchandise, therefore, cannot be consumed, for it is not made exclusively for my contemporaries. My service remains therefore indefinite, and in consequence, unpayable.

Why publish then? Is it to be understood, applauded? But yourself, *you*, great George Sand, you confess your solitude. Is there at this time, I don't say, admiration or sympathy, but the appearance of a little attention to works of art? Who is the critic who reads the book that he has to criticise? In ten years they won't know, perhaps, how to make a pair of shoes, they are becoming so frightfully stupid! All that is to tell you that, until better times (in which I do not believe), I shall keep *Saint-Antoine* in the bottom of a closet.

If I publish it, I would rather that it should be at the same time as another entirely different book. I am working now on one which will go with it. Conclusion: the wisest thing is to keep calm.

Why does not Duquesnel go to find General Ladmirault, Jules Simon, Thiers? I think that the proceeding concerns him. What a fine thing the censorship is! Let us be reassured, it will always exist, for it always has! Our friend Alexandre Dumas fils, to make an agreeable paradox, has boasted of its advantages in the preface to the *Dame aux Camelias,* hasn't he?

And you want me not to be sad! I think that we shall soon see abominable things, thanks to the inept stubbornness of the Right. The good Normans, who are the most conservative people in the world, incline towards the Left very strongly.

If they consulted the bourgeoisie now, it would make father Thiers king of France. If Thiers were taken away, it would throw itself in the arms of Gambetta, and I am afraid it will do that soon! I console myself by thinking that Thursday next I shall be fifty-one years old.

If you are not to come to Paris in February, I shall go to see you at the end of January, before going back to the Pan Monceau; I promise.

The princess has written me to ask if you were at Nohant. She wants to write to you.

My niece Caroline, to whom I have just given *Nanon* to read, is enchanted with it. What struck her was the "youth" of the book. The criticism seems true to me. It is a real *book* while Francia, although more simple, is perhaps more finished; more irreproachable as a work.

I read last week the Illustre Docteur Matheus, by Erckmann-Chatrian. How very boorish! There are two nuts, who have very plebeian souls.

Adieu, dear good master. Your old troubadour embraces you,

I am always thinking of Theo. I am not consoled for his loss.

CCXLVI. To GUSTAVE FLAUBERT, at Croissset Nohant,
8 December, 1872

Oh! well, then, if you are in the realm of the ideal about this, if you have a future book in your mind, if you are accomplishing a task of confidence and conviction, no more anger and no more sadness, let us be logical.

I myself arrived at a philosophical state of very satisfactory serenity, and I did not *overstate* the matter when I said to you that all the ill any one can do me, or all the indifference that any one can show me, does not affect me really any more and does not prevent me, not only from being happy outside of literature, but also from being literary with pleasure, and from working with joy.

You were pleased with my two novels? I am repaid, I think that they are *satisfactory,* and the silence which has invaded my life (it must be said that I have sought it) is full of a good voice that talks to me and is sufficient to me. I have not mounted as high as you in my ambition. You want to write for the ages. As for me, I think that in fifty years, I shall be absolutely forgotten and perhaps unkindly ignored. Such is the law of things that are not of first rank, and I have never thought myself in the first rank. My idea has been rather to act upon my contemporaries, even if only on a few, and to share with them my ideal of sweetness and poetry. I have attained this end up to a certain point; I have at least done my best towards it, I do still, and my reward is to approach it continually a little nearer.

That is enough for myself, but, as for you, your aim is greater, I see that clearly, and success is further off. Then you ought to put yourself more in accord with yourself, by being still calmer and more content than I am. Your momentary angers are good. They are the result of a generous temperament, and, as they are neither malicious nor hateful, I like them, but your sadness, your weeks of spleen, I do not understand them, and I reproach you for them. I have believed, I do still, that there is such a thing as too great isolation, too great detachment from the bonds of life. You have powerful reasons to answer me with, so powerful that they ought to give you the victory.

Search your heart, think it over, and answer me, even if only to dispel the fears that I have often on your account; I don't want you to exhaust yourself. You are fifty years old, my son is the same or nearly. He is in the prime of his strength, in his best development, you are too, if you don't heat the oven of your ideas too hot. Why do you say often that you wish you were dead? Don't you believe then in your own work? Do let yourself be influenced then by this or that temporary thing? It is possible, we are not gods, and something in us, something weak and unimportant sometimes, disturbs our theodicy. But the victory every day becomes easier, when one is sure of loving logic and truth. It gets to the point even of forestalling, of overcoming in advance, the subject of ill humor, of contempt or of discouragement.

All that seems easy to me, when it is a question of self control: the subjects of great sadness are elsewhere, in the spectacle of the history that is unrolling around us; that eternal struggle of barbarity against civilization is a great bitterness for those who have cast off the element of barbarity and find themselves in advance of their epoch. But, in that great sorrow, in these secret angers, there is a great stimulant which rightly raises us up, by inspiring in us the need of reaction. Without that, I confess, for my part, that I would abandon everything.

I have had a good many compliments in my life, in the time when people were interested in literature. I have always dreaded them when they came to me from unknown people; they made me doubt myself too much. I have made enough money to be rich. If I am not, it is because I did not care to be; I have enough with what Levy makes for me. What I should prefer, would be to abandon myself entirely to botany, it would be for me a Paradise on earth. But it must not be, that would be useful only to myself, and, if chagrin is good for anything it is for keeping us from egoism, one must not curse nor scorn life. One must not use it up voluntarily; you are enamoured of *justice,* begin by being just to yourself, you owe it to yourself to conserve and to develop yourself.

Listen to me; I love you tenderly, I think of you every day and on every occasion: when working I think of you. I have gained certain intellectual benefits which you deserve more than I do, and of which you ought to make a longer use. Consider too, that my spirit is often near to yours, and that it wishes you a long life and a fertile inspiration in true joys.

You promise to come; that is a joy and a feast day for my heart, and in my family.

Your old troubadour

CCXLVII. To GEORGE SAND 12 December 1872

Dear good master,

Don't take seriously the exaggerations about my *ire*. Don't believe that I am counting "on posterity, to avenge me for the indifference of my contemporaries." I meant to say only this: if one does not address the crowd, it is right that the crowd should not pay one. It is political economy. But, I maintain that a work of art (worthy of that name and conscientiously done) is beyond appraisal, has no commercial value, cannot be paid for. Conclusion: if the artist has no income, he must starve! They think that the writer, because he no longer receives a pension from the great, is very much freer, and nobler. All his social nobility now consists in being the equal of a grocer. What progress! As for me, you say to me "Let us be logical"; but that's just the difficulty.

I am not sure at all of writing good things, nor that the book of which I am dreaming now can be well done, which does not prevent me from undertaking it. I think that the idea of it is original, nothing more. And then, as I hope to spit into it the gall that is choking me, that is to say, to emit some truths, I hope by this means to *purge myself,* and to be henceforward more Olympian, a quality that I lack entirely. Ah! how I should like to admire myself!

Mourning once more: I headed the procession at the burial of father Pouchet last Monday. That gentle fellow's life was very beautiful, and I mourned him.

I enter today upon my fifty-second year, and I insist on embracing you today: I do it affectionately, since you love me so well.

CCXLVIII. To GUSTAVE FLAUBERT Nohant, 8 January, 1873

Yes, yes, my old friend, you must come to see me. I am not thinking of going to Paris before the end of the winter, and it is so hard to see people in Paris. Bring me *Saint-Antoine*.

I want to hear it, I want to live in it with you. I want to embrace you with all my soul, and Maurice does too.

Lina loves you too, and our little ones have not forgotten you. I want you to see how interesting and lovely my Aurore has become. I shall not tell you anything new about myself. I live so little in myself. This will be a good reason for you to talk about what interests me more, that is to say, about yourself. Tell me ahead so that I can spare you that horrid coach from Chateauroux to Nohant. If you could bring Tourgueneff, we should be happy, and you would have the most perfect travelling companion. Have you read Peres et Enfants? How good it is!

Now, I hope for you really this time, and I think that our air will do you good. It is so lovely here!

Your old comrade who loves you,

G. Sand

I embrace you six times for the New Year.

CCXLIX. To GEORGE SAND Monday evening, 3 February, 1873

Dear master,

Do I seem to have forgotten you and not to want to make the journey to Nohant? Not at all! But, for the last month, every time I go out, I am seized anew with the grippe which gets worse each time. I cough abominably, and I ruin innumerable pocket-handkerchiefs! When will it be over?

I have sworn not to step beyond my doorsill till I am completely well again, and I am still awaiting the good will of the members of the commission for the Bouilhet fountain! For nearly two months, I have not been able to get together in Rouen six citizens of Rouen! That is the way friends are! Everything is difficult, the least undertaking demands great efforts.

I am reading chemistry now (which I don't understand a bit), and the Raspail theory of medicine, not to mention the Potager moderne of Gressent and the Agriculture of Gasparin. In this connection, Maurice would be very kind, to compile his agronomical recollections, so that I may know what mistakes he made and why he made them.

What sorts of information don't I need, for the book that I am undertaking? I have come to Paris this winter with the idea of collecting some; but if my horrible cold continues, my stay here will be useless! Am I going to become like the canon of Poitiers, of whom Montaigne speaks, who for thirty years did not leave his room "because of his melancholic infirmity," but who, however, was very well "except for a cold which had settled on his stomach." This is to tell you that I am seeing very few people. Moreover whom could I see? The war has opened many abysses. I have not been able to get your article on Badinguet. I am planning to read it at your house.

As regards reading, I have just swallowed ALL the odious Joseph de Maistre. They have saddled us enough with this gentleman! And the modern socialists who have praised him beginning with the saint-simonians and ending with A. Comte. France is drunk with authority, no matter what they say. Here is a beautiful idea that I find in Raspail, *the physicians ought* to be *magistrates,* so they could force, etc.

Your romantic and liberal old dunce embraces you tenderly.

CCL. To GUSTAVE FLAUBERT Nohant, 5 February, 1873

I wrote to you yesterday to Croisset, Lina thinking that you had returned there. I asked you the little favor which you have already rendered me, namely, to ask your brother to give his patronage to my friend Despruneaux in his suit which is going to be appealed. My letter will probably be forwarded to you in Paris, and reach you as quickly as this one. It is only a question of writing a line to your brother, if that does not bother you.

Pray, what is this obstinate cough? There is only one remedy, a minimum dose, a half-centigram of acetate of morphine taken every evening after digesting your dinner, for a week at least. I do nothing else and I always get over it, I cure all my family the same way, it is so easy to do and so quickly done! At the end of two or three days one feels the good effect. I am awaiting your cure with impatience, for your sake first, and second for myself, because you will come and because I am hungry and thirsty to see you.

Maurice is at a loss to know how to answer your question. He has not made any mistake in his experiments, and knows indeed those that others make or could make; but he says that they vary infinitely and that each mistake is a special one for the conditions in which one works. When you are here and he understands really what you want, he can answer you for everything that concerns the center of France, and the general geology of the planet, if there is any opportunity to generalize. His reasoning has been this: not to make innovations, but to push to its greatest development what exists, in making use always of the method established by experience. Experience can never deceive, it may be incomplete, but never mendacious. With this I embrace you, I summon you, I await you, I hope for you, but will not however torment you.

But we love you, that is certain; and we would like to infuse in you a little of our Berrichon patience about the things in this world which are not amusing, we know that very well! But why are we in this world if it is not to learn patience.

Your obstinate troubadour who loves you.

G. Sand

CCLI. To George Sand Tuesday, March 12, 1873

Dear master,

If I am not at your house, it is the fault of the big Tourgueneff. I was getting ready to go to Nohant, when he said to me: "Wait, I'll go with you the first of April." That is two weeks off. I shall see him tomorrow at Madame Viardot's and I shall beg him to go earlier, as I am beginning to be impatient. I am feeling the *need* of seeing you, of embracing you, and of talking with you. That is the truth.

I am beginning to regain my equilibrium again. What is it that I have had for the past four months? What trouble was going on in the depths of my being? I don't know. What is certain, is, that I was very ill in an indefinable way. But now I am better. Since the end of January, *Madame Bovary* and *Salammbo* have belonged to me and I can sell them. I am doing nothing about it, preferring to do without the money other than to exasperate my nerves. Such is your old troubadour.

I am reading all sorts of books and I am taking notes for my big book which will take five or six years to write, and I am thinking of two or three others. There will be dreams for a long time, which is the principal thing.

Art continues to be "in the marasmus," as M. Prudhomme says, and there is no longer any place in this world for people with taste. One must, like the rhinoceros, retire into solitude and await one's death.

CCLII. TO GUSTAVE FLAUBERT, in Paris Nohant,
15 March, 1873

Well, my old troubadour, we can hope for you very soon.
I was worried about you. I am always worried about you. To tell
the truth, I am not happy over your ill tempers, and your
prejudices. They last too long, and in effect they are like an
illness, you recognize it yourself. Now, forget; don't you know
how to forget? You live too much in yourself and get to consider
everything in relation to yourself. If you were an egoist, and a
conceited person, I would say that it was your normal condition;
but with you who are so good and so generous, it is an anomaly,
an evil that must be combated. Rest assured that life is badly
arranged, painful, irritating for everyone, but do not neglect the
immense compensations which it is ungrateful to forget.

That you get angry with this or that person, is of little
importance if it is a comfort to you; but that you remain furious,
indignant for weeks, months, almost years, is unjust and cruel to
those who love you, and who would like to spare you all anxiety
and all deception.

You see that I am scolding you; but while embracing
you, I shall think only of the joy and the hope of seeing you
flourishing again. We are waiting for you with impatience, and
we are counting on Tourgueneff whom we adore also.

I have been suffering a good deal lately with a series of
very painful hemorrhages; but they have not prevented me from
amusing myself writing tales and from playing with my *little
children*. They are so dear, and my big children are so good to
me, that I shall die, I believe, smiling at them. What difference

does it make whether one has a hundred thousand enemies if one is loved by two or three good souls? Don't you love me too, and wouldn't you reproach me for thinking that of no account? When I lost Rollinat, didn't you write to me to love the more those who were left? Come, so that I may *overwhelm* you with reproaches; for you are not doing what you told me to do.

We are expecting you, we are preparing a mid-Lent fantasy; try to take part. Laughter is a splendid medicine. We shall give you a costume; they tell me that you were very good as a pastry cook at Pauline's! If you are better, be certain it is because you have gotten out of your rut and have distracted yourself a little. Paris is good for you, you are too much alone yonder in your lovely house. Come and work, at our house; how perfectly easy to send on a box of books!

Send word when you are coming so that I can have a carriage at the station at Chateauroux.

CCLIII. To GEORGE SAND Thursday, 20 March, 1873

Dear master,

The gigantic Tourgueneff is at this moment leaving here and we have just sworn a solemn oath. You will have us at dinner the 12th of April, Easter Eve.

It has not been a small job to get to that point, it is so difficult to succeed in anything, no matter what.

For my part nothing would prevent me from going tomorrow But our friend seems to me to enjoy very little liberty and I myself have engagements the first week in April.

I am going this evening to two costume balls! Tell me after that that I am not young.

A thousand affectionate greetings from your old troubadour who embraces you.

Read as an example of modern fetidness, in the last number of the Vie Parisienne, the article on Marion Delorme. It ought to be framed, if, however, anything fetid can be framed. But nowadays people don't look so closely.

CCLIV. To GUSTAVE FLAUBERT Nohant, 23 March, 1873

No, that giant does not do as he likes, I have noticed that. But he is one of the class that finds its happiness in being ruled and I can understand it, on the whole. Provided one is in good hands,—and he is.

Well, we are hoping still, but we are not absolutely counting on anyone but you. You cannot give me a greater pleasure than by telling me that you are going out among people, that you are getting out of a rut and distracting yourself, absolutely necessary, in these muddled days.

On the day when a little intoxication is no longer necessary for self-preservation, the world will be getting on very well. We haven't come to that yet.

That *fetid* thing is not worth the trouble of reading, I didn't finish it, one turns away from such things, one does not spoil one's sense of smell by breathing them. But I do not think that the man to whom one offers that in a censer would be satisfied with it.

Do come with the swallows and bring *Saint-Antoine*. It is Maurice who is going to be interested in that! He is more of a scholar than I am, I who will appreciate, thanks to my ignorance about many things, only the poetic and great side of it. I am sure of it, I know already that it is there.

Keep on going about, you must, and above all continue to love us as we love you.

Your old troubadour,

G. Sand

CCLV. To Gustave Flaubert Nohant, 7th April, 1873

I am writing to my friend General Ferri Pisani, whom you know, who *has charge* at Chateauroux, to reserve you a carriage which will be waiting for you on the 12th, at the station, at twenty minutes past three. You must leave Paris at ten minutes past nine o'clock by the *express*. Otherwise the trip is too long and stupid. I hope that the general will come with you, if there is any decision contrary to your promise send him a telegram to Chateauroux so that he shall not wait for you. He usually comes on horseback.

We are looking forward *impatiently* to seeing you.

Your old troubadour

G. Sand

CCLVI. To GEORGE SAND 23 April, 1873

It is only five days since we parted, and I am missing you like the devil. I miss Aurore and all the household down to Fadette. Yes, that is the way it is, one is so happy at your house! you are so good and so interesting.

Why can't we live together, why is life always so badly arranged? Maurice seems to me to be the type of human happiness. What does he lack? Certainly, he is no more envied by anyone than by me.

Your two friends, Tourgueneff and Cruchard philosophized about that from Nohant to Chateauroux, very comfortably borne along in your carriage at a smart pace by two horses. Hurrah for the postillions of La Chatre! But the rest of the trip was horrid because of the company we had in our car. I was consoled for it by strong drink, as the Muscovite had a flask full of excellent brandy with him. We both felt a little heavy hearted. We did not talk, we did not sleep.

We found here the barodetien folly in full flower again.

On the heels of this affair has developed during the last three days, Stoppfel! another bitter narcotic! Oh! Heavens! Heavens! what a bore to live in such times! How wise you are live so far from Paris!

I have begun my readings again, and, in a week I shall begin my excursions hereabouts to discover a countryside that may serve for my two good men. After which, about the 12th or the 15th, I shall return to my house at the water-side. I want very much, this summer, to go to Saint Gervais, to bleach my nose and to strengthen my nerves. For ten years I have been finding a pretext for doing without it. But it is high time to beautify myself, not that I have any pretensions at pleasing and seducing by my physical graces, but I hate myself too much when I look in my mirror. The older one grows, the more care one should take of oneself.

I shall see Madame Viardot this evening, I shall go early and we will talk of you.

When shall we meet again, now? How far Nohant is from Croisset!

Yours, dear good master, all my affection.

Gustave Flaubert

otherwise called the R. P. Cruchard of the Barnabites, director of the Ladies of Disillusion.

CCLVII. To George Sand

Dear master,

Cruchard should have thanked you sooner for sending him your last book; but his reverence is working like ten thousand negroes, that is his excuse. But it did not hinder him from reading "Impressions et Souvenirs." I already knew some of it, from having read it in *le Temps* (a pun).[42]

This is what was new to me and what struck me: (1) the first fragment; (2) the second in which there is a charming and just page on the Empress. How true is what you say of the proletariat! Let us hope that its reign will pass like that of the bourgeois, and for the same causes, as a punishment for the same folly and a similar egoism.

The *"Reponse a un ami"* I knew, as it was addressed to me.

The *"Dialogue avec Delacroix"* is instructive; two curious pages on what he thought of father Ingres.

I am not entirely of your opinion as regards the punctuation. That is to say that I would shock you by my exaggeration in that respect; but I do not lack, naturally, good reasons to defend my point of view.

"J'allume le fagot," etc., all of this long article charmed me.

---

[42] "Dans de temps" means also, "some time ago."

In the *"Idees d'un maitre d'ecole,"* I admire your pedagogic spirit, dear master, there are many pretty a b c phrases.

Thank you for what you say of my poor Bouilhet!

I adore your "Pierre Bonin." I have known people like him, and as these pages are dedicated to Tourgueneff it is the moment to ask you if you have read *"I'Abandonnee"?* For my part, I find it simply sublime. This Scythian is an immense old fellow.

I am not at such high-toned literature now. Far from it! I am hacking and re-hacking *"le Sexe faible."* I wrote the first act in a week. It is true that my days are long. I spent, last week, one of eighteen hours, and Cruchard is as fresh as a young girl, not tired, no headache. In short, I think that I shall be through that work in three weeks. After that, God knows what!

It would be funny if Carvalho's fantasticality was crowned with success!

I am afraid that Maurice has lost his wager, for I want to replace the three theological virtues by the face of Christ appearing in the sun. What do you think about it? When the correction is made and I have strengthened the massacre at Alexandria and clarified the symbolism of the fantastic beasts, *"Saint-Antoine"* will be finished forever, and I shall start at my two good fellows who were set aside for the comedy.

What a horrid way of writing is required for the stage! The ellipses, the delays, the questions and the repetitions have to be lavish, if movement is desired, and all that in itself is very ugly.

I am perhaps blinding myself, but I think that I am now writing something very quick and easy to play. We shall see.

Adieu, dear master, embrace all yours for me.

Your old good-for-nothing Cruchard, friend of Chalumeau. Note that name. It is a gigantic story, but it requires one to toe the mark to tell it suitably.

CCLVIII. To Gustave Flaubert Nohant, 4 July, 1873

I don't know where you are at present, Cruchard of my heart. I am addressing this to Paris whence I suppose it will be forwarded to you. I have been ill, your reverence, nothing except a stupid anemia, no legs, no appetite, continual sweat on the forehead and my heart as jumpy as a pregnant woman; it is unfair, that condition, when one gets to the seventies, I begin my seventieth spring tomorrow, cured after a half score of river baths. But I find it so comfortable to rest that I have not yet done an iota of work since I returned from Paris, and until I opened my ink-well again to write to you today. We reread your letter this morning in which you said that Maurice had lost his wager. He insists that he has won it as you are taking out the vertus theologales.

As for me, bet or no bet, I want you to keep the new version which is quite in the atmosphere, while the theological virtues are not.—Have you any news of Tourgueneff? I am worried about him. Madame Viardot wrote me, several days ago, that he had fallen and hurt his leg.—Yes, I have read l'Abandonnee, it is very beautiful as is all that he does. I hope that his injury is not serious! such a thing is always serious with gout.

So you are still working frantically? Unhappy one! you don't know the ineffable pleasure of doing nothing! And how good work will seem to me after it! I shall delay it however as long as possible. I am getting more and more of the opinion that nothing is worth the trouble of being said!

Don't believe a word of that, do write lovely things, and love your old troubadour who always cherishes you.

G. Sand

Love from all Nohant.

CCLIX. To George Sand Thursday

Why do you leave me so long without any news of yourself, dear good master? I am cross with you, there!

I am all through with the dramatic art. Carvalho came here last Saturday to hear the reading of *le Sexe faible,* and seemed to me to be satisfied with it. He thinks it will be a success. But I put so little confidence in the intelligence of all those rascals, that for my part, I doubt it.

I am exhausted, and I am now sleeping ten hours a night, not to mention two hours a day. That is resting my poor brain.

I am going to resume my readings for my wretched book, which I shall not begin for a full year.

Do you know where the great Tourgueneff is now?

A thousand affectionate greetings to all and to you the best of everything from your old friend.

CCLX. To GEORGE SAND Sunday ...

I am not like M. de Vigny, I do not like the "sound of the horn in the depth of the woods." For the last two hours now an imbecile stationed on the island in front of me has been murdering me with his instrument. That wretched creature spoils my sunlight and deprives me of the pleasure of enjoying the summer. For it is lovely weather, but I am bursting with anger. I should like, however, to talk a bit with you, dear master.

In the first place, congratulations on your seventieth year, which seems more robust to me than the twentieth of a good many others! What a Herculean constitution you have! Bathing in an icy stream is a proof of strength that bewilders me, and is a mark of a "reserve force" that is reassuring to your friends. May you live long. Take care of yourself for your dear grandchildren, for the good Maurice, for me too, for all the world, and I should add: for literature, if I were not afraid of your superb disdain.

Ha! good! again the hunting horn! The man is mad. I want to go and find the rural guard.

As for me, I do not share your disdain, and I am absolutely ignorant of, as you say, "the pleasure of doing nothing." As soon as I no longer hold a book, or am not dreaming of writing one, *a lamentable* boredom seizes upon me. Life, in short seems tolerable to me only by legerdemain. Or else one must give oneself up to disordered pleasure ... and even then!

Well, I have finished with *le Sexe faible,* which will be played, at least so Carvalho promises, in January, if Sardou's *l'Oncle Sam* is permitted by the censorship; if otherwise, it will be in November.

As I have been accustomed during the last six weeks to seeing things from a theatrical point of view, to thinking in dialogue, here I am starting to build the plot of another play! It will be called *le Candidat*. My written plot is twenty pages long. But I haven't anyone to show it to. Alas! I shall therefore leave it in a drawer and start at my old book. I am reading *l'Histoire de la Medecine* by Daremberg, which amuses me a great deal, and I have finished l'Essai sur les facultes de l'entendement by Gamier, which I think very silly. There you have my occupations. *Things* seem to be getting quieter. I breathe again.

I don't know whether they talk as much of the Shah in Nohant as they do around here. The enthusiasm has been immense. A little more and they would have proclaimed him Emperor. His sojourn in Paris has had, on the commercial shop-keeping and artisan class, a monarchical effect which you would not have suspected, and the clerical gentlemen are doing very well, very well indeed!

On the other side of the horizon, what horrors they are committing in Spain! So that the generality of humanity continues to be charming.

CCLXI. TO GUSTAVE FLAUBERT, at Croissset Nohant,
30 August, 1873

Where are you to be found now? where are you nestled?
As for me, I have just come from Auvergne with my whole
household, Plauchut included. Auvergne is beautiful, above all it
is pretty. The flora is always rich and interesting, the walking
rough, the living accommodations poor. I got through it all very
well, except for the elevation of two thousand meters at Sancy,
which combining an icy wind with a burning sun, laid me flat for
four days with a fever. After that I got into the running again,
and I am returning here to resume my river baths till the frost.

There was no more question of any work, of any
literature at all, than if none of us had ever learned to read. The
local poets pursued me with books and bouquets. I pretended to
be dead and was left in peace. I am square with them now that I
am home, by sending a copy of something of mine, it doesn't
matter what, in exchange. Ah! what lovely places I have seen
and what strange volcanic combinations, where we ought to
have heard your *Saint-Antoine* in a *setting* worthy of the subject!
Of what use are these pleasures of vision, and how are these
impressions transformed later? One does not know ahead, and,
with time and the easy ways of life, everything is met with again
and preserved.

What news of your play? Have you begun your book?
Have you chosen a place to study? Do tell me what is becoming
of my Cruchard, the Cruchard of my heart. Write to me even if
only a word! Tell me that you still love us as I love you and as
all of us here love you.

G. Sand

CCLXII. To GEORGE SAND Croisset, Friday,
5th September, 1873

On arriving here yesterday, I found your letter, dear good master. All is well with you then, God be praised!

I spent the month of August in wandering about, for I was in Dieppe, in Paris, in Saint-Gratien, in Brie, and in Beauce, hunting for a certain country that I had in mind, and I think that I have found it at last in the neighborhood of Houdan. But, before starting at my terrifying book, I shall make a last search on the road that goes from Loupe to Laigle. After that, good night.

The Vaudeville begins well. Carvalho up to now has been charming. His enthusiasm is so strong even that I am not without anxieties. One must remember the good Frenchmen who cried "On to Berlin," and then received such a fine drubbing.

Not only is the aforesaid Carvalho content with the *le Sexe faible,* but he wants me to write at once another comedy, the scenario of which I have shown him, and which he would like to produce a year from now. I don't think the thing is quite ready to be put into words. But on the other hand, I should like to be through with it before undertaking the story of my good men. Meanwhile, I am keeping on with my reading and note-taking.

You are not aware, doubtless, that they have forbidden Coetlogon's play formally, *because it criticised the empire.* That is the censorship's answer. As I have in the *le Sexe faible* a rather ridiculous general, I am not without forebodings. What a fine thing is Censorship! Axiom: All governments curse literature, power does not like another power.

When they forbade the playing of *Mademoiselle La Quintinie,* you were too stoical, dear master, or too indifferent. You should always protest against injustice and folly, you should bawl, froth at the mouth, and smash when you can. If I had been in your place with your authority, I should have made a grand row. I think too that Father Hugo was wrong in keeping quiet about le Roi s'amuse. He often asserts his personality on less legitimate occasions.

At Rouen they are having processions, but the effect is completely spoiled, and the result of it is deplorable for fusion! What a misfortune! Among the imbecilities of our times, that (fusion) is perhaps the greatest. I should not be surprised if we should see little Father Thiers again! On the other hand many Reds, from fear of the clerical reaction, have gone over to Bonapartism. One needs a fine dose of simplicity to keep any political faith.

Have you read the *Antichrist?* I find that indeed a beautiful book, aside from some faults of taste, some modern expressions applied to ancient things. Renan seems to me on the whole to have progressed. I passed all one evening recently with him and I thought him adorable.

CCLXIII. To GUSTAVE FLAUBERT, at Croissset Nohant,
3d October, 1873

The existence of Cruchard is a beautiful poem, so much in keeping, that I don't know if it is a fictitious biography or the copy for a real article done in good faith. I had to laugh a bit after the departure of all the Viardots (except Viardot) and the big Muscovite, who was charming although very much indisposed from time to time. He left very well and very gay, but regretting not to have been to see you. The truth is that he was ill just then. He has had a disordered stomach, like me, for some time. I get well by being moderate, and he does not! I excuse him; after these crises one is famished, and if it is because of an empty stomach that one has to fill up, he must be terribly famished. What a kind, excellent and worthy man! And what modest talent! Everyone adores him here and I give them the example. We adore you too, Cruchard of my heart. But you love your work better than your friends, and in that you are inferior to the real Cruchard, who at least adored our holy religion.

By the way, I think that we shall have Henry V. They tell me that I am seeing the dark side of things; I don't see anything, but I perceive the odor of sacristies that increases. If that should not last a long time, I should like our clerical bourgeois to undergo the scorn of those whose lands they have bought and whose titles they have taken. It would be a good thing.

What lovely weather in our country! I still go every day to dip into the cold rush of my little river and I feel better. I hope to resume tomorrow my work that has been absolutely abandoned for six months. Ordinarily, I take shorter holidays;

but the flowering of the meadow saffron always warns me that it is time to begin grubbing again. Here it is, let us grub. Love me as I love you.

My Aurore, whom I have not neglected, and who is world: well, sends you a big kiss. Lina, Maurice send affection.

G. Sand

CCLXIV. To GEORGE SAND Croisset, Thursday

Whatever happens, Catholicism will receive a terrible blow, and if I were a devotee, I should spend my time before a crucifix saying: "Maintain the Republic for us, O my God!"

But *they are afraid* of the monarchy. Because of itself and because of the reaction which would follow. Public opinion is absolutely against it. The reports of messieurs the prefects are disquieting; the army is divided into Bonapartists and Republicans; the body of big business in Paris has pronounced against Henry V. Those are the bits of information that I bring back from Paris, where I have spent ten days. In a word, dear master, I think now that *they* will be swamped! Amen!

I advise you to read the pamphlet by Cathelineau and the one by Segur also. It is curious! The basis is clearly to be seen. Those people think they are in the XIIth century.

As for Cruchard, Carvalho asked him for some changes which he refused. (You know that sometimes Cruchard is not easy.) The aforesaid Carvalho finally realized that it was impossible to change anything in *le Sexe faible* without distorting the real idea of the play. But he is asking to play *le Candidat* first, it is not finished but it delights him—naturally. Then when the thing is finished, reviewed and corrected, perhaps he won't want it. In short, if after *l'Oncle Sam, le Candidat* is finished, it will be played. If not, it will be *le Sexe faible*.

However, I don't care, I am so eager to start my novel which will take me several years. And moreover, the theatrical style is beginning to exasperate me. Those little curt phrases, this continual scintillation irritates like seltzer water, which is pleasing at first but shortly seems like nasty water. Between now and January I am going to compose dialogues in the best manner possible, after that I am coming back to serious things.

I am glad to have diverted you a little with the biography of Cruchard. But I find it is hybrid and the character of Cruchard is not consistent! A man with such an executive ability does not have so many literary preoccupations. The archeology is superfluous. It belongs to another kind of ecclesiastics. Perhaps there is a transition that is lacking. Such is my humble criticism.

They had said in a theatrical bulletin that you were in Paris; I had a mistaken joy about it, dear good master whom I adore and whom I embrace.

CCLXV. To Gustave Flaubert

Your poor old troubadour, just getting well from a cruel attack of rheumatism, during which he could not lie down, nor eat, nor dress without aid, is at last up again. He suffered liver trouble, jaundice, rash, fever, in short he was fit to be thrown out on a pile of rubbish.

Here he is up again, very feeble, but able to write a few lines and to say with you *amen* to the buried catholic dictatorships; it is not even Catholics that they should be called, those people are not. They are only clericals.

I note today in the papers that they have played *l'Oncle Sam*. I hear that it is bad, but it may very well be a success all the same. I think that your play is surely postponed and Carvalho seems as capricious too, to me, as hard to put your finger on as other theatrical managers.

All Nohant embraces you and I embrace you even more, but I cannot write any more.

G. Sand Monday

Hard work? When indeed can I start at it? I am *no good.*

CCLXVI. To George Sand January, 1874

As I have a quiet moment, I am going to profit by it by talking a little with you, dear good master! And first of all, embrace for me all your family and accept all my wishes for a Happy New Year!

This is what is happening now to your Father Cruchard.

Cruchard is very busy, but serene and very calm, which surprises everybody. Yes, that's the way it is. No indignations, no boiling over. The rehearsals of *le Candidat* have begun, and the thing will be on the boards the first of February. Carvalho seems to me very satisfied with it! Nevertheless he has insisted on my combining two acts in one, which makes the first act inordinately long.

I did this work in two days, and Cruchard has been splendid! He slept seven hours in all, from Thursday morning (Christmas Day) to Saturday, and he is only the better for it.

Do you know what I am going to do to complete my ecclesiastical character? I am going to be a godfather. Madame Charpentier in her enthusiasm for *Saint-Antoine* came to beg me to give the name Antoine to the child that she is expecting! I refused to inflict on this young Christian the name of such an agitated man, but I had to accept the honor that was done me. Can you see my old top-knot by the baptismal font, beside the chubby-cheeked baby, the nurse and the relatives? O civilization, such are your blows! Good manners, such are your exactions!

I went on Sunday to the civic funeral of Francois-Victor Hugo. What a crowd! and not a cry, not the least bit of disorder!

Days like that are bad for Catholicism. Poor father Hugo (whom I could not help embracing) was very broken, but stoical.

What do you think of *le Figaro*, which reproached him for wearing at his son's funeral, "a soft hat"?

As for politics, a dead calm. The Bazaine trial is ancient history. Nothing shows better the contemporary demoralization than the pardon granted to this wretched creature! Besides, the right of pardon if one departs from theology is a denial of justice. By what right can a man prevent the accomplishment of the law?

The Bonapartists should have let this alone; but not at all: they defended him bitterly, out of hatred for the 4th of September. Why do all the parties regard themselves as having joint interests with the rascals who exploit them? It is because all parties are execrable, imbecile, unjust, blind! An example: the history of Azor (what a name!). He robbed the ecclesiastics. Never mind! the clericals consider themselves attacked.

As regards the church. I have read in full (which I never did before) Lamennais' *Essai sur l'indifférence*. I know now, and thoroughly, all the great buffoons who had a disastrous influence on the XIXth century. To establish common sense or the prevailing mode and custom as the criterion of certitude, that is preparing the way for universal suffrage, which is, to my way of thinking, the shame of human kind.

I have just read also, *la Chretienne* by the Abbe Bautain. A curious book for a novelist. It smacks of its period of modern Paris. I gulped a volume by Garcin de Tassy on Hindustani literature, to get clean. One can breathe, at least, in that.

You see that your Father Cruchard is not entirely stupefied by the theatre. However, I haven't anything to complain of in the Vaudeville. Everyone there is polite and exact! How different from the Odeon!

Our friend Chennevieres is now our superior, since the theatres are in his division. The theatrical people are enchanted.

I see the Muscovite every Sunday. He is very well and like him better and better.

Saint-Antoine will be in galley proof at the end of January.

Adieu, dear master! When shall we meet? Nohant is very far away! and I am going to be, all this winter, very busy.

CCLXVII. To GUSTAVE FLAUBERT January, 1874

I am seized with a headache, but, although perfectly imbecile, I want to embrace you and thank you for having written to me on New Year's day. All Nohant loves you and smacks you, as they say in the country.

We wish you a magnificent success and we are glad that it is not to be at the cost of annoyances. However, that is hardly the way of the actors whom I have known, and at the Vaudeville I have found only those who were good natured. Have you a part for my friend Parade? And for Saint-Germain, who seemed to you idiotic one day when perhaps he had lunched too well, but who nevertheless is a fine addlepate, full of sympathy and spirit. And with real talent!

I am not reading all these horrid things that you feed on so as to sense better apparently the good things with which you sandwich them. I have stopped laughing at human folly, I flee it and try to forget it. As for admiration, I am always ready, it is the healthiest regime by far, and too, I am glad to know that I shall soon read *Saint-Antoine* again.

Keep in touch with your play and don't get ill this hateful winter.

Your old troubadour who loves you.

G. Sand

CCLXVIII. TO GEORGE SAND
Saturday evening, 7th February, 1874

I have at last a moment to myself, dear master; now let us talk a little.

I knew through Tourgueneff that you were doing very well. That is the main thing. Now I am going lo give you some news about that excellent Father Cruchard.

Yesterday I signed the final proof for *Saint-Antoine*....But the aforesaid old book will not be published until the first of April (like an April fool trick?) because of the translations. It is finished, I am not thinking any more about it! *Saint-Antoine* is relegated, as far as I am concerned, to the condition of a memory! However I do not conceal from you that I had a moment of great sadness when I looked at the first proof. It is hard to separate oneself from an old companion!

As for *le Candidat*, it will be played, I think, between the 2oth and the 25th of this month. As that play gave me very little trouble and as I do not attach great importance to it, I am rather calm about the results of it.

Carvalho's leaving irritated and disturbed me for several days. But his successor Cormon is full of zeal. Up to now I have nothing but praise for him, as for all the others in fact. The people at the Vaudeville are charming. Your old troubadour, whom you picture agitated and always angry, is gentle as a lamb and even good natured! First I made all the changes that *they* wanted, and then *they* put back the original text. But of my own accord I have cut out what seemed to me too long, and it goes well, very well. Delannoy and Saint-Germain have excellent wigs and play like angels. I think it will be all right.

One thing vexes me. The censorship has ruined the role of a little legitimist ragamuffin, so that the play, conceived in the spirit of strict unpartisanship, has now to flatter the reactionaries: a result that distresses me. For I don't want to please the political passions of anyone, no matter who it may be, having, as you know, an essential hatred of all dogmatism, of all parties.

Well, the good Alexander Dumas has made the plunge! Here he is an Academician! I think him very modest. He must be to think himself honored by honors.

CCLXIX. To GUSTAVE FLAUBERT Nohant, 15 February, 1874

Everything is going well, and you are satisfied, my troubadour. Then we are happy here over your satisfaction and we are praying for success, and we are waiting impatiently *Saint-Antoine* so as to read it again. Maurice has had a cold which attacks him every other day. Lina and I are well, little girls superlatively so. Aurore learns everything with admirable facility and docility; that child is my life and ideal. I no longer enjoy anything except her progress. All my past, all that I have been able to acquire or to produce, has no value in my eyes unless it can profit her. If a certain portion of intelligence and goodness was granted to me, it is so that she may have a greater share. You have no children, be therefore a litterateur, an artist, a master; that is logical, that is your compensation, your happiness, and your strength. And do tell us that you are getting on, that seems to us the main thing in life.—And keep well, I think that these rehearsals which make you go to and fro are good for you.

We all embrace you fondly.

G. Sand

CCLXX. To George Sand
Saturday evening, 28 February, 1874

Dear master,

The first performance of *le Candidat* is set for next Friday, unless it is Saturday, or perhaps Monday the 9th? It has been postponed by Delannoy's illness and by *l'Oncle Sam*, for we had to wait until the said Sam had come down to under fifteen hundred francs.

I think that my play will be very well given, that is all. For I have no idea about the rest of it, and I am very calm about the result, a state of indifference that surprises me greatly. If I were not harassed by people who ask me for seats, I should forget absolutely that I am soon to appear on the boards, and to expose myself, in spite of my great age, to the derision of the populace. Is it stoicism or fatigue?

I have been having and still have the grippe, the result of it for your Cruchard, is a general lassitude accompanied by a violent (or rather a profound) melancholy. While spitting and coughing beside my fire, I muse over my youth. I dream of all my dead friends, I wallow in blackness! Is it the result of a too great activity for the past eight months, or the radical absence of the feminine element in my life? But I have never felt more abandoned, more empty, more bruised. What you said to me (in your last letter) about your dear little girls moved me to the depths of my soul! Why haven't I that? I was born with all the affections, however! But one does not make one's destiny, one submits to it. I was cowardly in my youth, I had a fear of life! One pays for everything.

Let us speak of other things, it will be gayer.

H. M. the Emperor of all the Russias does not like the Muses. The censorship of the "autocrat of the north" had formally forbidden the transportation of *Saint-Antoine,* and the proofs were returned me from Saint Petersburg, last Sunday; the French edition even will be prohibited. That is quite a serious money loss to me. It would have taken very little for the French censorship to forbid my play. Our friend Chennevieres gave me a good boost. Except for him I should not be played. Cruchard does not please the temporal powers. Isn't it funny, this simple hatred of authority, of all government whatever, for art!

I am reading now books on hygiene. Oh! but they are comic! What assurance physicians have! what effrontery! what asses for the most part! I have just finished the Gaule poetique of Marchangy (the enemy of Beranger). This book gave me hysterics.

So as to retemper myself in something stronger, I reread the great, the most holy, the incomparable Aristophanes. There is a man, that fellow! What a world in which such work were produced!

CCLXXI. To Gustave Flaubert Nohant, March, 1874

Our two little girls cruelly ill with the grippe have taken up all my time, but I am following, in the papers, the course of your play. I would go to applaud it, my cherished Cruchard, if I could leave these dear little invalids. So it is on Wednesday that they are going to judge it. The jury may be good or stupid, one never knows!

I have started grubbing again after having rested from the long and successful novel published by the Revue. I shall send it to you when it is published in book form.

Don't you delay to give me the news on Thursday, I don't need to tell you that success and the lack of it prove nothing, and that it is a ticket in a lottery. It is agreeable to succeed; to a philosophical spirit it ought not to be very distressing to fail. As for me, without knowing the play, I predict a success on the first day. As for its continuance, that is always unknown and unforeseen from day to day.

We all embrace you very affectionately.

G. Sand

CCLXXII. TO GEORGE SAND
Thursday, one o'clock, 12 March, 1874

Speaking of *frosts,* this is one! People who want to flatter me insist that the play will do better before the real public, but I don't think so! I know the defects of my play better than anyone. If Carvalho had not, for a month, bored me to death with corrections that I have cut out, I would have made re-touches or perhaps changes which would perhaps have modified the final issue. But I was so disgusted with it that I would not have changed a line for a million francs. In a word, I am dished.

It must be said too that the hall was detestable, all fops and students who did not understand the material sense of the words. They made jokes of the poetical things. A poet says: "I am of 1830, I learned to read in Hernani, and I wanted to be Lara." Thereupon a burst of ironical laughter, etc.

And moreover I have fooled the public in regard to the title. They expected another Rabagas! The conservatives have been vexed because I did not attack the republicans. Similarly the communists would have liked some insults against the legitimists.

My actors played superbly, Saint-Germain among others; Delannoy who carries all the play, is distressed, and I don't know what to do to soften his grief. As for Cruchard, he is calm, very calm! He had dined very well before the performance, and after it he supped even better. Menu: two dozen oysters from Ostend, a bottle of champagne frappe, three slices of roast beef, a truffle salad, coffee and a chaser. Religion and the stomach sustain Cruchard.

I confess that I should have liked to make some money, but as my fall involves neither art nor sentiment I am profoundly unconcerned.

I tell myself: "well, it's over!" and I experience a feeling of freedom. The worst of it all is the scandal about the tickets. Observe that I had twelve orchestra seats and a box! (*Le Figaro* had eighteen orchestra seats and three boxes.) I did not even see the chief of the claque. One would say that the management of the Vaudeville had arranged for me to fail. Its dream is fulfilled.

I did not give away a quarter of the seats that I needed and I bought a great many for people who slandered me eloquently in the lobbies. The "bravos" of a devoted few were drowned at once by the "hushes." When they mentioned my name at the end, there was applause (for the man but not for the work) accompanied by two beautiful cat-calls from the gallery gods. That is the truth.

La Petite Presse of this morning is polite. I can ask no more of it. Farewell, dear good master, do not pity me, for I don't feel pitiable.

P. S.—A nice bit from my servant when he handed me your letter this morning. Knowing your handwriting, he said sighing: "Ah! the best one was not there last evening!" That is just what I think.

CCLXXIII To Georage Sand Wednesday, April, 1874

Thank you for your long letter about *le Candidat*. Now here are the criticisms that I add to yours: we ought to have: (1) lowered the curtain after the electoral meeting and put the entire half of the third act into the beginning of the fourth; (2) cut out the anonymous letter, which is unnecessary, since Arabelle informs Rousselin that his wife has a lover; (3) inverted the order of the scenes in the fourth act, that is to say, beginning with the announcement of the tryst between Madame Rousselin and Julien and, making Rousselin a little more jealous. The anxieties of his election turn him aside from his desire to go to entrap his wife. Not enough is made of the exploiters. There should be ten instead of three. Then, he gives his daughter. The end was there, and at the instant that he notices the blackguardism, he is elected. Then his dream is accomplished, but he feels no joy over it. In that manner there would have been moral progress.

I think, whatever you say about it, that the subject was good, but that I have spoiled it. Not one of the critics has shown me in what. But I know, and that consoles me. What do you think of La Rounat, who in his page implores me, "in the name of our old friendship," not to have my play printed, he thinks it so "silly and badly written"! A parallel between me and Gondinet follows.

The theatrical mystery is one of the funniest things of this age. One would say that the art of the theatre goes beyond the limits of human intelligence, and that it is a secret reserved for those who write like cab drivers. The *question of immediate success* leads all others. It is the school of demoralization. If my play had been sustained by the management, it could have made money like another. Would it have been the better for that?

The Tentation is not doing badly. The first edition of two thousand copies is exhausted. Tomorrow the second will be published. I have been torn in pieces by the petty journals and praised highly by two or three persons. On the whole nothing serious has appeared yet, nor will appear, I think. Renan does not write any more (he says) in the Debats, and Taine is busy getting settled at Annecy.

I have been *execrated* by the Messrs. Villemessant and Buloz, who will do all they can to be disagreeable to me. Villemessant reproaches me for not "having been killed by the Prussians." All that is nauseous!

And you beg me not to notice human folly, and to deprive myself of the pleasure of depicting it! But the comic is the only consolation of virtue. There is, moreover, a manner of taking it which is elevated; that is what I am aiming at with two good people. Don't fear that they are too realistic! I am afraid, on the contrary, that it may seem beyond the bounds of possibility, for I shall push the idea to the limit.

This little work that I shall start in six weeks will keep me busy for four or five years!

CCLXXIV. To GEORGE SAND April, 1874

As it would have necessitated a *struggle,* and as Cruchard has lawsuits in horror, I have withdrawn my play on the payment of five thousand francs, so much the worse! I will not have my actors hissed! The night of the second performance when I saw Delannoy come back into the wings with his eyes wet, I felt myself a criminal and said to myself: "Enough." (Three persons affect me: Delannoy, Tourgueneff and my servant!) In short, it is over. I am printing my play, you will get it towards the end of the week.

I am jumped on on all sides! *le Figaro* and le Rappel; it is complete! Those people to whom I lent money or for whom I did favors call me an idiot. I have never had less nerves. My stoicism (or pride) surprises myself even, and when I look for the causes, I ask myself, dear master, if you are not one of them.

I recall the first night of *Villemer,* which was a triumph, and the first night of *Don Juan de Village,* which was a failure. You do not know how much I admired you on those two occasions! The dignity of your character (a thing rarer still than genius) edified me! and I formulated within myself this prayer: "Oh! how I wish I could be like her, on a similar occasion." Who knows, perhaps your example has sustained me? Forgive the comparison! Well, I don't bat an eye-lid. That is the truth.

But I confess to regretting the *thousands of francs* which I should have made. My little milk-jug is broken. I should have liked to renew the furniture at Croisset, fooled again!

My dress rehearsal was deadly! Every reporter in Paris! They made fun of it all. I shall underline in your copy, all the passages that they seized on. Yesterday and the day before they did not seize on them any more. Oh! well, so much the worse! It is too late. Perhaps the *pride* of Cruchard has killed it.

And they have written articles on *my* dwellings, my *slippers,* my *dog.* The chroniclers have described my apartment where they saw "on the walls, pictures and bronzes." But there is nothing at all on the walls! I know that one critic was enraged because I did not go to see him; and a third person came to tell me so this morning, adding: "What do you want me to tell him?...But Messieurs Dumas, Sardou and even Victor Hugo are not like you.—Oh! I know it!—Then you are not surprised, etc."

Farewell, dear good adored master, friendly regards to yours. Kisses to the dear little girls, and all my love to you.

P.S. Could you give me a copy or the original of Cruchard's biography; I have no draft of it and I want to reread it to freshen up *my ideal.*

CCLXXV. To Gustave Flaubert, at Croissset Nohant,
10 April, 1874

Those who say that I do not think *Saint-Antoine*
beautiful! and excellent, lie about it, I do not need to tell you.
Let me ask you how I could have confided in the Levy clerks
whom I do not know! I remember, as for Levy himself, saying to
him last summer, that I found the thing superb and first class.

I would have done an article for you if I had not already
refused Maurice recently, to do one about Hugo's Quatre-vingt-
treize. I said that I was ill. The fact is, that I do not know how to
do articles, and I have done so many of them for Hugo that I
have exhausted my subject. I wonder why he has never done any
for me; for, really, I am no more of a journalist than he is, and I
need his support much more than he needs mine.

On the whole, articles are not of any use, now, no more
than are friends at the theatre. I have told you that it is the
struggle of one against all, and the mystery, if there is one, is to
turn on an electric current. The subject then is very important in
the theatre. In a novel, one has time to win the reader over. What
a difference! I do not say as you do that there is nothing
mysterious in that. Yes, indeed, there is something very
mysterious in one respect: namely that one cannot judge of one's
effect beforehand, and that the shrewdest are mistaken ten times
out of fifteen. You say yourself that you have been mistaken. I
am at work now on a play; it is not possible to know if I am
mistaken or not. And when shall I know? The day after the first
performance, if I have it performed, which is not certain. There
is no fun in anything except work that has not been read to any

one. All the rest is drudgery and *professional business,* a horrible thing. So make fun of all this *gossip;* the guiltiest ones are those who report it to you. I think it is very odd that they say so much against you to your friends. No one indeed ever says anything to me: they know that I would not allow it. Be valiant and *content* since *Saint-Antoine* is doing well and selling better. What difference does it make if they cut you up in this or that paper? In former times it meant something; in these days, nothing. The public is not the public of other days, and journalism has not the least literary influence. Every one is a critic and forms his own opinions. They never write articles about my novels. That doesn't make any difference to me.

I embrace you and we love you.

Your old troubadour.

CCLXXVI. To GEORGE SAND Friday evening, 1st May, 1874

Things are progressing, dear master, insults are accumulating! It is a concerto, a symphony in which each one is intent on his own instrument. I have been cut up beginning *le Figaro* up to *la Revue des Deux Mondes*, including *la Gazette de France* and *le Constitutionnel*. And *they* have not finished yet! Barbey d'Aurevilly has insulted me personally, and the good Saint-Rene Taillandier, who declares me "unreadable," attributes ridiculous words to me. So much for printing. As for speech, it is in accord. Saint-Victor (is it servility towards Michel Levy) rends me at the Brabant dinner, as does that excellent Charles Edmond, etc. On the other hand I am admired by the professors of the Faculty of Theology at Strasbourg, by Renan, and by the cashier at my butcher's! not to mention some others. There is the truth.

What surprises me, is that under several of these criticisms there is a *hatred* against me, against me personally, a deliberate slandering, the cause of which I am seeking. I do not feel hurt, but this avalanche of foolishness saddens me. One prefers inspiring good feelings to bad ones. As for the rest, I am not thinking any more about *Saint-Antoine*. That is over with!

I shall start, this summer, another book of about the same calibre; after that I shall return to the novel pure and simple. I have in my head two or three to write before I die. Just now I am spending my days at the Library, where I am accumulating notes. In a fortnight, I shall return to my house in the fields. In July I shall go to get rid of my congestion on the top of a Swiss mountain, obeying the advice of Doctor Hardy, the man who called me "a hysterical woman," a saying that I consider profound.

The good Tourgueneff is leaving next week for Russia, his trip will forcibly interrupt his frenzy for pictures, for our friend never leaves the auction rooms now! He is a man with a passion, so much the better for him!

I missed you very much at Madame Viardot's a fortnight ago. She sang *Iphigenie en Aulide*. I cannot tell you how beautiful it was, how transporting, in short how sublime. What an artist that woman is! What an artist! Such emotions console one for life.

Well! and you, dear good master, that play that they talk about, is it finished? You are going to fall back into the theatre! I pity you! After having put dogs on the boards at the Odeon, perhaps they are going to ask you to put on horses! That is where we are now!

And all the household, from Maurice to Fadet, how is it?

Kiss the dear little girls for me and let them return it to you from me.

Your old friend.

CCLXXVII. TO GUSTAVE FLAUBERT Nohant, 4th May, 1874

Let them say what they like, *Saint-Antoine* is a masterpiece, a magnificent book. Ridicule the critics, they are blockheads. The present century does not like lyricism. Let us wait for the reaction, it will come for you, and a splendid one. Rejoice in your insults, they are great promises for the future.

I am working still on my play, I don't at all know if it is worth anything and don't worry about it. I shall be told that when it is finished, and if it does not seem interesting I shall lock it up. It will have amused me for six weeks, that is the most certain thing for us about our profession.

Plauchut is the joy of the salons! happy old man! always content with himself and with others; that makes him as good as an angel, I forgive him all his graces.

You were happy at hearing the Diva Paulita, we had her, with Iphigenie, for two weeks in Nohant last autumn. Ah! yes, there is beauty and grandeur! Try to come to see us before going to Croisset, you would make us happy.

We all love you and all my dear world embraces you with a *great good heart*.

Your old troubadour always,

G. Sand

CCLXXVIII. To GEORGE SAND Croisset, Tuesday,
26th March, 1874

Dear good master,

Here I am back again in my solitude! But I shall not
remain in it long, for, in a short month, I shall go to spend three
weeks on the Righi, so as to breathe a bit, to relax myself, to
deneurasthenize myself! It is a long time since I took the air, I
am tired. I need a little rest. After that I shall start at my big book
which will take at least four years. It will have that good quality!

Le Sexe faible which was accepted at the Vaudeville
Carvalho, was returned to me by the said Vaudeville and
returned also by Perrin, who thinks the play off-color and
unconventional. "Putting a cradle and a nurse on the French
stage!" Think of it! Then, I took the thing to Duquesnel who has
not yet (naturally) given me any answer. How far the
demoralization which the theatres bring about extends! The
bourgeois of Rouen, my brother included, have been talking to
me of the failure of *le Candidat* in hushed voices (sic) and with a
contrite air, as if I had been taken to the assizes under an
accusation of forgery. *not to succeed is a crime* and success is
the criterion of well doing. I think that is grotesque in a supreme
degree.

Now explain to me why they put mattresses under certain
falls and thorns under others? Ah! the world is funny, and it
seems chimerical to me to want to regulate oneself according to
its opinion.

The good Tourgueneff must be now in Saint Petersburg; he sent me a favorable article on *Saint-Antoine* from Berlin. It is not the article, but he, that has given me pleasure. I saw him a great deal this winter, and I love him more and more. I saw a good deal of father Hugo who is (when the political gallery is absent) a charming, good fellow.

Was not the fall of the Broglie ministry pleasing to you? Very much so to me! but the next! I am still young enough to hope that the next Chamber will bring us a change for the better. However?

Ah, confound it! how I want to see you and talk a long time with you! Everything is poorly arranged in this world. Why not live with those one loves? The Abbey of Theleme[43] is a fine dream, but nothing but a dream. Embrace warmly the dear little girls for me, and entirely yours.

R. P. Cruchard

More Cruchard than ever. I feel like a good-for-nothing, a cow, damned, antique, deliquescent, in short calm and moderate, which is the last term in decadence.

---

[43] Cf. Rabelais' Gargantua.

CCLXXIX. To GEORGE SAND Kalt-Bad. Righi.
Friday, 3d July, 1874

Is it true, dear master, that last week you came to Paris? I went through it to go to Switzerland, and I read "in a sheet" that you had been to see les Deux Orphelines, had taken a walk in the Bois de Boulogne, had dined at Magny's, etc.; all of which goes to prove that, thanks to the freedom of the Press, one is not master of one's own actions. Whence it results that Father Cruchard is wrathful with you for not having advised him of your presence in the "new Athens." It seems to me that people are sillier and flatter there than usual. The state of politics has become drivel! They have tickled my ears with the return of the Empire. I don't believe in it! However...We should have to expatriate ourselves then. But how and where?

Is it for a play that you came? I pity you for having anything to do with Duquesnel! He had the manuscript of *le Sexe faible* returned to me by an agent of the theatrical management, without a word of explanation, and in the ministerial envelope was a letter from an underclerk, which is a gem! I will show it to you. It is a masterpiece of impertinence! People do not write in that way to a Carpentras urchin, offering a skit to the Beaumarchais theatre.

It is that very play *le Sexe faible* that, last year, Carvalho was so enthusiastic about! Now no one wants it any more for Perrin thinks it unconventional to put on the boards of the Theatre Francais, a nurse and a cradle. Not knowing what to do with it, I have taken it to the Cluny Theatre.

Ah! my poor Bouilhet did well to die! But I think that the Odeon could show more respect for his posthumous work.

Without believing in an Holbachic conspiracy, I think that they have been knocking me a bit too much of late; and they are so indulgent towards certain others.

The American Harrisse maintained to me the other day that Saint-Simon wrote badly. At that I burst out and talked to him in such a way that he will never more before me belch his idiocy. It was at dinner at the Princess's; my violence cast a chill.

You see that your Cruchard continues not to listen to jokes on religion! He does not become calm! quite the contrary!

I have just read la Creation naturelle by Haeckel, a pretty book, pretty book! Darwinism seems to me to be better expounded there than in the books of Darwin himself.

The good Tourgueneff has sent me news from the depths of Scythia. He has found the information he wanted for a book that he is going to do. The tone of his letter is frivolous, from which I conclude that he is well. He will return to Paris in a month.

A fortnight ago I made a little trip to Lower Normandy, where I have found at last a neighborhood suitable to place my two good men. It will be between the valley of the Orne and the valley of the Auge. I shall have to return there several times.

Beginning with September, then, I shall start that hard task! it makes me afraid, and I am overwhelmed by it in advance.

As you know Switzerland, it is useless for me to talk to you of it, and you would scorn me if I were to tell you that I am bored to extinction here. I came here obediently because they ordered me to, for the purpose of bleaching my face and calming my nerves! I don't think that the remedy will be efficacious; anyhow it has been deadly boring to me. I am not a man of nature, and I do not understand anything in a country where there is no history. I would give all these glaciers for the Vatican

Museum. One can dream there. Well, in three weeks I shall be glued to my green table! in a humble refuge, where it seems to me you never want to come!

CCLXXX. To GUSTAVE FLAUBERT Nohant, 6th July, 1874
(Yesterday, seventy years.)

I was in Paris from the 30th of May to the 10th of June, you were not there. Since my return here, I have been ill with the grippe, rheumatic, and often absolutely deprived of the use of my right arm. I have not the courage to stay in bed: I spend the evening with my children and I forget my little miseries which will pass; everything passes. That is why I was not able to write to you, even to thank you for the good letter which you wrote to me about my novel. In Paris I was overwhelmed by fatigue. That is the way I am growing old, and now I am beginning to feel it; I am not more often ill, now, illness *prostrates* me more. That is nothing, I have not the right to complain, being well loved and well cared for in my nest. I urge Maurice to go about without me, since my strength is not equal to going with him. He leaves tomorrow for Cantal with a servant, a tent, a lamp, and a quantity of utensils to examine the *micros* of his entomological *division* I am telling him that you are bored on the Righi. He cannot understand it.

The 7th

I am taking up my letter again, begun yesterday; I still find it very hard to move my pen, and even at this moment, I have a pain in my side, and I cannot...
Till tomorrow.

The 8th

At last, I shall be able perhaps today: for I am furious to think that perhaps you are accusing me of forgetting you, when I am prevented by weakness that is entirely physical, in which my affections count for nothing. You tell me that they *knock* you too much. I read only *le Temps* and it is a good deal for me even to open a paper to see about what it is talking. You ought to do as I do and *ignore* criticism when it is not serious, and even when it is. I have never been able to see what good it is to the author criticised. Criticism always starts from a personal point of view, the authority of which the artist does not recognize. It is because of that usurpation of powers in the intellectual order of things, that people get to discussing the Sun and the Moon; but that does not prevent them in the least from showing us their good tranquil faces.

You do not want to be a man of nature, so much the worse for you! therefore you attach too much importance to the details of human things, and you do not tell yourself that there is in you a *natural* force that defies the *ifs* and the *buts* of human prattle. We are of nature, in nature, by nature, and for nature. Talent, will, genius, are natural phenomena like the lake, the volcano, the mountain, the wind, the star, the cloud. What man dabbles in is pretty or ugly, ingenious or stupid; what he gets from nature is good or bad; but it is, it exists and subsists. One should not ask from the jumble of appreciation called *criticism,* what one has done and what one wants to do. Criticism does not know anything about it; its business is to gossip.

Nature alone knows how to speak to the intelligence in a language that is imperishable, always the same, because it does not depart from the eternally true, the absolutely beautiful. The hard thing, when one travels, is to find nature, because man has arranged it everywhere and has almost spoiled it everywhere; probably it is because of that that you are bored, it is because it is disguised and travestied everywhere. However, the glaciers are still intact, I presume.

But I cannot write further, I must tell you quickly that I love you, that I embrace you affectionately. Give me news of yourself. I hope to be on my feet in a few days. Maurice is waiting until I am robust before he goes: I am hurrying as much as I can! My little girls embrace you, they are superb. Aurore is devoted to mythology (George Cox, Baudry translation). You know that? An adorable work for children and parents. Enough, I can no more. I love you; don't have black ideas, and resign yourself to being bored if the air is good there.

CCLXXXI. To GEORGE SAND Righi, 14 July, 1874;

What? ill? poor, dear master! If it is rheumatism, do as my brother does, who in his character of physician, scarcely believes in medicine. Last year he went to the baths at Aix in Savoy, and in two weeks he was cured of the pains that had tormented him for six years. But to do that you would have to move, to resign your habits, Nohant and the dear little girls. You will remain at home and *you will be wrong.* You ought to take care of yourself ... for those who love you.

And as regard this, you send me, in your last letter, a horrid thing. Could I, for my part, suspect you of forgetting Cruchard! Come now, I have, first of all, too much vanity and next, too much faith in you.

You don't tell me how your play is getting on at the Odeon.

Speaking of plays, I am going again to expose myself to insults of the populace and the penny-a-liners. The manager of the Cluny Theatre, to whom I took *le Sexe faible,* has written me an admiring letter and is disposed to put on that play in October. He is reckoning on a great money success. Well, so be it! But I am recalling the enthusiasm of Carvalho, followed by an absolute chill! and all that increases my scorn for the so-called shrewd people who pretend to know all about things. For, in short, there is a dramatic work, declared by the managers of the Vaudeville and the Cluny "perfect," by the Theatre Francais "unplayable," and by the manager of the Odeon "in need of rewriting from one end to the other." Draw a conclusion now! and listen to their advice! Never mind, as these four gentlemen are the masters of your destinies because they have the money, and as they have more mind than you, never having written a line, you must believe them and submit to them.

It is a strange thing how much pleasure imbeciles find in floundering about in the work of another! in cutting it, correcting it, playing the pedagogue! Did I tell you that I was, because of that, very much at odds with a certain ———. He wanted to make over, sometime ago, a novel that I had recommended to him, which was not very good, but of which he is incapable of turning the least phrase. And I did not hide from him my opinion about him; inde irae. However, it is impossible for me to be so modest as to think that that good Pole is better than I am in French prose. And you want me to remain calm! dear master! I have not your temperament! I am not like you, always soaring above the miseries of this world. Your Cruchard is as sensitive as if he were divested of skin. And imbecility, self-sufficiency, injustice exasperate him more and more. Thus the ugliness of the Germans who surround me shuts off the view of the Righi!!! Zounds! What mugs!

God be thanked, "of my horrible sight I purge their States."

CCLXXXII. To GEORGE SAND Saturday, 26 September, 1874

Then, after having been bored like an ass on the top of the Righi, I returned home the first of August and started my book. The beginning was not easy, it was even "direful," and "methought" I should die of despair; but now things are going, I am all right, come what may! But one needs to be absolutely mad to undertake such a book. I fear that, by its very conception, it is radically impossible. We shall see, Ah! supposing I should carry it out well ... what a dream.

You doubtless know that once more I am exposing myself to the storms of the footlights (pretty metaphor) and that "braving the publicity of the theatre" I shall appear upon the boards of Cluny, probably, towards the end of December. The manager of that "little theatre" is enchanted with *le Sexe faible*. But so was Carvalho, which did not prevent him ... You know the rest.

Of course every one blames me for letting my play be given in such a joint. But since the others do not want that play and since I insist that it shall be presented to make a few sous for the Bouilhet heirs, I am forced to pass that over. I am keeping two or three pretty anecdotes about this to tell you when we meet. Why is the theatre such a general cause of delirium? Once one is on that ground, ordinary conditions are changed. If one has had the misfortune (slight) not to succeed, friends turn from one. They are very inconsiderate of one. They never salute one! I swear to you on my word of honor that that happened to me on account of le Candida. I do not believe in Holbachic conspiracies, but all that they have done to me since March amazes me. But, I decidedly don't bat an optic, and the fate of *le Sexe faible* disturbs me less than the least of the phrases of my novel.

Public intelligence seems to me to get lower and lower! To what depth of imbecility shall we descend? Belot's last book sold eight thousand copies in two weeks. Zola's Conquete de Plassans, seventeen hundred in six months, and there was an article about it. All the Monday-morning idiots have just been swooning away about M. Scribe's Une Chaine. France is ill, very ill, whatever they say; and my thoughts are more and more the color of ebony.

However, there are some pretty comic elements: (1) the Bazaine escape with the episode of the sentinel; (2) l'Histoire d'un Diamant by Paul de Musset (see the *Revue des Deux Mondes* for September); (3) the vestibule of the former establishment of Nadar near Old England [sic], where one can contemplate a life-size photograph of Alexander Dumas.

I am sure that you are finding me grouchy and that you are going to answer me: "What difference does all that make?" But everything makes a difference, and we are dying of humbug, of ignorance, of self-confidence, of scorn of grandeur, of love of banality, and imbecile babble.

"Europe which hates us, looks at us and laughs," said Ruy Blas. My Heavens, she has a right to laugh.

CCLXXXIII To Gustave Flaubert Nohant,
5th November, 1874

What, my Cruchard, you have been ill? That is what I feared, I who live in the woes of indigestion and yet hardly work at all, I am disquieted at your kind of life, the excess of intellectual expenditure and the seclusion. In spite of the charm that I have proved and appreciated at Croisset, I fear for you that solitude where you have no longer anyone to remind you that you must eat, drink and sleep, and above all walk. Your rainy climate makes you keep to the house. Here, where it does not rain enough, we are at least hustled out of doors by the beautiful warm sun and that Phoebus invigorates us, while our Phoebus-Apollo murders us.

But I am always talking to you as to a Cruchard philosophic and detached from his personality, to a Cruchard fanatical about literature and drunk with production. When, then, shall you be able to say to yourself: Lo! this is the time for rest, let us taste the innocent pleasure of living for life's sake, of watching with amazement the agitations of others and of not giving to them anything except the excess of our overflow. It does one good to ruminate over what one has assimilated in life, sometimes without attention and without discrimination.

Old friendships sustain us and all at once they distress us. I have just lost my poor blind Duvernet, whom you have seen at our house. He expired very quietly without suspecting it and without suffering. There is another great void about us and my nephew, the substitute, has been nominated for Chateauroux. His mother has followed him.

So we are all alone. Happily we love one another so much that we can live like that, but not without regret for the absent ones. Plauchut left us yesterday to return at Christmas. Maurice is already at work preparing a splendid performance of marionettes for us. And you, if you are in Paris, won't you come to keep the Christmas Eve revels with us? You will have finished your rehearsals, you will have had a success, perhaps you will be in the mood to return to material life, eating truffles?

Tell us about yourself, do not be ill, always love your old troubadour and his people who love you too.

G. Sand

CCLXXXIV. To George Sand
Wednesday, 2nd December, 1874

I am having remorse about you. It is a crime to let so long a time elapse without answering such a letter as your last. I was waiting to write to you until I had something definite to tell you about *le Sexe faible.* What is definite is that I took it away from the Cluny a week ago. The cast that Weinschenk proposed to me was odiously stupid and he did not keep the promises that he made. But, God be thanked, I withdrew in time. At present my play has been offered to the Gymnase. No news up to now from Montigny.

I am worrying like five hundred devils about my book, asking myself sometimes if I am not mad to have undertaken it. But, like Thomas Diafoirus, I am stiffening myself against the difficulties of execution which are frightful. I need to learn a heap of things about which I am ignorant. In a month I hope to finish with the agriculture and the gardening, and I shall only then be at the second third of my first chapter.

Speaking of books, do read *Fromont et Risler,* by my friend Daudet, and *les Diaboliques,* by my enemy Barbey d'Aurevilly. You will writhe with laughter. It is perhaps owing to the perversity of my mind, which likes unhealthy things, but the latter work seemed to me extremely amusing; it is the last word in the involuntary grotesque. In other respects, dead calm, France is sinking gently like a rotten hulk, and the hope of salvage, even for the staunchest, seems chimerical. You need to be here, in Paris, to have an idea of the universal depression, of the stupidity, of the decrepitude in which we are floundering.

The sentiment of that agony penetrates me and I am sad enough to die. When I am not torturing myself about my work, I am groaning about myself. That is the truth. In my leisure moments, all I do is to think of the dead, and I am going to say a very pretentious thing to you. No one understands me; I belong to another world. The men of my profession are so little of my profession! There is hardly anyone except Victor Hugo with whom I can talk of what interests me. Day before yesterday he recited by heart to me from Boileau and from Tacitus. That was like a gift to me, the thing is so rare. Moreover, the days when there are not politicians at his house, he is an adorable man.

CCLXXXV. To GUSTAVE FLAUBERT, at Croissset Nohant,
8th December, 1874

Poor dear friend,

I love you all the more because you are growing more
unhappy. How you torment yourself, and how you disturb
yourself about life! for all of which you complain, is life; it has
never been better for anyone or in any time. One feels it more or
less, one understands it more or less, one suffers with it more or
less, and the more one is in advance of the age one lives in, the
more one suffers. We pass like shadows on a background of
clouds which the sun seldom pierces, and we cry ceaselessly for
the sun which can do no more for us. It is for us to clear away
our clouds.

You love literature too much; it will destroy you and you
will not destroy the imbecility of the human race. Poor dear!
imbecility, that, for my part, I do not hate, that I regard with
maternal eyes: for it is a childhood and all childhood is sacred.
What hatred you have devoted to it! what warfare you wage on
it!

You have too much knowledge and intelligence, you
forget that there is something above art: namely, wisdom, of
which art at its apogee is only the expression. Wisdom
comprehends all: beauty, truth, goodness, enthusiasm, in
consequence. It teaches us to see outside of ourselves, something
more elevated than is in ourselves, and to assimilate it little by
little, through contemplation and admiration.

But I shall not succeed in changing you. I shall not even succeed in making you understand how I envisage and how I lay hold upon *happiness,* that is to say, the acceptation of life whatever it may be! There is one person who could change you and save you, that is father Hugo; for he has one side on which he is a great philosopher, while at the same time he is the great artist that you require and that I am not. You must see him often. I believe that he will quiet you: I have not enough tempest in me now for you to understand me. As for him, I think that he has kept his thunderbolts and that he has all the same acquired the gentleness and the compassion of age.

See him, see him often and tell him your troubles, which are great, I see that, and which turn too much to spleen. You think too much of the dead, you think that they have too soon reached their rest. They have not. They are like us, they are searching. They labor in the search.

Every one is well, and embraces you. As for me, I do not get well, but I have hopes, well or not, to keep on still so as to bring up my grandchildren, and to love you as long as I have a breath left.

G. Sand

CCLXXXVI. To GUSTAVE FLAUBERT, at Croissset Nohant, 16th January, 1875

I too, dear Cruchard, embrace you at the New Year, and wish that you may have a tolerable one, since you do not care to hear the myth happiness spoken of. You admire my serenity; it does not come from my depths, it comes from my necessity of thinking only of others. There is but a little time left, old age creeps on and death is pushing me by the shoulders.

I am as yet, if not necessary, at least extremely useful, and I shall go on as long as I have a breath, thinking, talking, working for them.

Duty is the master of masters, it is the real Zeus of modern times, the son of Time, and has become his master. It is that which lives and acts outside of all the agitations of the world. It does not reason, does not discuss. It examines without fear, it walks without looking behind it; Cronos, the stupid, swallowed stones, Zeus breaks them with the lightning, and the lightning is the will. I am not a philosopher, I am a servant of Zeus, who takes away half of their souls from slaves, but who leaves them entire to the brave.

I have no more leisure to think of myself, to dream of discouraging things, to despair of human-kind, to look at my past sorrows and joys and to summon death.

Mercy! If one were an egoist, one would see it approach with joy; it is so easy to sleep in nothingness, or to awaken in a better life! for it opens these two hypotheses, or to express it better, this antithesis.

But, for the one who must continue working, death must not be summoned before the hour when exhaustion opens the doors of liberty. You have had no children. It is the punishment of those who wish to be too independent; but that suffering is nevertheless a glory for those who vow themselves to Apollo. Then do not complain for having to grub, and describe your martyrdom to us; there is a fine book to be written about that.

You say that Renan is despairing; for my part, I don't believe that: I believe that he is suffering as are all those who look high and far ahead; but he ought to have strength in proportion to his vision. Napoleon shares his ideas, he does well if he shares them all. He has written me a very wise and good letter. He now sees relative safety in a wise republic, and I, too, think it still possible. It will be very bourgeois and not very ideal, but one has to begin at the beginning. We artists have no patience at all. We want the Abbey of Theleme at once; but before saying, "Do what you want!" one must go through with "Do what you can!" I love you and I embrace you with all my heart, my dear Polycarp. My children large and small join with me.

Come now, no weakness! We all ought to be examples to our friends, our neighbors, our fellow citizens. And how about me, don't you think that I need help and support in my long task that is not yet finished? Don't you love anyone, not even your old troubadour, who still sings, and often weeps, but who conceals himself when he weeps, as cats do when they die?

CCLXXXVII. To GEORGE SAND Paris, Saturday evening

Dear master,

I curse once more *the dramatic mania* and the pleasure that certain people have in announcing remarkable news! Someone had told me that you were *very* ill. Your good handwriting came to reassure me yesterday morning, and this morning I have received the letter from Maurice, so the Lord be praised!

What to tell you about myself? I am not stiff, I have ... I don't know what. Bromide of potassium has calmed me and given me eczema on the middle of my forehead.

Abnormal things are going on inside me. My psychic depression must relate to some hidden cause. I feel old, used up, disgusted with everything, and others bore me as I do myself.

However, I am working, but without enthusiasm: as one does a stint, and perhaps it is the work that makes me ill, for I have undertaken a senseless book.

I lose myself in the recollections of my childhood like an old man ... I do not expect anything further in life than a succession of sheets of paper to besmear with black. It seems to me that I am crossing an endless solitude to go I don't know where. And it is I who am at the same time the desert, the traveller, and the camel.

I spent the afternoon today at the funeral of Amedee Achard. The Protestant ceremonies were as inane as if they had been Catholic. *All Paris* and the reporters were there in force!

Your friend, Paul Meurice, came a week ago to ask me to "do the Salon" in le Rappel. I declined the honor, for I do not admit that anyone can criticise an art of which he does not know the technique! And then, what use is so much criticism!

I am reasonable. I go out every day, I exercise, and I come home tired, and still more irritated, that is the good I get out of it. In short, your troubadour (not very troubadourish) has become a sad bonehead.

It is in order not to bore you with my complaints that I write so rarely to you now, for no one has a livelier sense than I of my unbearableness.

Send me Flamarande; that will give me a little air.

I embrace you all, and especially you, dear master, so great, so strong, and so gentle. Your Cruchard, who is more and more cracked, if cracked is the right word, for I perceive that the contents are escaping.

CCLXXXVIII. To Gustave Flaubert 20th February

Then you are quite ill, dear old fellow? I am not worried about it, since it concerns only nerves and rheumatisms, and I have lived seventy years with all that nuisance in my body, and I am still healthy. But I am sad to know that you are bored, suffering, and your spirit turned to darkness as it necessarily is when one is ill.

I was sure that a moment would come when someone would prescribe walking to you. All your illness comes from the lack of exercise, a man of your strength and your complexion ought to have lived an athletic life.

Don't sulk then about the very wise order that condemns you to an hour's walk each day.

You fancy that the work of the spirit is only in the brain, you are very much mistaken, it is also in the legs.

Tell me that two weeks of this regime has cured you. It will happen, I am sure of it.

I love you, and I embrace you, as does every one of my brood.

Your old troubadour

CCLXXXIX. To GUSTAVE FLAUBERT Nohant,
25th March, 1875

Don't be worried about me, my Polycarp. I have nothing serious, a little grippe, and this right arm which hardly moves but which electricity will cure. One thinks that it is an effort.

I am much more worried about you, although you are ten times as strong as I am, but your morale is affected whereas mine takes what comes, in a cowardly way, if you like, but there is perhaps a philosophy in knowing how to be cowardly rather than angry.

Do write to me, tell me that you are going out of doors, that you are walking, that you are better.—I have finished going over the proofs of Flamarande. That is the most boring part of the task.

I shall send you the book when it is published. I know that you do not like to read bit by bit.

I am a little tired; however, I want to begin something else. Since it is not warm enough to go out, I get bored with not having anything on the stocks. Everything is going well in the nest, except for a few colds. Spring is so peevish this year! At last the pale sun will become the dear Phoebus-Appolo with the shining hair, and all will go well.

Aurore is getting so big that one is surprised to hear her laugh and play like a child, always good, and tender, the other is always very funny and facetious.

Tell us of yourself and always love us as we love you.

Your old troubadour

CCXC. To GUSTAVE FLAUBERT Nohant, 7th May, 1875

You leave me without news of you? You say that you prefer to be forgotten, rather than to complain ceaselessly, as it is very useless and since you will not be forgotten; complain then, but tell us that you are alive and that you still love us.

As you are much nicer, the more surly you are, I know that you are not rejoicing over the death of poor Michel. For me, it is a great loss in every way, for he was absolutely devoted to me and proved it all the time by his care and services without number.

We are all well here. I am better since it is not cold any more, and I am working a great deal. I am also doing many water colors, I am reading the Iliad with Aurore, who does not like any translation except Leconte de Lisle's, insisting that Homer is spoiled by approximate renderings.

The child is a singular mixture of precocity and childishness. She is nine years old and so large that one would think her twelve. She plays dolls with passion, and she is as *literary* as you or I, meanwhile learning her own language which she does not yet know.

Are you still in Paris in this lovely weather? Nohant is now *streaming* with flowers, from the tips of the trees to the turf; Croisset must be even prettier, for it is cool, and we are struggling with a drought that has now become chronic in Berry. But if you are still in Paris, you have that beautiful Pare Monceau under your eyes where you are walking, I hope, since you have to. Life is at the price of walking!

Won't you come to see us? Whether you are sad or gay, we love you the same here, and we wish that affection meant something to you, but we shall give it to you, and we give it to you without conditions.

I am thinking of going to Paris next month, shall you be there?

G. Sand

CCXCI. To GEORGE SAND Croisset, 10th May, 1875

A wandering gout, pains that go all over me, an invincible melancholy, the feeling of "universal uselessness" and grave doubts about the book that I am writing, that is what is the matter with me, dear and valiant master. Add to that worries about money with melancholic recollections of the past, that is my condition, and I assure you that I make great efforts to get out of it. But my will is tired. I cannot decide about anything effective! Ah! I have eaten my white bread first, and old age is not announcing itself under gay colors. Since I have begun hydrotherapy, however, I feel a little less like a *cow,* and this evening I am going to begin work without looking behind me.

I have left my apartment in the rue Murillo, and I have taken a larger one which is next to the one that my niece has just reserved on the Boulevard Reine Hortense. I shall be less alone next winter, for I cannot endure solitude.

Tourgueneff seemed to me, however, to be very well pleased with the two first chapters of my frightful book. But Tourgueneff loves me too much, perhaps to judge impartially. I am not going to leave my house for a long time now, for I *will* get ahead in my task, which weighs on my chest like a burden of a million pounds. My niece will come to spend all the month of June here. When she has gone away, I shall make a little archeological and geological excursion in Calvados, and that will be all.

No, I do not rejoice at Michel Levy's death, and I even envy him that death so quiet. Just the same, that man did me a great deal of harm. He wounded me deeply. It is true that I am endowed with an absurd sensitiveness; what scratches others tears me to pieces. Why am I not organized for enjoyment as I am for suffering!

The bit you sent me about Aurore who is reading Homer, did me good. That is what I miss: a little girl like that! But one does not arrange one's own destiny, one submits to it. I have always lived from day to day, without plans for the future and pursuing my end (one alone, literature) without looking to the right or to the left. Everything that was around me has disappeared, and now I find I am in a desert. In short, the element of distraction is absolutely lacking to me. One needs a certain vivacity to write good things! What can one do to get it again? How can one proceed, to avoid thinking continually about one's miserable person? The sickest thing in me is my humor: the rest doubtless would go well. You see, dear, good master, that I am right to spare you my letters. Nothing is as imbecile as the whiners.

CCXCII. To Gustave Flaubert
Thursday morning, 10th June, 1875

We are leaving, Lina and I, on Saturday morning, and up to then we shall be on the move. If you wanted to come to dine with us Friday at Magny's at six o'clock, at least we could say farewell. You should be free at nine o'clock, for we go to bed with the chickens in order to leave early the next day. What do you say?

I love you with all my heart.

CCXCIII. To Gustave Flaubert

Friend, I shall come at your call as soon as you say to me, "I have finished."

I love you, and I embrace you.

G. Sand

CCXCIV. To GUSTAVE FLAUBERT Nohant, 15 August

My poor, dear, old fellow,

I learn only today in a letter from that dear, lazy soul of a Tourgueneff, about the misfortune which has come to your niece. Is it then irreparable? Her husband is very young and intelligent, can't he begin over again, or take a position that will give him a living? They have no children, they do not need millions to live on, young and well as they both are. Tourgueneff tells me that your property has been affected by this failure. If it is *affected merely* you will bear this serious annoyance philosophically. You have no vices to satisfy, nor ambitions to appease. I am sure that you will accommodate your life to your resources. The hardest thing for you to bear, is the chagrin of that young woman who is as a daughter to you. But you will give her courage and consolation, it is the moment to be above your own worries, in order to assuage those of others. I am sure that as I write, you have calmed her mind and soothed her heart. Perhaps, too, the disaster is not what it seems at the first moment. There will be a change for the better, a new way will be found, for it is always so, and the worth of men is measured according to their energy, to the hopes which are always a sign of their force and intelligence. More than one has risen again bravely. Be sure that better days will come and tell them so continually, for it is true. Your moral and physical welfare must not be shaken by this rebuff. Think of healing those whom you love, and forget yourself. We shall be thinking of you, and we shall be suffering for you; for I am keenly affected at seeing that you have a new subject of sadness amidst your spleen.

Come, dear splendid old fellow, cheer up, do us a new successful novel, and think of those who love you, and whose hearts are saddened and torn by your discouragements. Love them, love us, and you will find once more your strength and your enthusiasm.

We all embrace you very tenderly. Do not write if it bores you, say to us only, "I am well, and I love you."

G. Sand

CCXCV. To GEORGE SAND Wednesday

Will you forgive my long delay, dear master? But I think that I must bore you with my eternal jeremiads. I repeat myself like a dotard! I am becoming too stupid! I am boring everybody. In short, your Cruchard has become an intolerable old codger, because he has been intolerant. And as I cannot do anything that I ought to do, I must, out of consideration for others, spare them the overflow of my bile.

For the last six months, especially, I don't know what has been the trouble with me, but I feel dreadfully ill, without being able to get to the root of the matter, and I know many people are in the same condition. Why? Perhaps we are suffering from the illness of France; here in Paris, where her heart beats, people feel better than at her extremities, in the provinces.

I assure you that every one now is suffering with some incomprehensible trouble. Our friend Renan is one of the most desperate, and Prince Napoleon feels exactly the way he does. But they have strong nerves. But, as for me, I am attacked by a well defined melancholia. I should be resigned to it, and I am not.

I work all the more, so as not to think about myself. But since I have undertaken a book that has absurd difficulties in its execution, the feeling of my powerlessness adds to my chagrin.

Don't tell me again that imbecility is sacred like childhood, for imbecility contains no germ. Let me believe that the dead do not "search any more," and that they are at rest. We are sufficiently tormented on earth to be at rest when we are beneath it! Ah! How I envy you, how I long to have your serenity! To say nothing of the rest! and your two dear little girls, whom I embrace as tenderly as I do—you.

CCXCVI. To GUSTAVE FLAUBERT, at Croissset Nohant,
7th September, 1875

You are distressed, you are discouraged, you distress me too. That is all right, I would rather have you complain than keep silent, dear friend. And I don't want you to stop writing to me.

I also have great and frequent sorrows. My old friends are dying before I do. One of the dearest, the one who brought up Maurice and whom I was expecting to help me to bring up my grandchildren, has just died, almost in an instant. That is a deep sorrow. Life is a succession of blows at one's heart. But duty is there: we must go on and do our tasks without saddening those who suffer with us.

I ask you absolutely to *will,* and not to be indifferent to the griefs which we are sharing with you. Tell us that calm has come and that the horizon has cleared.

We love you, sad or gay.

Give us news of yourself.

G. Sand

CCXCVII. To GUSTAVE FLAUBERT Nohant, 8th October, 1875

Well, well, your health has come back in spite of you, since you are sleeping all night. The sea air forces you to live and you have made progress, you have given up a work that would not have made a success. Do something more of earth earthy, which would reach everybody. Tell me what price they would sell Croisset for if they are obliged to sell it. Is it a house and garden, or is there a farm and grounds! If it is not beyond my means I might buy it and you should spend the rest of your life there. I have no money, but I should try to shift a little capital. Answer me seriously, I beg of you; if I can do it, it shall be done.

I have been ill all the summer, that is to say, that I have suffered continually, but I have worked all the more not to think of it. In fact they are to put on Villemer and Victorine at the Theatre Francais again. But there is nothing now in preparation.

I do not know at what time in the autumn or winter I shall have to go to Paris. I shall find you there ready and courageous, shan't I? If you have made, through goodness and devotion, as I think, a great sacrifice for your niece, who, in truth, is your real daughter, you will forget all about it and will begin your life again as a young man. Is one old when one does not choose to be? Stay at the seaside as long as you can. The important thing is to patch up the physical machine. Here with us it is as warm as in midsummer. I hope that you still have the sun down there. Study the life of the mollusc! They are creatures better endowed than one thinks, and, for my part, I should love to take a walk with Georges Pouchet! Natural history is the inexhaustible source of agreeable occupations for even those who seek only amusement in it, and if you actually attacked it you would be saved. But you must by all means save yourself, for you are somebody, and you cannot drop out of the running, as can a mere ruined grocer. We all embrace you with our best love.

G. Sand

CCXCVIII. To Gustave Flaubert, in Paris Nohant,
15 November, 1875

So you are there in Paris, and have you left your apartment at the rue Murillo? You are working? Good luck and good courage! The old man is coming to the top again! I know that they are rehearsing Victorine at the Theatre Francais; but I don't know whether I shall go to see that revival. I have been so ill all the summer and I am still suffering so much with intestinal trouble, that I do not know if I shall ever be strong enough to move in winter. Well, we shall see. The hope of finding you there will give me courage; that is not what will be lacking, but, since I passed my seventieth birthday, I have been very much upset, and I do not yet know if I shall get over it. I cannot walk any more, I who used to love to be on my feet so much, without risking atrocious pains. I am patient with these miseries, I work all the more, and I do water-colors in my hours of recreation.

Aurore consoles and charms me; I should like to live long enough to get her married. But God disposes, and one must take death and life as He wills.

Well, this is just to say to you that I shall go to embrace you unless the thing is *absolutely* impossible. You shall read me what you have begun. Meanwhile, give me news of yourself; for I shall not stir until the last rehearsals. I know my cast, I know that they will all do well, according to their capabilities, and, besides, that Perrin will look after them.

We all *kiss* you very tenderly, and we love you, Cruchard or not.

G. Sand

CCXCIX. To GEORGE SAND Paris, 11 December, 1875

Things are going a little better, and I am profiting by the occasion to write to you, dear, good, adorable master.

You know that I have abandoned my big novel in order to write a little *medieval* bit of nonsense, which won't run to more than thirty pages. It puts me in a more decent setting than that of modern times, and does me good. Then I am hunting for a contemporary novel, but I am hesitating among several embryonic ideas; I should like to do something concise and violent. The string of the necklace (that is to say, the main idea) is still to seek.

Externally my life is scarcely changed: I see the same people, I receive the same visits. My faithful ones on Sunday are first of all, the big Tourgueneff, who is nicer than ever, Zola, Alphonse Daudet, and Goncourt. You have never spoken to me of the first two. What do you think of their books?

I am not reading anything at all, except Shakespeare, whom am going through from beginning to end. That tones you up and puts new air into your lungs, just as if you were on a high mountain. Everything appears mediocre beside that prodigious felow.

As I go out very little, I have not yet seen Victor Hugo. However, this evening I am going to resign myself to putting on my boots, so that I can go to present my compliments to him. His personality pleases me infinitely, but his court! ... mercy!

The senatorial elections are a subject of diversion to the public of which I am a part. There must have occurred, in the corridors of the Assembly, dialogues incredibly grotesque and base. The XlXth century is destined to see all religions perish. Amen! I do not mourn any of them.

At the Odeon, a live bear is going to appear on the boards. That is all that I know about literature.

CCC. To GUSTAVE FLAUBERT, in Paris Nohant,
18th and 19th December, 1875

At last I discover my old troubadour who was a subject of chagrin and serious worry to me. Here you are yourself again, trusting in the very natural luck of external events, and discovering in yourself the strength to control them, whatever they may be, by effort. What is it that you call some one in *high finance?* For my part, I don't know; I am in relations with Victor Borie. He will do me a favor if he sees it to his interest. Must I write him?

Then you are going to start grubbing again? So am I; for since Flamarande I have done nothing but mark time, while waiting for something better. I was so ill all summer! but my strange and excellent friend Favre has cured me wonderfully, and I am taking a new lease on life.

What's our next move? For you, of course, *desolation,* and, for me, consolation. I do not know on what our destinies depend; you see them pass, you criticise them, you abstain from a literary appreciation of them, you limit yourself to depicting them, with deliberate meticulous concealment of your personal feelings. However, one sees them very clearly through your narrative, and you make the people sadder who read you. As for me, I should like to make them less sad. I cannot forget that my personal victory over despair was the work of my will and of a new way of understanding which is entirely opposed to what I had before.

I know that you criticise the intervention of the personal doctrine in literature. Are you right? Isn't it rather a lack of conviction than a principle of esthetics? One cannot have a philosophy in one's soul without its appearing. I have no literary advice to give you, I have no judgment to formulate on the author friends of whom you speak. I, myself have told the Goncourts all my thought; as for the others, I firmly believe that they have more education and more talent than I have. Only I think that they, and you especially, lack a definite and extended vision of life. Art is not merely painting. True painting, moreover, is full of the soul that wields the brush. Art is not merely criticism and satire: criticism and satire depict only one side of the truth.

I want to see a man as he is, he is not good or bad, he is good and bad. But he is something more ... nuance. Nuance which is for me the purpose of art, being good and bad, he has an internal force which leads him to be very bad and slightly good,—or very good and slightly bad.

I think that your school is not concerned with the substance, and that it dwells too much on the surface. By virtue of seeking the form, it makes the substance too cheap! it addresses itself to the men of letters. But there are no men of letters, properly speaking. Before everything, one is a man. One wants to find man at the basis of every story and every deed. That was the defect of *l'Education sentimentale,* about which I have so often reflected since, asking myself why there was so general a dislike of a work that was so well done and so solid. This defect was the absence of *action* of the characters on themselves. They submitted to the event and never mastered it. Well, I think that the chief interest in a story is what you did not want to do. If I were you, I would try the opposite; you are feeding on Shakespeare just now, and you are doing well! He is the author who puts men at grips with events; observe that by them, whether for good or for ill, the event is always conquered. In his works, it is crushed underfoot.

Politics is a comedy just now. We have had tragedy, shall we end with the opera or with the operetta? I read my paper conscientiously every morning; but aside from that moment, it is impossible for me to think of it or to be interested in it. All of it is absolutely void of any ideal whatsoever, and therefore I cannot get up any interest in any of the persons concerned in that scullery. All of them are slaves of fact because they have been born slaves of themselves.

My dear little girls are well. Aurore is a well-set-up girl, a beautiful upright soul in a strong body. The other one is grace and sweetness. I am always an assiduous and a patient teacher, and very little time is left to me to write *professionally,* seeing that I cannot keep awake after midnight and that I want to spend all my evening with my family; but this lack of time stimulates me and makes me find a true pleasure in digging away; it is like a forbidden fruit that I taste in secret.

All my dear world embraces you and rejoices to hear that you are better. Did I send you Flamarande and the pictures of my little girls? If not, send me a line, and I send you both.

Your old troubadour who loves you,

G. Sand

Embrace your charming niece for me. What a good and lovely letter she wrote me! Tell her that I beg her to take care of herself and to please get well quickly.

What do you mean! Littre a senator? It is impossible to believe it when one knows what the Chamber is. All the same it must be congratulated for this attempt at self-respect.

CCCI. To George Sand December, 1875

Your good letter of the 18th, so maternally tender, has made me reflect a great deal. I have reread it ten times, and I shall confess to you that I am not sure that I understand it. Briefly, what do you want me to do? Make your instructions exact.

I am constantly doing all that I can to enlarge my brain, and I work in the sincerity of my heart. The rest does not depend on me.

I do not enjoy making "desolation," believe me, but I cannot change my eyes! As for my "lack of convictions," alas! I choke with convictions. I am bursting with anger and restrained indignation. But according to the ideal of art that I have, I think that the artist should not manifest anything of his own feelings, and that the artist should not appear any more in his work than God in nature. The man is nothing, the work is everything! This method, perhaps mistakenly conceived, is not easy to follow. And for me, at least, it is a sort of permanent sacrifice that I am making to good taste. It would be agreeable to me to say what I think and to relieve Mister Gustave Flaubert by words, but of what importance is the said gentleman?

I think as you do, dear master, that art is not merely criticism and satire; moreover, I have never tried to do intentionally the one nor the other. I have always tried to go into the soul of things and to stick to the greatest generalities, and I have purposely turned aside from the accidental and the dramatic. No monsters and no heroes!

You say to me: "I have no literary advice to give you; I have no judgments to formulate on the authors, your friends, etc." Well? indeed! but I implore advice, and I am waiting for your judgments. Who, pray, should give them, and who, pray, should formulate them, if not you?

Speaking of my friends, you add "my school." But I am ruining my temperament in trying not to have a school! A priori, I spurn them, every one. The people whom I see often and whom you designate cultivate all that I scorn and are indifferently disturbed about what torments me. I regard as very secondary, technical detail, local exactness, in short the historical and precise side of things. I am seeking above all for beauty, which my companions pursue but languidly. I see them insensible when I am ravaged with admiration or horror. Phrases make me swoon with pleasure which seem very ordinary to them. Goncourt is very happy when he has seized upon a word in the street that he can stick in a book, and I am well satisfied when I have written a page without assonances or repetitions. I would give all the legends of Gavarni for certain expressions and master strokes, such as "the shade was *nuptial,* august and solemn!" from Victor Hugo, or this from Montesquieu: "the vices of Alexander were extreme like his virtues. He was terrible in his wrath. It made him cruel."

In short, I try to think well, *in order to* write well. But writing well is my aim, I do not deny it.

"I lack a well-defined and extended vision of life." You are right a thousand times over, but by what means could it be otherwise? I ask you that. You do not enlighten my darkness with metaphysics, neither mine nor that of others. The words religion or Catholicism on the one hand; progress, fraternity, democracy on the other, do not correspond to the spiritual needs of the moment. The entirely new dogma of equality which radicalism praises is experimentally denied by physiology and history. I do not see the means of establishing today a new principle, any more than of respecting the old ones. Therefore I am hunting, without finding it, that idea on which all the rest should depend.

Meanwhile I repeat to myself what Littre said to me one day: "Ah! my friend, man is an unstable compound, and the earth an inferior planet."

Nothing sustains me better than the hope of leaving it soon, and of not going to another which might be worse. "I would rather not die," as Marat said. Ah! no! enough, enough weariness!

I am writing now a little silly story, which a mother can permit her child to read. The whole will be about thirty pages, I shall have two months more at it. Such is my energy, I shall send it to you as soon as it appears (not my energy, but the little story).

CCCII. To GUSTAVE FLAUBERT, in Paris Nohant,
12th January, 1876

My cherished Cruchard,

I want to write to you every day; time is lacking absolutely. At last here is a free moment; we are buried under the snow; it is the sort of weather that I adore: this whiteness is like general purification, and the amusements of the house seem more intimate and sweeter. Can anyone hate the winter in the country? The snow is one of the most beautiful sights of the year!

It appears that I am not clear in my sermons; I have that much in common with the orthodox, but I am not of them; neither in my idea of equality, nor of authority, have I any fixed plan. You seem to think that I want to convert you to a doctrine. Not at all, I don't think of such a thing. Everyone sets off from a point of view, the free choice of which I respect. In a few words, I can give a resume of mine: not to place oneself behind an opaque glass through which one can see only the reflection of one's own nose. To see as far as possible the good, the bad, about, around, yonder, everywhere; to perceive the continual gravitation of all tangible and intangible things towards the necessity of the decent, the good, the true, the beautiful.

I don't say that humanity is on the way to the heights. I believe it in spite of everything; but I do not argue about it, it is useless because each one judges according to his own personal vision, and the general aspect is for the moment poor and ugly. Besides, I do not need to be sure of the safety of the planet and its inhabitants in order to believe in the necessity of the good and the beautiful; if the planet departs from that law it will perish; if the inhabitants discard it they will be destroyed. Other stars, other souls will pass over their bodies, so much the worse! But, as for me, I want to gravitate up to my last breath, not with the certitude nor the need of finding elsewhere a *good place,* but because my sole joy is in keeping myself with my family on an upward road.

In other words, I am fleeing the sewer, and I am seeking the dry and the clean, certain that it is the law of my existence. Being a man amounts to little; we are still near the monkey from which they say we proceed. Very well! a further reason for separating ourselves still more from it and for being at least at the height of the relative truth that our race has been admitted to comprehend; a very poor truth, very limited, very humble! well, let us possess it as much as we can and not permit anyone to take it from us. We are, I think, quite agreed; but I practice this simple religion and you do not practice it, since you let yourself become discouraged; your heart has not been penetrated with it, since you curse life and desire death like a Catholic who yearns for compensation, were it only the rest eternal. You are no surer than another of this compensation. Life is perhaps eternal, and therefore work is eternal. If this is so, let us do our day's work bravely. If it is otherwise, if the *moi* perishes entirely, let us have the honor of having done our stated task, it is our duty; for we have evident duties only toward ourselves and our equals. What we destroy in ourselves, we destroy in them. Our abasement lowers them, our falls drag them down; we owe it to them to remain erect so that they shall not fall. The desire for an early death, as that for a long life, is therefore a weakness, and I do not want you to admit any longer that it is a right. I thought that had it once; I believed, however, what I believe today; but I lacked strength, and like you I said: "I cannot help it." I lied to myself. One can help everything. One has the strength that one thinks one has not, when one desires ardently to *gravitate,* to mount a step each day, to say to oneself: "The Flaubert of tomorrow must be superior to the one of yesterday, and the one of day after tomorrow more steady and more lucid still."

When you feel you are on the ladder, you will mount very quickly. You are about to enter gradually upon the happiest and most favorable time of life: old age. It is then that art reveals itself in its sweetness; as long as one is young, it manifests itself with anguish. You prefer a well-turned phrase to all metaphysics. I also, I love to see condensed into a few words what elsewhere fills volumes; but these volumes, one must have understood them completely (either to admit them or to reject them) in order to find the sublime resume which becomes literary art in its fullest expression; that is why one should not scorn the efforts of the human mind to arrive at the truth.

I tell you that, because you have excessive prejudices *as to words*. In truth, you read, you dig, you work much more than I and a crowd of others do. You have acquired learning that I shall never attain. Therefore you are a hundred times richer than all of us; you are a rich man, and you complain like a poor man. Be charitable to a beggar who has his mattress full of gold, but who wants to be nourished only on well-turned phrases and choice words. But brute, ransack your own mattress and eat your gold. Nourish yourself with the ideas and feelings accumulated in your head and your heart; the words and the phrases, *the form* to which you attach so much importance, will issue by itself from your digestion. You consider it as an end, it is only an effect. Happy manifestations proceed only from an emotion, and an emotion proceeds only from a conviction. One is not moved at all by the things that one does not believe with all one's heart.

I do not say that you do not believe: on the contrary, all your life of affection, of protection, and of charming and simple goodness, proves that you are the most convinced individual in the world. But, as soon as you handle literature, you want, I don't know why, to be another man, one who should disappear, one who destroys himself, who does not exist! What an absurd mania! what a false rule of *good taste!* Our work is worth only what we are worth.

Who is talking about putting yourself on the stage? That, in truth, is of no use, unless it is done frankly by way of a chronicle. But to withdraw one's soul from what one does, what is that unhealthy fancy? To hide one's own opinion about the characters that one puts on the stage, to leave the reader therefore uncertain about the opinion that he should have of them, that is to desire not to be understood, and from that moment, the reader leaves you; for if he wants to understand the story that you are telling him, it is on the condition that you should show him plainly that this one is a strong character and that one weak.

L'Education sentimentale has been a misunderstood book, as I have told you repeatedly, but you have not listened to me. There should have been a short preface, or, at a good opportunity, an expression of blame, even if only a happy epithet to condemn the evil, to characterize the defect, to signalize the effort. All the characters in that book are feeble and come to nothing, except those with bad instincts; that is what you are reproached with, because people did not understand that you wanted precisely to depict a deplorable state of society that encourages these bad instincts and ruins noble efforts; when people do not understand us it is always our fault. What the reader wants, first of all, is to penetrate into our thought, and that is what you deny him, arrogantly. He thinks that you scorn him and that you want to ridicule him. For my part, I understood you, for I knew you. If anyone had brought me your book without its being signed, I should have thought it beautiful, but strange, and I should have asked myself if you were immoral, skeptical, indifferent or heart-broken. You say that it ought to be like that, and that M. Flaubert will violate the rules of good taste if he shows his thought and the aim of his literary enterprise. It is false in the highest degree. When M. Flaubert writes well and seriously, one attaches oneself to his personality. One wants to sink or swim with him. If he leaves you in doubt, you lose interest in his work, you neglect it, or you give it up.

I have already combated your favorite heresy, which is that one writes for twenty intelligent people and does not care a fig for the rest. It is not true, since the lack of success irritates you and troubles you. Besides, there have not been twenty critics favorable to this book which was so well written and so important. So one must not write for twenty persons any more than for three, or for a hundred thousand.

One must write for all those who have a thirst to read and who can profit by good reading. Then one must go straight to the most elevated morality within oneself, and not make a mystery of the moral and profitable meaning of one's book. People found that with *Madame Bovary*. If one part of the public cried scandal, the healthiest and the broadest part saw in it a severe and striking lesson given to a woman without conscience and without faith, to vanity, to ambition, to irrationality. They pitied her; art required that, but the lesson was clear, and it would have been more so, it would have been so for everybody, if you had wished it, if you had shown more clearly the opinion that you had, and that the public ought to have had, about the heroine, her husband, and her lovers.

That desire to depict things as they are, the adventures of life as they present themselves to the eye, is not well thought out, in my opinion. Depict inert things as a realist, as a poet, it's all the same to me, but, when one touches on the emotions of the human heart, it is another thing. You cannot abstract yourself from this contemplation; for man, that is yourself, and men, that is the reader. Whatever you do, your tale is a conversation between you and the reader. If you show him the evil coldly, without ever showing him the good he is angry. He wonders if it is he that is bad, or if it is you. You work, however, to rouse him and to interest him; you will never succeed if you are not roused yourself, or if you hide it so well that he thinks you indifferent. He is right: supreme impartiality is an anti-human thing, and a novel ought to be human above everything. If it is not, the public is not pleased in its being well written, well composed and conscientious in every detail. The essential quality is not there: interest. The reader breaks away likewise from a book where all the characters are good without distinctions and without weaknesses; he sees clearly that that is not human either. I believe that art, this special art of narration, is only worth while through the opposition of characters; but, in their struggle, I prefer to see the right prevail. Let events overwhelm the honest men, I agree to that, but let him not be soiled or belittled by them, and let him go to the stake feeling that he is happier than his executioners.

15th January, 1876

It is three days since I wrote this letter, and every day I have been on the point of throwing it into the fire; for it is long and diffuse and probably useless. Natures opposed on certain points understand each other with difficulty, and I am afraid that you will not understand me any better today than formerly. However, I am sending you this scrawl so that you can see that I am occupied with you almost as much as with myself.

You must have success after that bad luck which has troubled you deeply. I tell you wherein lie the certain conditions for your success. Keep your cult for form; but pay more attention to the substance. Do not take true virtue for a commonplace in literature. Give it its representative, make honest and strong men pass among the fools and the imbeciles that you love to ridicule. Show what is solid at the bottom of these intellectual abortions; in short, abandon the convention of the realist and return to the time reality, which is a mingling of the beautiful and the ugly, the dull and the brilliant, but in which the desire of good finds its place and its occupation all the same.

I embrace you for all of us.

G. Sand

CCCIII. To GUSTAVE FLAUBERT Nohant, 6th March, 1876

I am writing to you in a hurry this morning because I have just received news from M. Perrin of the first performance of the revival of the *Mariage de Victorine,* a play of mine, at the Theatre Francais.

I have neither the time to go there, nor the wish to leave like that at a moment's notice, but I should have liked to send some of my friends there, and he does not offer me a single seat for them. I am writing him a letter that he will receive tomorrow, and I am asking him to send you at least one orchestra seat. If you do not get it, please understand that it was not my fault. I shall have to say the same thing to five or six other people.

I embrace you therefore in a hurry, so as not to lose the post.

Give me news of your niece and embrace her for me.

G. Sand

CCCIV. To GUSTAVE FLAUBERT, at Paris Nohant,
8th March, 1876

You scorn Sedaine, you great profane soul! That is where the doctrine of form destroys your eye! Sedaine is not a writer, that is true, although he falls but little short of it, but he is a man, with a heart and soul, with the sense of moral truth, the direct insight into human feelings. I don't mind his out-of-date reasonings and dry phraseology! The right thought is always there, and it penetrates you deeply!

My dear old Sedaine! He is one of my well-beloved papas, and I consider le Philosophe sans le savior far superior to Victorine; it is such a distressing drama and so well carried out! But you only look for the well-turned phrase, that is one thing— only one thing, it is not all of art, it is not even half of it, it is a quarter at most, and if three-quarters are beautiful, one overlooks the part that is not.

I hope that you will not go to seek for your countryside before the good weather; here, we have been pretty well spared; but for the past three days there has been a deluge, and it makes me ill. I should not have been able to go to Paris. Your niece is better, God be praised! I love you and I embrace you with all my soul.

G. Sand

Do tell M. Zola to send me his book. I shall certainly read it with great interest.

CCCV. To GEORGE SAND Wednesday, 9th March, 1876

Complete success, dear master. The actors were recalled after each act, and warmly applauded. The public was pleased and from time to time cries of approval were heard. All your friends who had come at your summons were sorry that you were not there.

The roles of Antoine and Victorine were especially well played. Little Baretta is a real treasure.

How were you able to make Victorine from le Philosophe sans le savoir? That is beyond me. Your play charmed me and made me weep like an idiot, while the other bored me to death, absolutely bored me to death; I longed to get to the end. What language! the good Tourgueneff and Madame Viardot made saucer-eyes, comical to behold. In your work, what produced the greatest effect is the scene in the last act between Antoine and his daughter. Maubant is too majestic, and the actor who plays Fulgence is inadequate. But everything went very well, and this revival will have a long life.

The gigantic Harrisse told me that he was going to write to you immediately. Therefore his letter will arrive before mine. I should have started this morning for Pont-l'Eveque and Honfleur to see a bit of the country that I have forgotten, but the floods stopped me.

Read, I beg of you, the new novel by Zola, Son Excellence Rougon: I am very anxious to know what you think of it.

No, I do not *scorn* Sedaine, because I do not scorn what I do not understand. He is to me, like Pindar, and Milton, who are absolutely closed to me; however, I quite understand that the citizen Sedaine is not exactly of their calibre.

The public of last Tuesday shared my error, and Victorine, independently of its real worth, gained by contrast. Madame Viardot, who has naturally good taste, said to me yesterday, in speaking of you: "How was she able to make one from the other?" That is exactly what I think.

You distress me a bit, dear master, by attributing esthetic opinions to me which are not mine. I believe that the rounding of the phrase is nothing. But that *writing well* is everything, because "writing well is at the same time perceiving well, thinking well and saying well" (Buffon). The last term is then dependent on the other two, since one has to feel strongly, so as to think, and to think, so as to express.

All the bourgeois can have a great deal of heart and delicacy, be full of the best sentiments and the greatest virtues, without becoming for all that, artists. In short, I believe that the form and the matter are two subtleties, two entities, neither of which can exist without the other.

This anxiety for external beauty which you reproach me with is for me a *method*. When I discover a bad assonance or a repetition in one of my phrases, I am sure that I am floundering in error; by dint of searching, I find the exact expression which was the only one and is, at the same time, the harmonious one. The word is never lacking when one possesses the idea.

Note (to return to the good Sedaine) that I share all his opinions and I approve his tendencies. From the archeological point of view, he is curious and from the humanitarian point of view very praiseworthy, I agree. But what difference does it make to us today? Is it eternal art? I ask you that.

Other writers of his period have formulated useful principles also, but in an imperishable style, in a more concrete and at the same time more general manner.

In short, the persistence of the Comedie Francais in exhibiting that to us as "a masterpiece" had so exasperated me that, having gone home in order to get rid of the taste of this milk-food, I read before going to bed the *Medea* of Euripides, as I had no other classic handy, and Aurora surprised Cruchard in this occupation.

I have written to Zola to send you his book. I shall tell Daudet also to send you his Jack, as I am very curious to have your opinion on these two books, which are very different in composition and temperament, but quite remarkable, both of them.

The fright which the elections caused to the bourgeois has been diverting.

CCCVI. To GUSTAVE FLAUBERT, at Croissset Nohant,
15th March, 1876

I should have a good deal to say about the novels of M.
Zola, and it would be better to say it in an article than in a letter,
because there is a general question there which must be
formulated with a refreshed brain. I should like to read M.
Daudet's book first, the book you spoke of to me, the title of
which I cannot recall. Have the publisher send it to me collect, if
he does not want to give it to me; that is very simple. On the
whole, the thing that I shall not gainsay, meanwhile making a
philosophical criticism of the method, is that Rougon is a *strong*
book, as you say, and worthy of being placed in the first rank.

That does not change anything in my way of thinking,
that art ought to be the search for the truth, and that truth is not
the picture of evil. It ought to be the picture of good and evil. A
painter who sees only one is as false as he who sees only the
other. Life is not crammed with monsters only. Society is not
formed of rascals and wretches only. The honest people are not
the minority, since society exists in a certain order and without
too many unpunished crimes. Imbeciles dominate, it is true, but
there is a public conscience which weighs on them and obliges
them to respect the right. Let people show up and chastise the
rascals, that is good, it is even moral, but let them tell us and
show us the opposite; otherwise the simple reader, who is the
average reader, is discouraged, saddened, horrified, and
contradicts you so as not to despair.

How are you? Tourgueneff wrote me that your last work
was very remarkable: then you are not *done for,* as you pretend?

Your niece continues to improve, does she not? I too am better, after cramps in my stomach that made me blue, and continued with a horrible persistence. Physical suffering is a good lesson when it leaves one freedom of spirit. One learns to endure it and to conquer it. Of course one has some moments of discouragement when one throws oneself on the bed; but, for my part, I always think of what my old curé used to say to me, when he had the gout: *that will pass, or I shall pass.* And thereupon he would laugh, content with his joke.

My Aurore is beginning history, and she is not very well pleased with these killers of men whom they call heroes and demigods. She calls them horrid fellows.

We have a confounded spring; the earth is covered with flowers and snow, one gets numb gathering violets and anemones.

I have read the manuscript of *l'Etrangere.* It is not as *decadent* as you say. There are diamonds that sparkle brightly in this polychrome. Moreover, the decadences are transformations. The mountains in travail roar and scream, but they sing beautiful airs, also.

I embrace you and I love you. Do have your legend published quickly, so that we may read it.

Your old troubadour,

G. Sand

CCCVII. To Gustave Flaubert 30th March, 1876

Dear Cruchard,

I am enthusiastic about Jack, and I beg you to send my thanks to M. Daudet. Ah, yes! He has talent and heart! and how well all that is done and *seen!*

I am sending you a volume of old things that have just been collected. I embrace you, and I love you.

Your old troubadour,

G. Sand

CCCVIII. To GEORGE SAND Monday evening, 3rd April, 1876

I have received your volume this morning, dear master. I have two or three others that have been loaned to me for a long time; I shall send them off, and I shall read yours at the end of the week, during a little two-days' trip that I am forced to take to Pont-l'Eveque and to Honfleur for my Histoire d'un coeur simple, a trifle now "on the stocks," as M. Prudhomme would say.

I am very glad that Jack has pleased you. It is a charming book, isn't it? If you knew the author you would like him even better than his book. I have told him to send you Risler and Tartarin. I am sure in advance that you would thank me for the opportunity of reading these two books.

I do not share in Tourgueneff's severity as regards Jack, nor in the immensity of his admiration for Rougon. The one has charm, the other force. But neither one is concerned *above all* else with what is for me the end of art, namely, beauty. I remember having felt my heart beat violently, having felt a fierce pleasure in contemplating a wall of the Acropolis, a perfectly bare wall (the one on the left as you go up to the Propylaea). Well! I wonder if a book independently of what it says, cannot produce the same effect! In the exactness of its assembling, the rarity of its elements, the polish of its surface, the harmony of its ensemble, is there not an intrinsic virtue, a sort of divine force, something eternal as a principle? (I speak as a Platonist.) Thus, why is a relation necessary between the exact word and the musical word? Why does it happen that one always makes a verse when one restrains his thought too much? Does the law of numbers govern then the feelings and the images, and is what seems to be the exterior quite simply inside it? If I should continue a long time in this vein, I should blind myself entirely, for on the other side art has to be a good fellow; or rather art is what one can make it, we are not free. Each one follows his path, in spite of his own desire. In short, your Cruchard no longer knows where he stands.

But how difficult it is to understand one another! There are two men whom I admire a great deal and whom I consider real artists, Tourgueneff and Zola. Yet they do not admire the prose of Chateaubriand at all, and even less that of Gautier. Phrases which ravish me seem hollow to them. Who is wrong? And how please the public when one's nearest friends are so remote? All that saddens me very much. Do not laugh.

CCCIX. To GEORGE SAND Sunday evening... 1876

You *ought* to call me inwardly, dear master, "a confounded pig,"—for I have not answered your last letter, and I have said nothing to you about your two volumes, not to mention a third that I received this morning from you. But I have been, for the last two weeks, entirely taken up by my little tale which will be finished soon. I have had several errands to do, various readings to finish up with, and a thing more serious than all that, the health of my poor niece worries me extremely and, at times, disturbs my brain, so that I do not know at all what I am doing! You see that my cup is bitter! That young woman is anemic to the last degree. She is wasting away. She has been obliged to leave off painting, which is her sole distraction. All the usual tonics do no good. Three days ago, by the orders of another physician, who seems to me more learned than the others, she began hydrotherapy. Will he succeed in making her digest and sleep? in building up her strength? Your poor Cruchard takes less and less pleasure in life, and he even has too much of it, infinitely too much. Let us speak of your books, that will be better.

They have amused me, and the proof is that I have devoured with one gulp and one after another, Flamarande and the Deux Freres. What a charming woman is Madame Flamarande, and what a man is M. Salcede. The narrative of the kidnapping of the child, the trip in the carriage, and the story of Zamora are perfect passages. Everywhere the interest is sustained and at the same time progressive. In short, what strikes me the most in these two novels (as in all yours, moreover), is the natural order of the ideas, the talent, or rather the genius for narrative. But what an abominable wretch is your M. Flamarande! As for the servant who tells the story and who is evidently in love with Madame, I wonder why you did not show more plainly his personal jealousy.

Except for the count, all are virtuous persons in that story, even extraordinarily virtuous. But do you think them really true to life? Are there many like them? It is true that while reading, one accepts them because of the cleverness of the execution; but afterwards?

Well, dear master, and this is to answer your last letter, this is, I think what separates us essentially. You, on the first bound, in everything, mount to heaven, and from there you descend to the earth. You start from a priori, from the theory, from the ideal. Thence your pity for life, your serenity, and to speak truly, your greatness.—I, poor wretch, I am stuck on the earth as with soles of lead; everything disturbs me, tears me to pieces, ravages me, and I make efforts to rise. If I should take your manner of looking at the whole of life I should become laughable, that is all. For you preach to me in vain. I cannot have another temperament than my own; nor another esthetics than what is the consequence of it. You accuse me of not letting myself go, according to nature. Well, and that discipline? that virtue? what shall we do with it? I admire M. Buffon putting on cuffs when he wrote. This luxury is a symbol. In short I am trying simply to be as comprehensive as possible. What more can one exact?

As for letting my personal opinion be known about the people I put on the stage: no, no, a thousand times no! I do not recognize the right to that. If the reader does not draw from a book the moral that should be found there, the reader is an imbecile or the book is false from the point of view of accuracy. For, the moment that a thing is true, it is good. Obscene books likewise are immoral only because they lack truth. Things are not "like that" in life.

And observe that I curse what they agree to call realism, although they make me one of its high priests; reconcile all that.

As for the public, its taste disgusts me more and more. Yesterday, for instance, I was present at the first night of the Prix Martin, a piece of buffoonery that, for my part, I think full of wit. Not one of the witty things in the play produced a laugh, and the denouement, which seems out of the ordinary, passed unperceived. Then to look for what can please seems to me the most chimerical of undertakings. For I defy anyone to tell me by what means one pleases. Success is a consequence and must not be an end. I have never sought it (although I desire it) and I seek it less and less.

After my little story, I shall do another,—for I am too deeply shaken to start on a great work. I had thought first of publishing Saint-Julien in a periodical, but I have given the plan up.

CCCX. TO GEORGE SAND Friday evening...1876

Ah! thank you from the bottom of my heart, dear master! You have made me pass an exquisite day, for I have read your last volume, *la Tour de Percemont.—Marianne* only to-day; as I had many things to finish, among others my tale of Saint-Julien, I had shut up the aforesaid volume in a drawer so as not to succumb to the temptation. As my little story was finished last night, I rushed upon your book when morning came and devoured it.

I find it perfect, two jewels! *Marianne* moved me deeply and two or three times I wept. I recognized myself in the character of Pierre. Certain pages seemed to me fragments of my own memoirs, supposing I had the talent to write them in such a way! How charming, poetic and true to life all that is! *La Tour de Percemont* pleased me extremely. But *Marianne* literally enchanted me. The English think as I do, for in the last number of the *Athenaeum* there is a very fine article about you. Did you know that? So then, for this time, I admire you completely and without the least reserve.

There you are, and I am very glad of it. You have never done anything to me that was not good; I love you tenderly!

CCCXI. To Gustave Flaubert Sunday, Nohant,
5th April, 1876.

Victor Borie is in Italy, what must I write him? Are you the man to go to find him and explain the affair to him? He is somewhere near Civita-Vecchia, very much on the go and perhaps not easy to catch up with.

I am sure that he would receive you with open arms, for, although a financier to his finger-tips he has remained very friendly and nice to us. He does not tell us if he is on his mountain of alum for long. Lina is writing to him and will know soon, shall she tell him that you are disposed to go to meet him, or that you will wait until his return to Paris? anyway until the 20th of May he will get letters addressed to him at the Hotel Italy in Florence. We shall have to be on the watch, for he writes *at long intervals*.

I have not the time to say any more to you today. People are coming in. I have read *Fromont et Risler;* I charge you to thank M. Daudet, to tell him that I spent the night in reading it and that I do not know whether I prefer Jack or Risler; it is interesting, I might almost say *gripping*.

I embrace you and I love you, when will you give me some Flaubert to read?

G. Sand

CCCXII. To GEORGE SAND Monday evening

Dear master,

Thanks to Madame Lina's kind note, I betook myself to V. Borie's yesterday and was most pleasantly received. My nephew went to carry him the documents today. Borie has promised to look after the affair; will he do it?

I think that he is in just the position to do me indirectly the greatest service that any one could do me. If my poor nephew should get the capital which he needs in order to work, I could get back a part of what I have lost and live in peace the rest of my days.

I presented myself to Borie under your recommendation, and it is to you that I owe the cordiality of his reception. I do not thank you (of course) but you can tell him that I was touched by his kind reception (and stimulate his zeal if you think that may be useful).

I have been working a great deal lately. How I should like to see you so as to read my little medieval folly to you! I have begun another story entitled Histoire d'un coeur simple. But I have interrupted this work to make some researches on the period of Saint John the Baptist, for I want to describe the feast of Herodias.

I hope to have my readings finished in a fortnight, after which I shall return to Croisset from which spot I shall not budge till winter,—my long sessions at the library exhaust me. Cruchard is weary.

The good Tourgueneff leaves this evening for Saint Petersburg. He asks me if I have thanked you for your last book? Could I be guilty of such an oversight?

You will see by my *Histoire d'un coeur* simple where you will recognize your immediate influence, that I am not so obstinate as you think. I believe that the moral tendency, or rather the human basis of this little work will please you!

Adieu, dear good master. Remembrances to all yours.

I embrace you very tenderly.

Your old Gustave Flaubert

CCCXIII. To Maurice Sand Tuesday evening, 27th

All I can say to you, in the first place, my dear friend, is, that your book has made me pass a sleepless night. I read it instantly, at one fell swoop, only stopping to fill my good pipe from time to time and then to resume my reading.

When the impression is a little less fresh I shall take up your book again to find the flaws in it. But I think that there are very few. You must be content? It ought to please? It is dramatic and as amusing as possible!

Beginning with the first page I was charmed with the sincerity of the description. And at the end I admired the composition of the whole, the logical way the events were worked out and the characters related.

Your chief character, Miss Mary, is too hateful (to my taste) to be anything but an exact picture. That is one of the choicest parts of your book, together with the homelife, the life in New York?

Your good savage makes me laugh out loud when he is at the Opera.

I was struck by the house of the missionaries (Montaret's first night). You make it seem real.

Naissa scalping, and then wiping her hands on the grass, seemed to me especially well done. As well as the disgust that she inspires in Montaret.

I venture a timid observation: it seems to me that the flight of father Athanasius and of Montaret, when they escape from their prison, is not perfectly clear? Is not the material explanation of the event too short?

I do not care for, as language, two or three ready-made locutions, such as "break the ice." You can see that I have read you attentively! What a pedagogue I make, eh! I am telling you all that from memory, for I have lent your book, and it has not been returned to me yet. But my recollection of it is of a thing very well done.

Don't you agree with me that a play of very great effect could be made from it for a boulevard theatre?
By the way, how is Cadio going?

Tell your dear mamma that I adore her.

Harrisse, from whom I have received a letter today, charges me to remember him to her, and, for my part, I charge you to embrace her for me.

And I grasp your two hands heartily and say "bravo" to you again, and faithfully yours.

Gustave Flaubert

CCCXIV. To MADAM MAURICE SAND
Thursday evening, 25th May, 1876

Dear Madam,

I sent a telegram to Maurice this morning, asking for news of Madam Sand.

I was told yesterday that she was very ill, why has not Maurice answered me?

I went to Plauchut's this morning to get details. He is in the country, at Le Mans, so that I am in a state of cruel uncertainty.

Be good enough to answer me immediately and believe me, dear madam,

Your very affectionate,
Gustave Flaubert
4 rue Murillo, Parc Monceau

CCCXV. To Madam Lina Sand

Dear Madam,

Your note of this morning reassures me a little. But that of last night had absolutely upset me.

I beg you to give me very frequent news of your dear mother-in-law.

Embrace her for me and believe that I am

Your very devoted

Gustave Flaubert

Beginning with the middle of next week, about Wednesday or Thursday, I shall be at Croisset.

Saturday morning, 3d June, 1876.

CCCXVI. To Maurice Sand Croisset, Sunday, 24 June, 1876

You had prepared me, my dear Maurice, I wanted to write to you, but I was waiting till you were a little freer, more alone. Thank you for your kind thought.

Yes, we understood each other, yonder! (And if I did not remain longer, it is because my comrades dragged me away.) It seemed to me that I was burying my mother the second time. Poor, dear, great woman! What genius and what heart! But she lacked nothing, it is not she whom we must pity.

What is to become of you? Shall you stay in Nohant? That good old house must seem horribly empty to you! But you, at least, are not alone! You have a wife...a rare one! and two exquisite children. While I was with you, I had, over and above my grief, two desires: to run off with Aurore and to kill M. Marx.[44] There you have the truth, it is unnecessary to make you see the psychology of the thing. I received yesterday a very sympathetic letter from good Tourgueneff. He too loved her. But then, who did not love her? If you had seen in Paris the anguish of Martine![45] That was distressing.

Plauchut is still in Nohant, I suppose. Tell him that I love him because I saw him shed so many tears.

And let yours flow, my dear friend, do all that is necessary not to console yourself,—which would, moreover, be impossible. Never mind! In a short time you will feel a great joy

---

[44] A reporter for *le Figaro*.
[45] George Sand's maid.

in the idea alone that you were a good son and that she knew it absolutely. She used to talk of you as of a blessing.

And when you shall have rejoined her, when the great-grand-children of the grandchildren of your two little girls shall have joined her, and when for a long time there shall have been no question of the things and the people that surround us,—in several centuries,— hearts like ours will palpitate through hers! People will read her books, that is to say that they will think according to her ideas and they will love with her love. But all that does not give her back to you, does it? With what then can we sustain ourselves if pride desert us, and what man more than you should have pride in his mother!

Now dear friend, adieu! When shall we meet now? How I should feel the need of talking of her, insatiably!

Embrace Madam Maurice for me, as I did on the stairway at Nohant, and your little girls.

Yours, from the depths of my heart,

Your Gustave Flaubert

CCCXVII. To Maurice Sand Croisset,
Tuesday, 3rd October, 1876

Thank you for your kind remembrance, my dear friend. Neither do I forget, and I dream of your poor, dear mamma in a sadness that does not disappear. Her death has left a great emptiness for me. After you, your wife and the good Plauchut, I am perhaps the one who misses her most! I need her.

I pity you the annoyances that your sister causes you. I too have gone through that! It is so easy moreover to be good! Besides that causes less evil. When shall we meet? I want so much to see you, first just to see you—and second to talk of her.

When your business is finished, why not come to Paris for some time? Solitude is bad under certain conditions. One should not become intoxicated with one's grief, however much attraction one finds in doing so.

You ask me what I am doing. This is it: this year I have written two stories, and I am going to begin another so as to make the three into one volume that I want to publish in the spring. After that I hope to resume the big novel that I laid aside a year ago after my financial disaster. Matters are improving in that direction, and I shall not be forced to change anything in my way of living. If I have been able to start at work again, I owe it partly to the good counsel of your mother. She had found the best way to bring me back to respect myself.

In order to get the quicker at work, I shall stay here till New Year's Day,—perhaps later than that. Do try to put off your visit to Paris.

Embrace your dear little girls warmly for me, my respects to Madam Maurice, and—sincerely yours, ex imo.
Gustave Flaubert

CCCXVIII. To MAURICE SAND Saint-Gratien par Sannois, 20th August, 1877

Thank you for your kind remembrance, my dear Maurice. Next winter you will be in Passy, I hope,—and from time to time we can have a good chat. I even count on seeing myself at your table by the side of your friends whose "idol" I am.

You speak to me of your dear and illustrious mamma! Next to you I do not think that any one could think of her more often than I do! How I miss her! How I need her!

I had begun un coeur simple solely on account of her, only to please her. She died while I was in the midst of this work. Thus it is with our dreams.

I still continue not to find diversion in existence. In order to forget the weight of it, I work as frantically as possible.

What sustains me is the indignation that the Imbecility of the Bourgeois affords me! Summed up at present by the large party of law and order, it reaches a dizzy height!

Has there been anything in history more inept than the 16th of May? Where is there an idiot comparable to the Bayard of modern times?

I have been in Paris, or rather at Saint-Gratien, for three days. Day after tomorrow I leave the princess, and in a fortnight I shall make a little trip to Lower Normandy for the sake of literature. When we meet I shall talk a long time with you, if you are interested, about the terrible book that I am in the process of concocting. I shall have enough work in it to take me three or four years. Not less!

Don't leave me so long without news. Give a long look for me at the little corner of the holy ground!...My regards to your dear wife, embrace the dear little girls and sincerely yours, my good Maurice,

Your old friend
Gustave Flaubert

CCCXIX. TO MAURICE SAND Tuesday morning, April, 1880

My dear Maurice,

No! Erase Cruchard and Polycarp and replace those words by what you like.

The Public ought not to have all of us,—let us reserve something for ourselves. That seems to me more decent (quod decet). You do not speak of a *complete edition?* Ah! your poor dear mamma! How often I think of her! And what need I have of her! There is not a day when I do not say: "If she were there, I should ask her advice."

I shall be at Croisset till the 8th or the 10th of May. So, my old fellow, when you wish to come there, you will be welcome. I embrace you all from the oldest to the youngest.

Cruchard for you,
Polycarp for the human race,
Gustave Flaubert for Literature